Africa's Media Image in the 21st Century

Africa's Media Image in the 21st Century is the first book in over twenty years to examine the international media's coverage of sub-Saharan Africa. It brings together leading researchers and prominent journalists to explore representation of the continent, and the production of that image, especially by international news media. The book highlights factors that have transformed the global media system, changing whose perspectives are told and the forms of media that empower new voices.

Case studies consider questions such as: how have new media changed whose views are represented? Do Chinese or diaspora media offer alternative perspectives for viewing the continent? How do foreign correspondents interact with their audiences in a social media age? What is the contemporary role of charity groups and PR firms in shaping news content? They also examine how recent high-profile events and issues have been covered by the international media, from the Ebola crisis and Boko Haram to debates surrounding the "Africa Rising" narrative and neo-imperialism.

The book makes a substantial contribution by moving the academic discussion beyond the traditional critiques of journalistic stereotyping, Afro-pessimism, and "darkest Africa" news coverage. It explores the news outlets, international power dynamics, and technologies that shape and reshape the contemporary image of Africa and Africans in journalism and global culture.

Mel Bunce is a Senior Lecturer in Journalism at City University London, where she researches and teaches in the areas of global media, news production, and ethics. A former journalist from New Zealand, Mel has researched the work of foreign correspondents in Sudan, Uganda, Kenya, Senegal, and Nigeria.

Suzanne Franks is Professor of Journalism at City University London, where she is Head of Department and convenes a module on Humanitarian Communication. A former BBC TV current affairs journalist, she has made several films about Africa. Her publications include *Reporting Disasters: Famine, Aid, Politics and the Media* (2013).

Chris Paterson researches and teaches at the University of Leeds, UK. He wrote in the original *Africa's Media Image* (1992), has co-edited five books, and has authored *The International Television News Agencies* (2011) and *War Reporters under Threat: The United States and Media Freedom* (2014).

Communication and Society

Series Editor: James Curran

This series encompasses the broad field of media and cultural studies. Its main concerns are the media and the public sphere: on whether the media empower or fail to empower popular forces in society; media organisations and public policy; the political and social consequences of media campaigns; and the role of media entertainment, ranging from potboilers and the human-interest story to rock music and TV sport.

Media Perspectives for the 21st Century
Edited by Stylianos Papathanassopoulos

Journalism After September 11
Second Edition
Edited by Barbie Zelizer and
Stuart Allan

Media and Democracy
James Curran

Changing Journalism
Angela Phillips, Peter Lee-Wright and
Tamara Witschge

Misunderstanding the Internet
James Curran, Natalie Fenton and Des
Freedman

Critical Political Economy of the Media
An Introduction
Jonathan Hardy

Journalism in Context
Practice and Theory for the Digital Age
Angela Phillips

News and Politics
The Rise of Live and Interpretive
Journalism
Stephen Cushion

Gender and Media
Representing, Producing, Consuming
Tonny Krijnen and Sofie Van Bauwel

Misunderstanding the Internet
Second edition
James Curran, Natalie Fenton and Des
Freedman

Africa's Media Image in the 21st Century
From the "Heart of Darkness" to
"Africa Rising"
Edited by Mel Bunce, Suzanne Franks
and Chris Paterson

Africa's Media Image in the 21st Century

From the "Heart of Darkness" to "Africa Rising"

Edited by Mel Bunce,
Suzanne Franks,
and Chris Paterson

Routledge
Taylor & Francis Group

LONDON AND NEW YORK

First published 2017
by Routledge
2 Park Square, Milton Park, Abingdon, Oxon OX14 4RN

and by Routledge
711 Third Avenue, New York, NY 10017

Routledge is an imprint of the Taylor & Francis Group, an informa business

© 2017 selection and editorial material, Mel Bunce, Suzanne Franks and
Chris Paterson; individual chapter, the contributors

British Library Cataloguing-in-Publication Data
A catalogue record for this book is available from the British Library

Library of Congress Cataloging-in-Publication Data
Names: Bunce, Melanie, editor. | Franks, Suzanne, editor. | Paterson, Chris,
    editor.
Title: Africa's media image in the 21st century: from the "heart of
    darkness" to "Africa rising" / edited by Mel Bunce, Suzanne Franks and
    Chris Paterson.
Description: London; New York: Routledge, 2016. | Series: Communication
    and society | Includes bibliographical references and index.
Identifiers: LCCN 2015048198
Subjects: LCSH: Africa—In mass media. | Africa—Press coverage—
    History—21st century. | Journalism—Technological innovations.
Classification: LCC P96.A37.A58 2016 | DDC 070.4/49960331—dc23
LC record available at http://lccn.loc.gov/2015048198

ISBN: 978-1-138-96231-6 (hbk)
ISBN: 978-1-138-96232-3 (pbk)
ISBN: 978-1-315-65951-0 (ebk)

Typeset in New Baskerville
by Swales & Willis Ltd, Exeter, Devon, UK

Contents

List of figures   ix
List of tables   x
Notes on contributors   xi
Foreword by Beverly Hawk   xvi

Introduction: a new *Africa's Media Image*?   1
MEL BUNCE, SUZANNE FRANKS, AND CHRIS PATERSON

PART I
Framing Africa   15

1 **The international news coverage of Africa: beyond the
   "single story"**   17
   MEL BUNCE

2 **Media perspectives: in defence of Western journalists in Africa** 30
   MICHELA WRONG

3 **Reporting and writing Africa in a world of unequal encounters**   33
   FRANCIS B. NYAMNJOH

4 **Media perspectives: how does Africa get reported? A letter
   of concern to *60 Minutes***   38
   HOWARD W. FRENCH

5 **How not to write about writing about Africa**   40
   MARTIN SCOTT

6   Bringing Africa home: reflections on discursive practices of
    domestication in international news reporting on Africa
    by Belgian television   52
    STIJN JOYE

7   The image of Africa from the perspectives of the African
    diasporic press in the UK   61
    OLATUNJI OGUNYEMI

PART II
The image makers   71

8   Mediating the distant Other for the distant audience: how do
    Western correspondents in East and Southern Africa
    perceive their audience?   73
    TOUSSAINT NOTHIAS

9   Media perspectives: television reporting of Africa: 30 years on   83
    ZEINAB BADAWI

10 Foreign correspondents in sub-Saharan Africa: their
    socio-demographics and professional culture   86
    PAULO NUNO VICENTE

11 Media perspectives: reflecting on my father's legacy in
    reporting Africa   96
    SALIM AMIN

12 Media perspectives: we're missing the story: the media's
    retreat from foreign reporting   99
    ANJAN SUNDARAM

13 Instagram as a potential platform for alternative
    Visual Culture in South Africa   102
    DANIELLE BECKER

14 Media perspectives: social media and new narratives:
    Kenyans tweet back   113
    H. NANJALA NYABOLA

15 A "New Ghana" in "Rising Africa"?   116
    RACHEL FLAMENBAUM

PART III
Development and humanitarian stories   127

16 Media perspectives: is Africa's development
    story still stuck on aid?   129
    ELIZA ANYANGWE

17 AIDS in Africa and the British media: shifting
    images of a pandemic   132
    LUDEK STAVINOHA

18 Media perspectives: a means to an end? Creating a
    market for humanitarian news from Africa   143
    HEBA ALY

19 It was a "simple", "positive" story of African self-help
    (manufactured for a Kenyan NGO by advertising
    multinationals)   147
    KATE WRIGHT

20 Media perspectives: Africa for Norway: challenging
    stereotypes using humour   158
    NICKLAS POULSEN VIKI

21 Bloggers, celebrities, and economists: news coverage
    of the Millennium Villages Project   161
    AUDREY ARISS, ANYA SCHIFFRIN, AND MICHELLE CHAHINE

PART IV
Politics in the representation of Africa   175

22 Africa through Chinese eyes: new frames or the same
    old lens? African news in English from China Central
    Television, compared with the BBC   177
    VIVIEN MARSH

23 **Media perspectives: new media and African engagement**
    with the global public sphere   190
    SEAN JACOBS

24 **Shifting power relations, shifting images**   193
    HERMAN WASSERMAN

25 **Communicating violence: the media strategies of**
    Boko Haram   200
    ABDULLAHI TASIU ABUBAKAR

26 **Perceptions of Chinese media's Africa coverage**   211
    JAMES WAN

27 **New imperialisms, old stereotypes**   214
    CHRIS PATERSON

28 **Nollywood news: African screen media at the**
    intersections of the global and the local   223
    NOAH TSIKA

    Index   232

Figures

1.1   Newswire articles: subjects with biggest change   21

1.2   Tone of newspaper articles   25

5.1   Number of studies of US and UK news coverage of Africa published annually (January 1990 – April 2014)   42

5.2   Number of peer-reviewed studies of US and UK news coverage of Africa that include a focus on different media   44

5.3   Number of studies examining representations of different African countries within different media   45

10.1   Type of news media organisation   87

10.2   Internet access frequency among foreign correspondents   91

10.3   Audience feedback frequency among foreign correspondents   92

13.1   iseeadifferentyou (2015)   107

13.2   *Instagenic* exhibition   108

17.1   BBC coverage of "AIDS in Africa"   134

17.2   "AIDS in Africa" in the press   137

21.1   Number of articles by type and country   165

21.2   Tone of articles   166

Tables

1.1	Newswire articles in sample	19
1.2	Newspaper articles in sample	20
1.3	Subject of newswire stories	21
1.4	Breakdown of newswire stories on domestic politics	23
1.5	Subjects within newswire stories	24
1.6	Tone of newspaper articles by publication	26
5.1	Number of studies of US and UK news coverage to include an analysis of different countries or locations within Africa	43
7.1	Frequency of frames in the *African Voice*	66
7.2	Diversity of sources in the *African Voice*	68
21.1	Breakdown of publications	170
22.1	Categories for comparison of British and Chinese news about Africa	180
22.2	Framing analysis	182
22.3	Top five frames in the analysis of three key issues on the BBC's and CCTV's African news programmes	186

Contributors

Abdullahi Tasiu Abubakar is a lecturer in Journalism at City University London. He was awarded his PhD from the University of Westminster in London and he has worked for the BBC World Service and many Nigerian newspapers, including the *Daily Trust* as Editor-at-Large. Abdullahi has written on media, culture, and public diplomacy.

Heba Aly is the Managing Editor of the humanitarian news outlet IRIN. A Canadian–Egyptian multimedia journalist, she has reported from conflict zones in the Middle East, Africa, and Central Asia for the Canadian Broadcasting Corporation, the Christian Science Monitor, and Bloomberg News, among others. In 2008, she received a grant from the Pulitzer Center on Crisis Reporting for her work in northern Sudan.

Salim Amin is Chairman of Camerapix, The Mohamed Amin Foundation, and Africa24 Media. He is a documentary producer, Young Global Leader at the World Economic Forum, fellow of the African Leadership Initiative, and member of the Aspen Global Leadership Network. He has been named one of the "100 Most Influential Africans" by *New African* magazine and hosts a talk show, "The Scoop".

Eliza Anyangwe is a freelance writer and editor covering Africa and international development at *The Guardian* and CNN International. She is also the founder of the Nzinga Effect, a platform to celebrate and share the stories of African women.

Audrey Ariss leads research and design at the Center for Open Data Enterprise in Washington, DC. She has previously worked as a Google Policy Fellow, a researcher at The GovLab, a consultant, and an editorial assistant. Audrey holds a Masters in International Affairs and Quantitative Methods from Columbia University and a BA from the University of Oxford.

Zeinab Badawi is a BBC TV World News journalist and the Chair of the Royal African Society. Badawi was born in Sudan and grew up in the UK. An award-winning reporter, she spent ten years as co-presenter of *Channel 4 News* and is now a presenter of *BBC World News Today* and the interview show *HARDtalk*.

Danielle Becker is a lecturer in Art History and Visual Studies at Stellenbosch University and the University of Cape Town, South Africa. She is currently completing her doctoral research at UCT and has spoken at various international conferences.

Mel Bunce is a Senior Lecturer in Journalism at City University London, where she researches and teaches in the areas of global media, news production, and ethics. A former journalist from New Zealand, Mel was awarded her PhD from the University of Oxford for research on foreign correspondents in sub-Saharan Africa. She convenes the Humanitarian News Research Network at City University.

Michelle Chahine is a writer living in Santa Monica, California. She is currently the Digital Media Editor for MariaShriver.com and the non-profit organisation A Woman's Nation. She has a Bachelor of Fine Arts from Boston University and a Masters in International Affairs from Columbia University. Her website is michellechahine.com.

Rachel Flamenbaum is a doctoral candidate in Linguistic Anthropology at the University of California, Los Angeles. She is interested in issues of language, new media, and political economy. Her current research examines the consequences of asymmetrical socialisation into digital literacies among marginalised and elite students in Ghana, West Africa.

Suzanne Franks is Professor of Journalism at City University London, where she is Head of Department and convenes a module on Humanitarian Communication. She is a former BBC TV current affairs journalist and has made several films about Africa. Her recent publications include *Reporting Disasters: Famine, Aid, Politics and the Media* (Hurst & Co, 2013).

Howard W. French is an associate professor at Columbia University and was *New York Times* bureau chief for Central America and the Caribbean; West and Central Africa; and China. He has written three books, including *China's Second Continent: How a Million Migrants Are Building a New Empire in Africa* (Alfred Knopf, 2014).

Sean Jacobs is on the International Affairs faculty of The New School in New York City. He was born and grew up in Cape Town, where he completed his undergraduate education. He also studied at Northwestern University (MA) and the University of London (PhD) and held fellowships at New York University, Harvard, and The New School. Jacobs founded the website Africasacountry.com.

Stijn Joye is an assistant professor at Ghent University, Belgium, where he is a member of research groups Centre for Cinema and Media Studies, Centre for Journalism Studies, and Health, Media & Society. His areas of research and publication include international news, representation of distant suffering, and artistic imitation in film.

Vivien Marsh is a doctoral candidate at the University of Westminster and a former longstanding BBC multimedia global news journalist, serving latterly as World Service Asia-Pacific news editor. Her paper on CCTV's African news, "Mixed messages, partial pictures?", has been published recently in the *Chinese Journal of Communication*.

Toussaint Nothias is a lecturer in the Center for African Studies at Stanford University, and a research associate of the Programme in Comparative Media Law and Policy at the University of Oxford. He completed his PhD at the University of Leeds. His work has appeared in *Visual Communication, Communication, Culture & Critique*, and *African Journalism Studies*.

H. Nanjala Nyabola is a Kenyan writer, humanitarian advocate, and political analyst. She holds two masters degrees from the University of Oxford, where she studied as a Rhodes Scholar, and a J.D. from Harvard Law School. Her work has been published in *Al Jazeera English, Foreign Affairs, The Guardian*, and *The African Security Review*, among others.

Francis B. Nyamnjoh is Professor of Social Anthropology at the University of Cape Town, South Africa. His books include: *Africa's Media, Democracy and the Politics of Belonging* (Zed Books, 2005) and *Insiders & Outsiders: Citizenship and Xenophobia in Contemporary Southern Africa* (Zed Books, 2006).

Olatunji Ogunyemi is Principal Lecturer in Journalism, University of Lincoln, and convenes the Media of Diaspora Research Group. He publishes in journals and in edited books and is the author of *What Newspapers, Films, and Television Do Africans Living in Britain See and Read? The Media of the African Diaspora* (The Edwin Mellen Press, 2012).

Chris Paterson researches and teaches at the University of Leeds, UK. He wrote in the original *Africa's Media Image* (Praeger, 1992), has co-edited five books, and has authored *The International Television News Agencies* (Peter Lang, 2011) and *War Reporters under Threat: The United States and Media Freedom* (Pluto Press, 2014).

Anya Schiffrin is the Director of the International Media, Advocacy and Communications specialisation at Columbia University's School of International Affairs. She writes on journalism and development as well as the media in Africa and the extractive sector. Her recent book is *Global Muckraking: 100 Years of Investigative Reporting from Around the World* (New Press, 2014).

Martin Scott is a lecturer in Media and International Development, University of East Anglia, and author of *Media and Development* (Zed Books, 2014). He has published articles on topics including digital humanitarianism, celebrity humanitarianism, international news coverage, and representations of Africa.

Ludek Stavinoha is Lecturer in Media and International Development at the University of East Anglia. He completed his PhD at the University of Strathclyde and his research and published work focuses on media coverage of the global HIV/AIDS pandemic and the political economy of access to medicines.

Anjan Sundaram is an award-winning journalist who has reported from Africa and the Middle East for *The New York Times* and the Associated Press. He is the author of *Bad News: Last Journalists in a Dictatorship* (Doubleday, 2016) and *Stringer: A Reporter's Journey in the Congo* (Doubleday, 2014).

Noah Tsika is Assistant Professor of Media Studies at Queens College, City University of New York. His books include *Nollywood Stars: Media and Migration in West Africa and the Diaspora* (Indiana University Press, 2015) and he has published articles on African media in the journals *African Studies Review, Black Camera,* and *The Velvet Light Trap.*

Paulo Nuno Vicente is a researcher and Assistant Professor in Journalism and Digital Media at NOVA University of Lisbon, Portugal. As a journalist and documentary filmmaker he has worked extensively in the so-called "global South". He is also a founder and director of Bagabaga Studios, a new media production house.

Nicklas Poulsen Viki is the President of SAIH (the solidarity organisation of students and academics in Norway). He holds a Masters in Community Psychology from the University of Oslo, where his master's thesis focused on intercultural dialogue. Nicklas is a student activist interested in education, academic freedom, and the power of language.

James Wan is a journalist and editor of the website African Arguments. He is a fellow of the China–Africa Reporting Project hosted by the journalism department at University of the Witwatersrand, South Africa. He was previously Senior Editor at Think Africa Press.

Herman Wasserman is Professor of Media Studies and Director of the Centre for Film and Media Studies, University of Cape Town, South Africa. He has published widely on media in post-apartheid South Africa. He is Editor-in-Chief of the journal *African Journalism Studies.*

Kate Wright is Senior Lecturer in Journalism and News Media at the University of Roehampton in London. She is a former BBC journalist who publishes on international news and is currently writing a book for Peter Lang called *Who's Reporting Africa Now? Journalists, Non-Governmental Organisations and Multimedia*.

Michela Wrong, a former reporter for Reuters, the BBC World Service, and the *Financial Times*, is the author of three non-fiction books on Africa. Her first novel, *Borderlines*, was published this summer and is set in the Horn of Africa. She writes regularly for *Foreign Policy* and *The Spectator* magazines.

Foreword

Beverly Hawk

Poor news coverage is not a victimless crime. News shapes our assumptions about one another, prescribes the symbols with which we analyse events, informs international investment, and guides policy discussion. Africa coverage touches every discipline, influences political analysis of international issues, and shapes daily interactions among news consumers. The media image of Africa moulds many critical aspects of our lives, wherever we may live. Africa coverage provides us with the vocabulary we use in our policy discussions and identifies the issues deserving of attention in those discussions.

The publication in 1992 of the original *Africa's Media Image* anthology was a landmark event for journalism, the discipline of African Studies, and communication scholarship, and it marked a new collaboration between journalists and the academic researchers who would often critique them. That collection of research and experience brought together courageous and insightful scholars, journalists, editors, and Africa specialists to present their varied analyses. With this mix of expertise and experience, the collection crackled with conflict. The book was awarded the Sigma Delta Chi Award for research about journalism by the US Society of Professional Journalists, and the debates introduced in the book have created a lively literature that continues to shape the field.

Topics of food aid, the Cold War, African agency, censorship, and the historic contributions of the African American Press contributed to the breadth of the volume. Issues raised by the scholarship in *Africa's Media Image* continue to shape research and debate today, particularly its analysis of metaphors of Africa coverage and the vocabulary and symbols they employ. The works presented in *Africa's Media Image* showed that metaphors used to frame African stories were Western and often colonial, not African at all. Contributors found that Africa as the primitive archetype with its language of tribal bloodshed was often contrasted in US news coverage with African democracy movements that were presented in the vocabulary of the American Civil Rights Movement, presenting a dichotomy of primitive and modern. Well-meaning journalists chose familiar story frames that robbed the events they reported of their context: standard journalistic practice, then, provided a distorted image of the continent.

In recent decades, African university scholars and communications professionals have staked their claim to authority over the presentations of their lives and their meaning. By magnifying African voices, technological advances in communication are transforming information about Africa and consequently the image of Africa around the world. With Africa as the motive force in African news, the continent has an opportunity to claim agency over its image.

Today's news media are under more pressure than ever, with less money to fund their work, fewer bureaus to feed their content, greater danger for their correspondents, and a relentless 24/7 news cycle that places impossible demands on standards of accuracy. Further, today's international communication is shaped by social media that offer more freedom but less oversight and present daily opportunities for the manipulation of readers and viewers.

The provocative works of research and comment presented in this new volume assess change and continuity in Africa's portrayal. Leaders in the field of media research and Africa specialists with expertise in the complexity of African societies and politics have joined together to create a new collection of research, one that is sure to shape the field for years to come.

Beverly Hawk
Editor, *Africa's Media Image*, Praeger, 1992

Introduction

A new *Africa's Media Image?*

Mel Bunce, Suzanne Franks, and Chris Paterson

Africa's Media Image in the 21st Century: From the "Heart of Darkness" to "Africa Rising" is the first book in a generation to assess in detail and from multiple perspectives the way that sub-Saharan Africa is reported in the international media. Beverly Hawk edited an *Africa's Media Image* in 1992: this focused, primarily from a US angle, upon the way that the media represented Africa. It was seen as a groundbreaking work and it won the Sigma Delta Chi Award for journalism research from the Society of Professional Journalists. Since that time there has been a revolution not only in the media but also in the way Africa is reported and understood. This book seeks to examine the issue on an even wider canvas.

It has become a well-rehearsed argument that Africa has historically suffered in a multitude of ways from the prevalence of negative and stereotypical representation by a Northern media system over which the continent has had no influence and no input (De B'béri & Louw 2011). The emergence of increasingly participatory and indigenous information flows, in combination with a healthy cynicism and debate about traditional media and apparent decreases in dependence on Northern sources, all imply a more autonomous and confident region of the world actively inventing new ways to communicate.

Africa's changing media image

Who tells Africa's story has always mattered, and has always been a matter for contestation. Research from the 1970s through to the 1990s demonstrated that international representations of Africa were narrow, laden with stereotypes, and highly dependent on Cold War frames and portrayals of an improvised, often savage, "other". Heather Brookes' analysis of the *Daily Telegraph*'s and *Guardian*'s coverage of Africa in 1990, to give one example, found that Africa was represented in the UK press as a "homogenous block with violence, helplessness, human rights abuses and lack of democracy as its main characteristics" (1995: 465; see also Fair & Parks 2001: 49; Crawford 1996: 32).

The landmark 2005 essay by Binyavanga Wainaina, "How to write about Africa", satirically commented on the problematic language and imagery used by authors and reporters in the global North when they wrote about Africa. Wainaina's essay clearly struck a chord. It quickly became one of the most read pieces ever published in *Granta* magazine and helped to popularise critical reflection about Africa's representation. It has since become an important touchstone in the literature. We commend the reader to consult the original text (Wainaina 2005), but this is a brief sample of Wainaina's pointed instructions to those writing about Africa:

> In your text, treat Africa as if it were one country. It is hot and dusty with rolling grasslands and huge herds of animals and tall, thin people who are starving. Or it is hot and steamy with very short people who eat primates.

Prominent journalists have been among the most vocal critics of the news industry structures that incentivise and reinforce Afro-pessimism. For example, famed news agency photographer Mohammed Amin (whose son writes in this book) told Paterson in 1995 – shortly before his death in a hijacking – that encouraging his London editors to invest in covering routine politics in Africa for their own sake was a constant struggle:

> [T]here's a mentality. Nigeria – those elections a few years ago [1993] – and I was talking to my editor, wanting us to put in a crew in Nigeria. And the response was, "Is there going to be trouble?" Well, my answer was, "There's a reasonably good chance there will be trouble, but this is an important country. Should we not be covering the election? If there's trouble, of course we cover the trouble as well." "Well," they said, ".... If there are dead bodies in the streets of Lagos we've got to go in there." Now, you know, I'm sick of that sort of an attitude! I wonder if the same editor would think like that if there's coming elections in Britain or France or America – that you've got to wait until there are dead bodies in the streets. ... [T]hey think like that about Africa.[1]

The power of the image

Media representations matter. The negative content and imagery that Wainaina satirises has important implications for global flows of finance, trade, tourism (Schorr 2011). Moreover – and perhaps most importantly – such negative and "othering" representations inform intercultural relations. As discourse theorists note, language plays a central role in the perpetuation of norms, values, and stereotypes; and it can operate to support and perpetuate oppression by the powerful (e.g. Said 1978; Spivak &

Guha 1988). Forms of "Afro-pessimism", in particular, represent the African continent as a failed and passive site, in need of outside intervention (Momoh 2003; De B'Béri & Louw 2011; Nothias 2014). Audience research suggests that these representations do have an impact on how international audiences perceive Africa (Borowski 2012; International Exchange 1988).

In her powerful and widely disseminated TED Talk "The danger of a single story", the much-celebrated Nigerian author Chimamanda Ngozi Adichie (2009) describes going to college in the United States and meeting her roommate. The roommate, who only knew about Nigeria from popular culture, expected Adichie to be poor, unable to work appliances, and to enjoy "tribal music". Reflecting on the encounter, Adichie points to the role that Western literature and popular media play in shaping these preconceptions:

> [I]f all I knew about Africa were from popular images, I too would think that Africa was a place of beautiful landscapes, beautiful animals, and incomprehensible people, fighting senseless wars, dying of poverty and AIDS, unable to speak for themselves and waiting to be saved by a kind, white foreigner . . . .

Adichie's powerful indictment of the single, stereotypical story becoming the only story can be viewed online (Adichie 2009).

A changing narrative

Since the publication of Hawk's *Africa's Media Image*, and Wainaina's important essay, there have been many important and profound changes in the media representation of Africa. Several scholars have concluded (Nothias 2014; Ojo 2014; Bunce, in this volume) that the mainstream international print coverage of Africa shows signs of becoming more positive in tone and varied in its subject matter. The exemplar of this new, positive reporting is the now-famous *Economist* cover image of a child flying a rainbow-coloured, Africa-shaped kite, accompanied by the words, "Africa Rising". The cover story, published in December 2011, described the continent's growing middle class, widespread technological innovation, and significant economic development. A series of similar, positive articles followed in quick succession: *TIME* magazine, *The New York Times*, and other agenda-setting publications heralded a shift in both events and growth statistics "on the ground" and noted that the media image of the continent was becoming more positive. A stream of optimistic books further underlined the new narrative of growth and transformation: Hunter-Gault's (2006) *New News Out of Africa: Uncovering Africa's Renaissance*, Vijay Mahajan's (2009) *Africa Rising: How 900 Million African Consumers Offer More Than You Think*, and Dayo Olopade's (2014) *The Bright Continent*.

The concept of "Africa Rising" was warmly welcomed by politicians, civil society advocates, diaspora groups, and business professionals, all eager to embrace a more positive image for the continent. Kenyan President Uhuru Kenyatta declared, "Africa is the world's newest and most promising frontier of limitless opportunity .... Gone are the days when the only lens to view our continent was one of despair and indignity" (Baker & Santora 2015). However, it has also raised concern among commentators who suggest that these new narratives – although more positive – perpetuate a neo-colonial framing of the continent by presenting Africa as a site for international intervention and resource extraction. As Bach writes, "Africa Rising" narratives may constitute "an invitation to call back the ghosts of explorers, soldiers, traders and settlers who each in their own way once 'discovered' Africa" (2013: 11). The meaning and implications of these new representations require further research and several contributions featured in this volume are a starting point in this debate.

New image makers

When Hawk and her contributors wrote in 1992, the global media landscape was dominated by "West to the rest" information flows: a relatively small number of traditional, legacy media outlets, supplied by a few international news agencies, produced international news for audiences in the global North, and this news was then disseminated around the world. Concern with the dominance of Northern media producers sparked the UNESCO New World Information Order (NWIO) debates of the 1970s (McBride 1980) and it continues to inform the post-colonial critiques noted above that suggest Africa's global image is constructed through the Western gaze.

In the past twenty years, however, important structural changes in the media system have seen the introduction of significant, alternative, (often) non-Western perspectives. Traditional news outlets have systematically cut their foreign news budgets over the last two decades, leading to a radical reduction in the number of Western foreign correspondents posted abroad (Carroll 2007; Utley 1997). Rather than expensive foreign correspondents, many news outlets now rely on cheaper, locally contracted journalists who were born and raised in the country they report on. This is particularly the case at the major newswires (AFP, AP, Reuters), who provide the majority of the world's raw news content (Boyd-Barrett & Rantanen 2001) and are important producers of international news about Africa (Bunce 2013; Paterson 2011). At these outlets, local journalists are generally the frontline reporters, who discover events and relay them to regional bureaus – for example, in Nairobi or Johannesburg – where staff are a mixture of local and international journalists. As a result, the news is not always or only made by Western journalists but rather, "news production today is a site

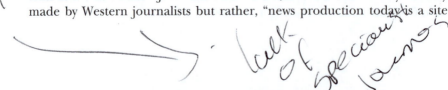
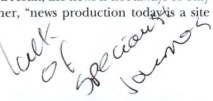

of struggle where journalists from diverse backgrounds contest the way in which news events should be framed" (Bunce 2015: 43).

Another significant development, discussed in several of the contributions to this volume, is the introduction and expansion of major new international media organisations, most notably Doha-based Al Jazeera and the Chinese news agency Xinhua, that have an alternative perspective on events in Africa. Al Jazeera, for example, has been set up with the specific and articulated goal of giving a "voice to the voiceless" and telling stories from the perspective of the subaltern (Figenschou 2010: 86). These media organisations are fascinating case studies, as they seek to balance the desire to tell stories in new ways with building credibility among traditional media consumers.

A final, extremely important transformation in the media system since Hawk's collection, is the introduction of technologies that allow local audiences to reclaim their representation. The power of Twitter in particular to challenge Western coverage started to be noted in earnest in 2012 when CNN ran a report about an attempted terrorist attack that many found sensationalist. The Kenyan Twittersphere responded with critique and parody under the hashtag #SomeonetellCNN. Eventually the East African foreign correspondent for CNN apologised, and the story was withdrawn. The hashtag was resurrected during the 2013 Kenyan election, as Nyabola discusses in this volume. Mohammed Ademo (2013), writing for *Columbia Journalism Review*, discuses the impact of this technology:

> [W]hat's new is social media's role in empowering Africans to own the narrative and protest against what they saw as stereotypical coverage of their stories ... as more Africans start to use social media, it is playing an increasingly important role in allowing them to partake in conversations about their future, and to protest unfair representations.

Alongside innovations in technology, changes in the humanitarian sector and geo-political landscape have also had important implications for Africa's media image. Historically much of the international reporting of Africa has been through the focus of aid and development. Just as the tropes for framing Africa have frequently been through disaster coverage – stories of war, famine, and crisis – so what has followed from that is the emphasis in reporting upon how *Western actors* are *responding* and *reacting*, usually through some kind of aid or related intervention. Allied to this is the increasing role that NGOs and large aid agencies have themselves come to play in storytelling (Franks 2010). Sometimes this manifests itself through a close involvement with journalists seeking to report, from practical assistance with transport or security to well-informed local knowledge and the provision of obliging interviewees for media outlets. Reporting with the assistance of an aid agency is sometimes vital for news organisations, but NGOs naturally expect something in return. There have been many critiques and even satires of these complicated relationships – such as the comedian Jane Bussman's account *The Worst Date Ever, or How It Took a Comedy Writer to Expose Africa's Secret War* (Bussman 2010).

On other occasions, since the emergence of digital platforms and especially social media, the NGOs, just like many other organisations, are now able to take a direct role themselves in telling the story. This has taken a range of innovative new forms as the technological possibilities have extended and NGOs have developed increasingly sophisticated communications operations that can sometimes circumvent or at least lessen the necessity for engaging with legacy media and journalists at all.

This emergence of different voices with the flowering of citizen journalism and diverse content creation indicates how NGOs in common with others have thus found a voice through using new media. Flows of production today are in multiple directions. So on the one hand we see plenty of content produced in Africa that is then exported overseas, for example by youth culture, religious groups, or a wide variety of bloggers. And on the other hand, though similarly, the wide diaspora of Africans based elsewhere are also producing their own media (e.g. Mabweazara 2013; the chapter by Ogunyemi in this volume).

Africa and geo-politics

What economist Jim O'Neill famously termed the fast-rising BRIC countries (to become BRICS in 2010) and, later, MINT countries, signalled the rise of two booming African economies of South Africa and Nigeria. By 2012 Nigerian GDP was surpassing that of South Africa. A useful starting point in situating the African continent as an increasingly autonomous actor on the world stage (and thereby driving its own global image rather than being driven by an externally constructed one), is the growth of a substantial middle class around the continent (McKinsey 2010), even in some of those countries that are consistently ranked among the very poorest in the world. In modern malls in most African cities, for example, the scores of middle-class families who are shopping and dining make for a stark contrast to persistent urban and rural poverty.

But should the presence of a thriving – if still minority – middle class, along with indications even of reverse migration – middle-class families returning to Africa from adopted homes in North America and Europe (e.g. Okome 2014) – and a booming communication sector in many countries (especially Nigeria, Kenya, and South Africa) justify a universal "Afro-optimism", or do these forces perhaps offer a narrative of an Africa that works for them, while leaving an impoverished and often hungry majority out of the story?

Most financial flow into Africa is now no longer in development aid but in remittances from a vast, and largely thriving, diaspora (BBC 2013), and this flow is substantially facilitated by the unprecedented uptake of mobile telephony across the continent and across nearly all levels of wealth (Wakunuma-Zoer & Litho, 2009; Wasserman, 2011). That dramatic facilitation of communication in Africa enabled by mobile telephony and, increasingly, internet access, has vastly increased the potential for counter-narratives to circulate in Africa, and for journalists to access a broader story (e.g. Akinfemisoye 2013).

As we highlighted earlier, a longstanding trope of external media coverage of Africa is that of a continent beset by conflict. Indeed, in the two decades since the first *Africa's Media Image* a genocide engulfed Rwanda, with nearly 800,000 murders occurring over the course of a few months in 1994. The world paid little attention to that unfathomable tragedy, which contributed significantly to an even greater tragedy unfolding over a longer period in the civil wars of the Democratic Republic of Congo, Africa's fourth most populous country. There, the direct and indirect effects of war have claimed as many as several million lives (although counts vary widely). Those wars also resulted in an epidemic of rape, which itself has increasingly become a controversy in assessments of Western reporting, with some suggesting that this once-neglected tragedy came eventually to dominate the external image of the DRC (Buss 2014; Seay 2011).

But DRC's wars have also been fuelled by the demand for mineral resources (Prunier 2008). While many critiques of the telling of Africa's story highlight the propensity of Western editors to prefer stories of violence, few journalists dug deeply into Central African conflict. Several who have done so appear in this volume: Wrong, Sundaram, and French. That ongoing search for wealth in Africa by those from outside problematises the counter-narrative of an increasingly autonomous continent free of external shackles. In particular, the vast extraction of wealth from Africa by non-African corporate and state entities – with little evidence of resulting prosperity for most Africans – strikes many as a continuation of the imperial project, a neo-imperialism, as Fuchs (2010) argues, which is substantially sustained by the contemporary corporate transnational media.

Imperial processes are certainly underway in contemporary Africa, as some of the authors in this volume address. But the interpretation of such processes remains highly contentious. Are these evolving foreign interventions exploitative or cooperative, and does a discourse of neo-imperialism itself support a neo-colonial media image of Africa as a continent and one fifth of the world's population incapable of autonomy? Struggles for resources and political influence in Africa do continue to be significantly driven by external forces, whether through the shady affiliations to Middle Eastern extremist groups of violent non-state organisations in Somalia and northern Nigeria, or through the investments of international corporations in African labour, resources, consumer markets, and increasingly vast tracts of land (Hall 2013). At the time of writing, Europe is reluctantly taking a new interest in Africa in response to the ever-increasing and desperate migration of thousands of the poorest Africans to Europe as a response to poverty, political repression, and environmental change.

Africa's Media Image: a new version

In compiling this collection, the editors have organised the book around four complementary thematic parts. Like Beverly Hawk's original *Africa's Media Image*, there is a blend of recent and innovative academic research, combined with shorter commentary essays, from a range of journalists and writers who are all involved in some aspect of the reporting and production of news about Africa to international audiences. Each of the four parts features a combination of these two types of contribution.

The opening section is focused around how Africa is portrayed today in the international media. In each of the chapters the author addresses the way that contemporary media coverage seeks to frame the audience's understanding of Africa. As Scott notes, many scholarly studies of Africa-related news content have been based on small samples, and they have disproportionately focused on elite news outlets, such as *The New York Times*, as well as high-profile events (most notably, violent conflict in Darfur and Rwanda). In addition, many studies do not include temporal or regional comparisons, and so struggle to place their findings in context and interpret them. Problematically, researchers have often drawn on the results of this limited research to reach generalised conclusions about "the news coverage of Africa". In this collection we offer a wider range of research that covers more than the same handful of sources and demonstrates that in the 21st century there are many different versions of news out of Africa.

Alongside traditional content analyses of the coverage, this opening part includes more discursive discussion from Stijn Joye contrasting the way that news about Africa is domesticated for European audiences, while a chapter from Ola Ogunyemi reflects upon the way that the media reporting on Africa engages with diaspora audiences based abroad. But there are also commentaries criticising the record of mainstream media, including a contribution from Howard French, who in 2015 organised an open letter to CBS signed by 200 interested writers and experts critiquing the US media framing of Africa. Over the years many commentators have raised their voice in opposition to the way Africa is framed for international audiences. In some ways these are echoes of the same arguments first put forward by Edward Said in *Orientalism* and formulated in the landmark MacBride Report (1980). In more recent years we have seen well-known interventions by writers such as Binjavanga Wainaina and Chimamanda Adichie (quoted earlier). And many others have also engaged with this debate from a range of angles: H. Nanjala Nyabola (2014) and Laura Seay (2012), for example, are both highly critical of Western reporting; Patrick Gathara (2014) responds to argue that frequently indigenous African reporting about the continent does not offer a better analysis and is liable to make similar errors. We have included in this collection a piece from journalist and writer Michela Wrong, who has engaged with this topic on several occasions. Here she takes a different tack and criticises those complaining about Western journalists, emphasizing the difficulties that they might encounter in reporting stories from Africa. Anthropologist Francis Nyamnjoh's chapter invites us to take a further step back to explore what constitutes "authentic" description, whether by journalist or academic researcher.

The second part of the book focuses upon the *making* of news about Africa. It includes a range of contributions by journalists and media producers who are creating today's reporting from and about Africa: Salim Amin is a television entrepreneur with multimedia interests in East Africa, Zeinab Badawi is a television presenter for the BBC's international TV service who was already writing about the problematic coverage of Africa in 1986, while Anjun Sundaram and H. Nanjala Nyabola are both digital natives with extensive networks across Africa. There are other contributions, by researchers Toussaint Nothias and Paolo Vicente, that discuss the authors' extensive investigations of the contemporary reporters and correspondents who cover Africa for the international media. As a counterpoint to this, there are other chapters that reflect upon the making of news – and, more broadly, a new "image" of Africa – via emerging digital and social media platforms, from Rachel Flamenbaum, who focuses upon Ghana, and from Danielle Becker, whose research is about Instagram in South Africa.

In Part III, we have covered the changing way that stories of aid and development have been used as a focus in the reporting on Africa. Although critics may have reservations about this, NGOs, with their stake in the "development industry", remain significant players in African economies, and in some cases they are specifically involved in the way news is reported. Eliza Anyangwe, formerly of the Guardian Development Network and now with CNN, criticises the recurring emphasis upon the aid narrative and the way that distorts much reporting. Nicklas Poulsen Viki is himself part of an innovative NGO based in Norway called "Radiatoraid", which has used imaginative ways to change the familiar "white saviour/helpless black victim" story of Africa by turning it around through the production of humorous "counter-narratives". Heba Aly has been involved in the dissemination of "humanitarian news" and presents some observations on how this has developed, with respect to news about Africa. Three US-based writers tackle the issues raised in the diverse media representation of an ambitious development scheme – the Millennium Village Project – which was introduced in 2004 across ten sub-Saharan countries. Kate Wright analyses in detail the complicated relationship between an NGO and the promotion of a news story in Kenya, while Ludek Stavinoha focuses on the reporting of the AIDS pandemic in Africa.

The final part focuses upon the media representation of both political and geo-political forces within Africa. Several chapters examine how in a changing global environment the competing interests at a regional, national, and international level, attempting to gain influence in the continent, have engaged with media interests. Three of the chapters in this section are particularly concerned with contrasting dimensions of the emerging role of China in Africa, with specific reference to the way that the Chinese media have invested in and reported news about Africa. Another chapter presents research from Nigeria about the media strategies of the Boko Haram group, one of a growing number of non-state political actors able to operate across national borders. In contrast to this, there is a chapter examining the role of the Nigerian film industry as an influential global player that is increasingly significant in shaping the global image of Africa.

It is over twenty years since the first collection of *Africa's Media Image* (Hawk 1992) was published, and stories about both Africa and the media have changed enormously in that period. Together these four parts, comprising 28 chapters, offer a huge range of perspectives, analyses, and opinions on the media representation of Africa in the 21st century. They present the views of well-established scholars as well as emerging researchers, combined with news producers and participants directly involved in the reporting of Africa on a range of media platforms. The collection also includes writers who are knowledgeable about a wide diversity of locations across the continent and who represent multiple viewpoints.

The aim of this collection is to contribute to an updating of our understanding of the way that news about Africa for international audiences is made and how it is framed. In a world of political and technological upheavals, where newsmaking itself has undergone a revolution, we hope that this book will provide a much-needed reassessment and reinterpretation of how Africa's media image is produced and interpreted in the digital age. Our intention is to inspire yet further research and analysis and indeed to act as a starting point for a second wave of reflection and writing about how the African continent and people of Africa are reported and represented to the world.

Note

1 Interview with C. Paterson, November 1995.

Bibliography

Ademo, M. (2013) "In Kenya's election, reporting what's there, not what's assumed", *Columbia Journalism Review*, 6 March.

Adichie, C. N. (2009) "The danger of a single story", TED Talk, available at https://www.ted.com/talks/chimamanda_adichie_the_danger_of_a_single_story?language=en [accessed 25/11/2015].

Akinfemisoye, M. O. (2013) "Challenging hegemonic media practices: of 'alternative' media and Nigeria's democracy", *Ecquid Novi: African Journalism Studies*, 34(1): 7–20.

Bach, D. (2013) "Africa in international relations: the frontier as concept and metaphor", *South African Journal of International Affairs*, 20(1): 2–22.

Baker, P. & Santora, M. (2015) "Obama in Kenya: an upbeat tone, but notes of discord, too", *New York Times*, 25 July.

BBC (2013) "Africans' remittances outweigh Western aid", 17 April, available at http://www.bbc.co.uk/news/world-africa-22169474 [accessed 09/03/2016].

Borowski, R. (2012) "Young people's perceptions of Africa", *Race Equality Teaching*, 30(3): 24–27.

Boyd-Barrett, O. & Rantanen, T. (2001) "News agency foreign correspondents", in J. Tunstall (ed.), *Media Occupations and Professions: A Reader*, Oxford: Oxford University Press.

Brookes, H. (1995) "'Suit, tie and a touch of juju' – the ideological construction of Africa: a critical discourse analysis of news on Africa in the British press", *Discourse and Society*, 6(4): 461–494.

Bunce, M. (2013) *Reporting from "the field": foreign correspondents and the international news coverage of East Africa*, unpublished PhD thesis, University of Oxford, Oxford.

Bunce, M. (2015) "International news and the image of Africa: new storytellers, new narratives?", in J. Gallagher (ed.), *The Image of Africa: Creation, Negotiation and Subversion*, Manchester: Manchester University Press.

Buss, D. (2014) "Seeing sexual violence in conflict and post-conflict societies", in D. Buss, J. Lebert, B. Rutherford, D. Sharkey, and O. Abinam (eds.), *Sexual Violence in Conflict and Post-Conflict Societies: International Agendas and African Contexts*, London: Routledge.

Bussman, J. (2010) *The Worst Date Ever, or How It Took a Comedy Writer to Expose Africa's Secret War*, London: Pan.

Carroll, J. (2007) "Foreign news coverage: the US media's undervalued asset", working paper, 2007/1, Cambridge, MA: Joan Shorenstein Center on the Press, Politics and Public Policy, Harvard University.

Crawford, N. (1996) "Imag(in)ing Africa", *The International Journal of Press/Politics*, 1(2): 30–44.

De B'Béri, B. E. & Louw, E. (2011) "Special issue: the Afropessimism phenomenon", *Critical Arts*, 25: 335–466.

Fair, J. E. (1993) "War, famine, and poverty: race in the construction of Africa's media image", *Journal of Communication Inquiry*, 17: 5–22.

Fair, J. E. & Parks, L. (2001) "Africans on camera: television news coverage and aerial imaging of Rwandan genocide", *Africa Today*, 48(2): 34–57.

Figenschou, T. U. (2010) "A voice for the voiceless? A quantitative content analysis of Al-Jazeera English's flagship news", *Global Media and Communication*, 6(1): 85–107.

Franks, S. (2010) "The neglect of Africa and the power of aid", *International Communication Gazette*, 72(1): 71–84.

Fuchs, C. (2010) "New imperialism information and media imperialism?", *Global Media and Communication*, 6(1): 33–60.

Gathara, P. (2014) "If Western journalists get Africa wrong, who gets it right?", at http://www.theguardian.com/world/2014/jan/24/africa-media-who-gets-right [accessed 09/03/2016].

Hall, R. (2013) "Farming and food in Africa and the mounting battle over land, water and resource rights", *GREAT Insights*, 3(1), December 2013 – January 2014.

Hawk, B. (ed.) (1992) *Africa's Media Image*, New York: Praeger.

Hunter-Gault, C. (2006) *New News Out of Africa: Uncovering Africa's Renaissance*, Oxford: Oxford University Press.

International Exchange on Communication and Development between Africa and Europe (1988) *The Image of Africa* (final report), Rome.

Jones, B. (2014) "Of sunsets, savagery and soccer: framing Africa during the final days of the 2010 World Cup", in T. Chari and M. Namo (eds.) (2014), *African Football, Identity Politics and Global Media Narratives: The Legacy of the FIFA 2010 World Cup*, London: Palgrave Macmillan.

Keane, F. (2004) "Trapped in a time warped narrative", *Neiman Reports*, Fall.

Kleinman, A. & Kleinman, J. (1996) "The appeal of experience; the dismay of images: cultural appropriations of suffering in our times", *Daedalus*, 125(1): 1–24.

Kuper, A. & Kuper, J. (2001) "Serving the new democracy: must the media 'speak softly'? Learning from South Africa", *International Journal of Public Opinion Research*, 13(4): 355–376.

Mabweazara, H. M. (2013) "'Pirate' radio, convergence and reception in Zimbabwe", *Telematics and Informatics*, 30(3): 232–241.

Mahajan, V. (2009) *Africa Rising: How 900 Million African Consumers Offer More Than You Think*, Upper Saddle River, NJ: Pearson Education.

Mbembe, J. A. (2001) *On the Postcolony*, London: University of California Press.

McBride, S. (1980) *One World, Many Voices*, Paris: UNESCO.

McKinsey (2010) *Lions on the Move: The Progress and Potential of African Economies*, McKinsey Global Institute, June.

Momoh, A. (2003) "Does Pan-Africanism have a future in Africa? In search of the ideational basis of Afro-pessimism", *African Journal of Political Science*, 8: 31–57.

Mudimbe, V. Y. (1988) *The Invention of Africa: Gnosis, Philosophy and the Order of Knowledge*, Indianapolis, IN: Indiana University Press.

Nothias, T. (2014) "'Rising', 'hopeful', 'new': visualizing Africa in the age of globalization", *Visual Communication*, 13(3): 323–339.

Nyabola, N. (2014) "Why do Western media get Africa wrong?", at http://www.aljazeera.com/indepth/opinion/2014/01/why-do-western-media-get-africa-wrong-20141152641935954.html?utm=from_old_mobile [accessed 09/03/2016].

Ojo, T. (2014) "Africa in the Canadian media: the *Globe and Mail*'s coverage of Africa from 2003 to 2012", *Ecquid Novi: African Journalism Studies*, 35(1): 43–57.

Okome, M. O. (2014) "Thinking about return migration to Africa: theories, praxes, general tendencies & African particularities", *Ìrìnkèrindò: A Journal of African Migration*, 7(June): 1–22.

Olopade, D. (2014) *The Bright Continent*, New York: Houghton Mifflin Harcourt.

Paterson, C. (2011) *The International Television News Agencies: The World from London*, New York: Peter Lang.

Prunier, G. (2008) *Africa's World War: Congo, the Rwandan Genocide, and the Making of a Continental Catastrophe*, New York: Oxford University Press.

Said, E. (1978) *Orientalism*, New York: Vintage Books.

Schorr, V. (2011) "Economics of Afro-pessimism: the economics of perception in African Foreign Direct Investment", *Nokoko*, 2, Fall, Institute of African Studies, Carleton University.

Seay, L. (2011) "Do we have the Congo rape crisis all wrong?", *The Atlantic*, 24 May, at http://www.theatlantic.com/international/archive/2011/05/do-we-have-the-congo-rape-crisis-all-wrong/239328/ [accessed 09/03/2016].

Seay, L. (2012) "How not to write about Africa", *Foreign Policy*, 25 April.

Spivak, G. & Guha, R. (eds.) (1988) *Selected Subaltern Studies*, Foreword by Edward Said, Oxford: Oxford University Press.

Utley, G. (1997) "The shrinking of foreign news: from broadcast to narrowcast", *Foreign Affairs*, 76(2): 2–10.

Wainaina, B. (2005) "How to write about Africa", *Granta*, 92: 91–95.

Wakunuma-Zoer, K. J. & Litho, P. K. (2009) "ICTization beyond urban male elites: issues of gender equality and empowerment", in O. F. Mudhai, W. J. Tettey, and F. Banda (eds.), *African Media and the Digital Public Sphere*, New York: Palgrave Macmillan.

Wasserman, H. (2011) "Mobile phones, popular media, and everyday African democracy: transmissions and transgressions", *Popular Communication*, 9(2): 146–158.

Part I

Framing Africa

The international news coverage of Africa

Beyond the "single story"

Mel Bunce

In 1994, Christopher Hitchens visited sub-Saharan Africa and wrote a grim report about the continent:

> [R]un the rule across Africa and see if you can find, anywhere in the entire foresaken continent, anything like a success story. ... The famines, plagues, and epidemics are, from old-style locusts to ultra-modern aids, the most sweeping and devastating. ... Human life is at its nastiest, most brutish, and shortest. (*Vanity Fair*, December 1994)

Such dramatic and negative reporting on Africa was not unusual for the period. A large body of research has concluded that the international news coverage of sub-Saharan Africa in the 1990s was sporadic, simplistic, racist, and overwhelmingly negative in its subject matter and tone (e.g. Hawk 1992). Academics have described this negative coverage as a form of "Afro-pessimism", as it suggests that Africa has little or no prospect of positive developments (Schmidt & Garrett 2011: 423; Evans 2011: 400; De B'Béri and Louw 2011). In her popular TED Talk, Chimamanda Ngozi Adichie noted the danger of this negative, "single story" of Africa: "The problem with stereotypes is not that they are untrue, but that they are incomplete. They make one story become the only story" (Adichie 2009).

In the early 2010s, however, the international media started to tell new stories about sub-Saharan Africa. Leading outlets like *The Economist* published cover stories about an economically vibrant "Rising Africa" with burgeoning consumption, investment opportunities, and technological innovation. The new, positive narrative was quickly adopted by international think tanks and diaspora groups; as Michela Wrong (2015) writes, "'Africa Rising' has become the obligatory catch phrase applied to the continent. ... It is fashionable, these days, to be upbeat about Africa."

This seemingly seismic shift in the continent's meta-narrative has been widely noted and discussed in the media, online fora, and conferences – but it has not been systematically researched. We know there have been a handful of high-profile stories that are distinctive and more positive in tone than historical representations of Africa (see e.g. Nothias 2014). But we do not know if these stories are now commonplace in mainstream day-to-day coverage, or if they remain the exception.

This chapter contributes to our knowledge by presenting the results of a content analysis comparing two large samples of news content, one from the early 1990s and one from the 2010s.[1] The results find that, taken as a whole, news coverage of Africa has become significantly more positive in tone. In addition, there has been a decrease in stories that focus exclusively on humanitarian disaster, and an increase in stories about business and sport. These results suggest that we may finally be moving beyond a reductive and negative "single story" dominating the international news coverage of the continent. It is important to note, however, that these changes have not been made uniformly across the news industry. Representations of Africa in the media are diverse and multifaceted, and it is no longer possible – if it ever was – to speak of "*The* representation of Africa". Even within one publication, content can range from texts and images that are reductive and stereotypical through to those that are challenging, self-reflective, and critical.

Methods

This chapter asks whether the day-to-day international news coverage of Africa has moved beyond the Afro-pessimism that dominated reports in the 1990s. Afro-pessimism is an amorphous term, but we can understand it as referring to (at least) two different aspects of news content. First, there are stories that focus exclusively on issues or events that are unambiguously negative: for example, famine, disease, conflict, and poverty (e.g. Moeller 1999). Second, we can think of Afro-pessimism as referring to the tone in which stories are reported, and the negative evaluation of events, issues, and policy in Africa. The methods are developed to explore both of these aspects of news content.

Topic within news agency reports

The international newswires are the most important producers of day-to-day international news coverage on Africa. The "big three" – AFP, AP, and Reuters – are "the basic organizational foundations on which the international system operates", employing the majority of all foreign correspondents in the world (Williams 2011: 67). These agencies are particularly important in the African context because the vast majority of news outlets in the world do not have foreign correspondents on the continent; they rely heavily on the newswires for the raw content of news they republish (Bunce 2013).

The research examined the AFP, AP, and Reuters news coverage of eight countries: Nigeria, Ethiopia, Zaire/DRC, Tanzania, Kenya, Uganda, Ghana, and Mozambique. These are chosen as they are the eight most populous countries in sub-Saharan Africa, excluding South Africa and Sudan.[2] They also represent a range of (1) economy sizes, (2) geographic areas (East, West, South, and Central), and (3) languages (Anglophone, Francophone, Lusophone). Articles about these eight countries were collected on two days per month (the 4th and the 18th) – a total of 24 days – throughout the full calendar years of 1994 and 2013.[3] Factiva was searched for stories with a "major mention" of each country on these dates. Stories were excluded if they were fewer than 40 words long, or had more than two other countries listed in the title or first paragraph. This process resulted in a total sample of 892 articles, as seen in Table 1.1.

Each article was coded for its subject, from a list of 13 subjects (see Appendix). If an article addressed two subjects equally, both were coded. This resulted in a total data set of 1,061 subjects – 543 derived from articles published in 1994, and 518 derived from articles published in 2013. A second coder "double coded" a randomly selected 10 per cent of all the newswire articles and had an inter-coder reliability score of 0.9 (Cohen's kappa).

Tone of newspaper articles

To supplement the analysis of subjects within newswire stories, a second analysis examined the tone of articles in leading international newspapers. While news agencies provide important raw content of news, newspapers continue to play an important role framing news about Africa for audiences (Scott 2009); the headlines they select underline particular aspects of events or a story, and they place this in a wider context and provide analysis. Four newspapers were selected from different corners of the Anglophone world: *The Guardian* (UK), *The New York Times* (US),

Table 1.1 Newswire articles in sample

	1994				2013			
	AFP	AP	Reuters	Total	AFP	AP	Reuters	Total
Ethiopia	4	1	15	20	14	8	5	27
Ghana	5	0	25	30	9	5	22	36
Kenya	13	1	40	54	34	15	57	106
Mozambique	26	2	27	55	11	3	15	29
Nigeria	49	9	103	161	58	28	51	137
Tanzania	5	2	18	25	7	0	22	29
Uganda	8	1	23	32	6	7	28	41
Zaire/DROC	30	5	41	76	26	0	8	34
Total	**140**	**21**	**292**	**453**	**165**	**66**	**208**	**439**

The Globe and Mail (Canada), and *The Sydney Morning Herald* (Australia). Using the Lexis-Nexis database, these newspapers were searched for all stories containing "Africa" in the headline, in the years 1994 and 2013. Stories were excluded if: (1) they were specifically about South Africa (the goal was to explore the tone of news associated with the more general concept of "Africa"); (2) they listed two or more additional regions in their headline; (3) they comprised letters to the editor; (4) they consisted of obituaries; or (5) their total length was fewer than 40 words. This process resulted in a sample of 426 articles, as seen in Table 1.2. Each article in the sample was then coded for its overall tone, either "negative", "positive", or "mixed/neutral". A second coder "double coded" a randomly selected 10 per cent of the sample, producing an inter-coder reliability score of 0.85 (Cohen's kappa).

Limitation of methods

One limitation of the above methods was the need to reduce the time period and outlets under scrutiny in order to render the sample manageable. Whether the years 1994 and 2013 are representative of a wider "era" of reporting requires further research. However, this research design has tried to mitigate the impact of anomalous events by analysing a large sample spread over a full 12 months; canvassing a range of publications; and looking at coverage of multiple countries within sub-Saharan Africa. In addition, during the analysis of the data, events that received significant or unusual coverage were noted, and are reported in the results.

Results: topics in news agency reporting

There were many substantive changes in the international news coverage of Africa represented by the two samples (Table 1.3 and Figure 1.1). Between the 1994 and 2013 sample, there was a decrease in reporting on many of the subjects traditionally associated with Afro-pessimism – most notably, humanitarian reporting. At the same time, there was a significant increase in economic, business, and financial stories, which have been associated

Table 1.2 Newspaper articles in sample

	1994	2013	Total
Guardian	36	140	176
New York Times	42	75	117
Globe & Mail	46	43	89
Sydney Morning Herald	24	20	44
Total	**148**	**278**	**426**

Table 1.3 Subject of newswire stories[a]

Subjects	1994	2013	% change
Business	111 (20.4%)	189 (36.5%)	16.1%
Humanitarian	94 (17.3%)	10 (1.9%)	−15.4%
Domestic Politics	136 (25%)	57 (11%)	−14%
Conflict	63 (11.6%)	97 (18.7%)	7.1%
Sports	16 (2.9%)	43 (8.3%)	5.4%
Crime	32 (5.9%)	46 (8.9%)	3%
IR	55 (10.1%)	43 (8.3%)	−1.8%
Accident/Crash	14 (2.6%)	13 (2.5%)	−0.1%
Other	22 (4.1%)	20 (3.9%)	−0.2%
Total	**543**	**518**	

Note

a   Subjects with fewer than ten articles are included in "Other".

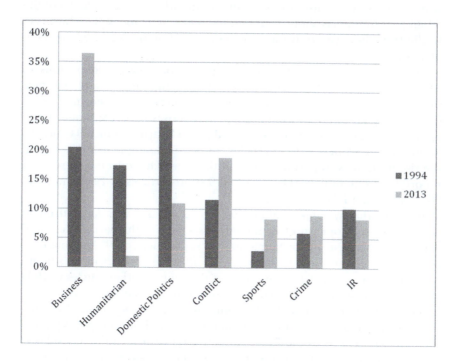

Figure 1.1 Newswire articles: subjects with biggest change

with more positive "Africa Rising" narratives. One subject bucks this trend, however: the reporting of conflict and crime, which increased between the two periods.

Business reporting is generally considered a positive form of news content, as it tends to focus on growth and business opportunities and, in this sense, may provide the "sprouts of hope" that Keane suggests have historically been missing from the international news coverage of Africa (2004: 8). The rise in business reporting was the single biggest change between the two samples. In 1994, approximately one-fifth of subjects in reports were business related (111 of 543), while in 2013, business reporting was a much higher one-third or so of all subjects (189 of 518). It is important to note that this rise in business reporting was not uniform across the news agencies, however. The biggest change – by a very large margin – took place at the Reuters newswire. In fact, the changes in business reporting at this one newswire largely explain the rise in business reporting across the total sample. In 1994, 28.9 per cent of the Reuters output was business related; in 2013, business reporting had grown enormously, and occupied a remarkable 68.4 per cent of all subjects reported by Reuters on these eight countries. The prominence of business reporting was also not consistent across the countries in the sample. In 2013, for example, 20 of the 32 subjects in reports about Tanzania (62.5 per cent) focused on business. In the DRC, however, only four articles focused on business (9.8 per cent of all subjects).

Sports reporting is also associated with more positive depictions of Africa, as it tends to depict African countries competing on a global stage on equal terms as other countries, and draws attention to "normal" everyday pursuits, far removed from humanitarian crises (Chari & Namo 2014). Sports constituted 2.9 per cent of the subjects (16 articles) in 1994 and this figure rose to 8.3 per cent (43 articles) of the total sample in 2013. As with the rise in business reporting, much of this is explained by the increase in reporting at one outlet: AFP published 9 sports articles in 1994 and 31 in 2013 (see Table 1.5).

Between the two news samples, there was also a very large drop in coverage of the topic most commonly associated with "dark Africa" and Afro-pessimism discourses: humanitarian reporting. In 1994, humanitarian stories accounted for 17.3 per cent of all subjects. In 2013, this figure was only 1.9 per cent. A large number of the humanitarian articles in 1994 came from Zaire, where journalists reported on the refugee crisis that followed the Rwandan genocide. An additional four stories about Tanzania focused on refugees from the Rwandan genocide. But even putting aside the coverage related to the Rwandan genocide (which can be considered an extreme and anomalous event), there were 33 stories on humanitarian issues in 1994, compared with only 10 in 2013. The 1994 humanitarian stories included articles on drought, famine, and disease – and they came from seven of the eight countries. The ten humanitarian stories in 2013, by contrast, addressed a much more limited range of crises: eight of the ten articles were about refugees and the remaining two were about flooding in

Mozambique. There were no news articles in the 2013 sample of 439 articles that focused on famine, drought, or disease.

Between the 1994 and 2013 samples, there was also a decline in reporting on domestic politics: it was the subject of 136 stories in 1994, and only 57 in 2013. Domestic political reporting is not obviously or necessarily associated with either positive or negative issues. However, it is worth noting that the reason for this decline was primarily a decrease in reports on corruption, oppression, strikes, and protests that would likely be considered "negative" by most readers (Table 1.4). General politics (policy announcements, cabinet reshuffles, and so on) remained relatively stable between the two periods, as did reporting on elections.

One difference in the subjects covered in 1994 and 2013 does not fit the observation that the topics within African news coverage have become more positive: there was an increase in reports on both conflict and crime. In 1994, there were 63 reports on conflict, primarily in Mozambique and Nigeria. In 2013, there were 97 reports, including stories from Nigeria, Kenya, and the Democratic Republic of Congo. The quantities of conflict reporting varied between the newswires. While AFP and AP increased their conflict reporting between 1994 and 2013, Reuters slightly decreased theirs from 10 per cent of subjects in 1994 to 9 per cent in 2013.

Results: tone of newspaper articles

The tone of newspaper articles was substantively and consistently more positive in the 2013 sample than it was in 1994. More than half (52.7 per cent) of the newspaper articles in 1994 were coded as negative. Examples included, "Hunger persists in Africa, U.S. antipoverty group says" (*Globe and Mail*, 14/10/1994) and "Africa dissolves in dusty mirage" (*Sydney Morning Herald*, 27/7/1994). In the 2013 sample, the proportion of negative articles was much lower, at 31.7 per cent.

Between the two samples, there was also a substantive rise in positive reporting: from only 10.8 per cent of stories in 1994, to 29 per cent in 2013. Positive stories touched on a range of topics including business ("In Africa,

Table 1.4 Breakdown of newswire stories on domestic politics

	1994	%	2013	%	Change
Elections	29	5.3%	25	4.8%	−0.5%
Corruption or oppression	55	10.1%	25	4.8%	−5.3%
Strikes or protests	38	7.0%	2	0.4%	−6.6%
General	14	2.6%	5	1.0%	−1.6%
Total	**136**	**25.0%**	**57**	**11.0%**	**−14.0%**

Table 1.5 Subjects within newswire stories

	1994			2013		
	AFP	AP	Reuters	AFP	AP	Reuters
Business	10 (5.9%)	0 (0%)	101 (28.9%)	16 (8.2%)	6 (7.7%)	167 (68.4%)
Dom Politics	39 (22.9%)	7 (30.4%)	90 (25.7%)	20 (10.2%)	14 (17.9%)	23 (9.4%)
Conflict	27 (15.9%)	1 (4.3%)	35 (10%)	53 (27%)	22 (28.2%)	22 (9%)
Humanitarian	39 (22.9%)	9 (39.1%)	46 (13.1%)	7 (3.6%)	2 (2.6%)	1 (0.4%)
IR	24 (14.1%)	2 (8.7%)	29 (8.3%)	22 (11.2%)	10 (12.8%)	11 (4.5%)
Crime	9 (5.3%)	2 (8.7%)	21 (6%)	26 (13.3%)	8 (10.3%)	12 (4.9%)
Sports	9 (5.3%)	0 (0%)	7 (2%)	31 (15.8%)	9 (11.5%)	3 (1.2%)
Accident	6 (3.5%)	1 (4.3%)	7 (2%)	9 (4.6%)	0 (0%)	4 (1.6%)
Other	7 (4.1%)	1 (4.3%)	14 (4%)	12 (6.1%)	7 (9%)	1 (0.4%)
Total	**170**	**23**	**350**	**196**	**78**	**244**

Blackberry finds touched on a land of growth", *Globe and Mail*, 27/11/2013); sports ("Africa's sleeping giants start to stir", *NYT*, 11/10/2013); and social and political commentary pieces, like the distinctly Australian article in the *Sydney Morning Herald* – "Africa's fair-dinkum feminism" (13/1/2013).

All the newspapers had a higher portion of positive stories in 2013 than they did in 1994 (see Table 1.6). The most dramatic transformation, however, was at *The Guardian*, where only 8 per cent of articles about Africa in 1994 were positive. In 2013, this had risen to 33 per cent. In the same period, negative articles almost halved, from 61 to 32 per cent. Remarkably, this meant that, in 2013, *The Guardian* published more positive news stories (46 in total) than negative stories (45 in total) with Africa in the headline.

The 2013 news sample was also more positive than previous studies of international news content about Africa. Schraeder and Endless (1998), for example, researched *The New York Times* between 1955 and 1995, and found that 73 per cent of stories could be categorised as presenting a negative image of African politics and society.[4] Interestingly, however, the rates of "positive" reporting in these mainstream Western newspapers were not as positive as the diaspora media content analysed by Ogunyemi (see Chapter 7 in this book). Studying the content of the magazine *The Voice*, Ogunyemi finds that 30 per cent of stories were negative, 46 per cent positive, and the

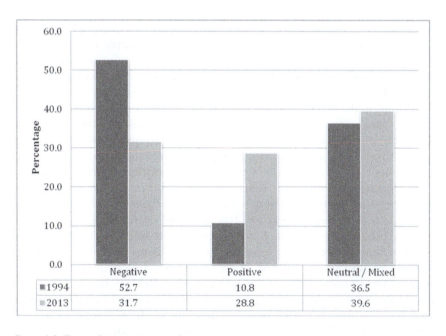

Figure 1.2 Tone of newspaper articles

Table 1.6 Tone of newspaper articles by publication

	Negative		Positive		Neutral/Mixed	
	1994	*2013*	*1994*	*2013*	*1994*	*2013*
Guardian	22 (61%)	45 (32%)	3 (8%)	46 (33%)	11 (31%)	49 (35%)
NY Times	22 (52%)	29 (39%)	5 (12%)	20 (27%)	15 (36%)	26 (36%)
G & M	25 (54%)	12 (28%)	3 (7%)	8 (19%)	18 (39%)	23 (54%)
SMH	9 (42%)	2 (10%)	5 (21%)	6 (30%)	10 (42%)	12 (60%)
Total	78 (53%)	88 (32%)	16 (11%)	80 (29%)	54 (37%)	110 (40%)

remaining 24 per cent mixed/neutral. This amounts to significantly more positive reporting, across a range of news genres, as compared with the newspaper content in the current study.

Conclusion

Many of the findings in this content analysis suggest that the international news coverage of Africa has become less negative. The analysis found that there was a decrease in reporting on humanitarian issues – stories on famine, refugee crises, and natural disasters – as well as on stories on political oppression and corruption. At the same time, there was a significant increase in business reporting and a smaller increase in sports reporting. In addition, the framing of news stories within newspapers has, across the board, become more positive. A remarkable example of this was *The Guardian* newspaper, which in 2013 published more positive stories than negative stories with Africa in the headline. This is a sharp contrast with historical research on Africa's international news coverage.

Although the tone of coverage has become more positive, and the subjects have moved away from such a focus on humanitarian issues, it is wrong to conclude that we have moved beyond Afro-pessimism to an era in which Afro-optimism and "Africa Rising" dominate the news agenda. First, the results found an increase in reporting on conflict, which now constitutes a greater proportion of reporting than it did in the sample from the 1990s. Second, the findings were not consistent across the publications. For example, while business reporting has increased overall, this was primarily because it has gone up at the Reuters newswire. In addition, while AFP was found to have increased its reporting on sport between the two samples, the other news outlets had not. These differences reflect the varying positions of the outlets in the wider media market: Reuters has increased its emphasis on business reporting in its competition with Bloomberg, while AFP has set itself the goal of becoming the leading agency for sports (Bunce 2013). This is an important reminder of the extent to which news is a socially constructed product, mediated by the markets, rather than a simple mirror of events in the world.

On 18 October 2013, AFP published two stories about Ethiopia. The first was about an astronomy research project: "Ethiopia sets sights on stars with space programme". The second focused on severe political oppression: "Ethiopian political prisoners tortured". Audiences following the news that day were exposed to two very different aspects of Ethiopia: a burgeoning research and science field, and a political crackdown. This represents neither a straightforward Afro-pessimism that scholars have suggested dominated news in the 1990s, nor an Afro-optimism that many have said has replaced it in the 2010s. This diversity asks audiences to engage with a more complicated world – one that is neither "all growth" nor "all negative".

Notes

1 This research was funded by a British Academy grant. The author is indebted to research assistant Aljosha Karim Schapals, who worked on the content analysis.
2 South Africa is excluded because it has long been regarded as "exceptional" on the continent, receiving considerably more diverse news coverage than other countries (El Zein & Cooper 1992: 136, 140); Sudan is excluded because it broke into two countries during the time period under analysis.
3 The original research design compared 1993 and 2013: a neat 20-year gap. However, a pilot study found that the Nigerian general election occupied the vast majority of that country's newswire coverage in 1993. Because Nigeria is the most reported-on country in the sample, by a considerable margin, this skewed the results, and 1994 was selected as the base year instead. In the history books, 1994 may be considered an exceptional year, as it included both the Rwandan genocide and the end of Apartheid in South Africa. However, neither of these countries was included in the newswire sample. It is also worth noting that the Rwandan genocide received relatively little media attention (Melvern 2007).
4 It is worth noting that Schraeder and Endless limited their study to the "hard news" section of *The New York Times*, which may be more inclined towards negative reporting. In addition to the hard news, the present study included all the sections of the newspapers.

References

Adichie, C. (2009) "The danger of a single story", TED Talk, at https://www.ted.com/talks/chimamanda_adichie_the_danger_of_a_single_story?language=en [accessed 25/11/2015].

Bunce, M. 2013. *Reporting from 'the field': foreign correspondents and the international news coverage of East Africa*, unpublished doctoral thesis, University of Oxford, Oxford.

Chari, T. & Namo, M. (eds) (2014) *African Football, Identity Politics and Global Media Narratives: The Legacy of the FIFA 2010 World Cup*, London: Palgrave Macmillan.

De B'Béri, B. E. & Louw, P. E. (2011) "Afropessimism: a genealogy of discourse", *Critical Arts*, 25(3): 335–346.

El Zein, H. & Cooper, A. (1992) "New York Times coverage of Africa, 1976–1990", in B. Hawk (ed.), *Africa's Media Image*, London: Praeger.

Evans, M. (2011) "Rainbow warriors: Afropessimism online", *Critical Arts*, 25(3): 397–422.

Hawk, B. (ed.) (1992) *Africa's Media Image*, New York: Praeger.

Hitchens, C. (1994) "African Gothic", *Vanity Fair*, December.

Keane, F. (2004) "Trapped in a time-warped narrative", *Nieman Reports*, 15 September.

Melvern, L. (2007) "Missing the story: the media and the Rwandan genocide", in A. Thompson (ed.), *The Media and the Rwandan Genocide*, London: Pluto.

Moeller, S. (1999) *Compassion Fatigue: How the Media Sell Disease, Famine, War and Death*. London: Routledge.

Nothias, T. (2013) "Definition and scope of Afro-pessimism: mapping the concept and its usefulness for analyzing news media coverage of Africa", *Leeds African Studies Bulletin*, 74: 54–62.

Nothias, T. (2014) "'Rising', 'hopeful', 'new': visualizing Africa in the age of globalization", *Visual Communication*, 13(3): 323–339.

Schmidt, S. & Garrett, J. (2011) "Reconstituting pessimistic discourses", *Critical Arts: South-North Cultural and Media Studies*, 25(3): 423–440.

Schraeder, P. & Endless, B. (1998) "The media and Africa: the portrayal of Africa in the 'New York Times' (1955–1995)", *Issues: A Journal of Opinion*, 26(2): 29–35.

Scott, M. (2009) "Marginalized, negative or trivial? Coverage of Africa in the UK press", *Media, Culture & Society*, 31(4): 533–557.

Williams, K. (2011) *International Journalism*, London: Sage.

Wrong, M. (2015) "'The Looting Machine', by Tom Burgis", *The New York Times*, 20 March.

Appendix: Subjects for coding

1 International Relations
2 Conflict/violent unrest
3 Domestic politics

   a   General
   b   Elections
   c   Corruption/political oppression
   d   Strikes/protests

4 Accident/crash
5 Crime
6 Business, finance, investment
7 Culture/media/arts
8 Environment/wildlife
9 Travel/tourism
10 Sports
11 Humanitarian crises
12 Development
13 Other

Chapter 2

Media perspectives
In defence of Western journalists in Africa[1]

Michela Wrong

A few years ago, baffled by unfolding events in Darfur, I went to listen to an academic speak at London's Frontline Club. A recognised expert on Sudan, he began by decrying the Western media's simplistic portrayal of Khartoum-supported "Arab" raiders driving "black African" farmers off their land. "It's a lot more complicated than that," he said, calling for a more nuanced, multilayered analysis.

After an hour and a half of contextualisation and qualification, I still had no answer to the questions that had prompted me to buy a ticket: "Why is this happening?", "What are the various players' motives?", and "What can be done to stop the killing?" Expressions in the audience suggested I wasn't alone. If there was anyone from the Foreign Office or Ministry of Defence there, hoping to glean tips for policy recommendations, they must have left frustrated.

I was reminded of that evening reading an article headlined "Why do we continually misunderstand conflict in Africa?" by Dr Lucy Hovil (2014), a researcher at the International Refugee Rights Initiative. It came hard on the heels of "Why do Western media get Africa wrong?", penned by Nanjala Nyabola (2014), based at the Harvard Law School.

The two women separately took issue with media coverage of events in the Central African Republic, where reporters have spoken of "sectarian" clashes between Christian and Muslims, and South Sudan, where the media has highlighted the "ethnic" form recent violence has taken.

Hovil argues that "reductive" interpretations of conflict lead to doomed peace formulas based on simplistic diagnoses of problems. Nyabola is more interested in language, arguing that it is impossible for a Western reporter who only speaks English to capture the essence of what it means to be a multilingual, multi-identity South Sudanese in war. "Africa just isn't being heard right."

These are two fine, thought-provoking articles. It's never a bad thing for journalists parachuting into unfamiliar war zones to be reminded to keep minds open, assumptions on a tight leash, and to faithfully record what people on the ground actually say, rather than are expected to say. Many of us will have crossed paths with that reporter who writes most of his articles before the wheels of the plane touch down.

Yet the essays triggered a surge of impatience on my part. Articles attacking the Western media's one-dimensional coverage have become almost as obligatory a part of African conflicts as stalemated peace talks and UN funding appeals. Their writers usually just skirt shy of accusing the journalists concerned of racism, but that lacuna is helpfully filled by readers in the "Comments" section.

There's surely an element of the Straw Man argument about these pieces. To put it bluntly, just how stupid do these writers think readers are? Most of us can grasp the notion that not every German was a Nazi in WW2 and not every Frenchman joined the Resistance. We can also guess that Northern Ireland's Troubles were more than purely religious in nature and that Yugoslavia's Civil War can't be boiled down to Serbs versus Croats/Bosnians. We encounter "one-dimensional" references to these conflicts every day, but we grasp the notion that their true causes were rich and various.

I also wonder if a certain Panglossian wishful thinking is at play. Slap the messenger, because the message itself can be so distasteful. The truth is that in many conflicts, the causes of the violence may well be myriad and complex – aren't they always? – but the way in which those tensions find expression once demagogic politicians and their propagandists get to work can be crude in the extreme. In South Sudan, soldiers loyal to Salva Kiir decided which men to drag from their homes and shoot by asking "What is your name?" in Dinka, a language alien to the Nuer (AFP, 2013). In Rwanda in 1994, the killers manning the road blocks worked on the basis of identity cards distinguishing Tutsis from Hutus. Not much nuance there.

The academics seem to have little idea of how journalists actually work. I'm guessing that neither Lucy Hovil nor Nanjala Nyabola writes their articles bouncing around in the back of an army jeep, jolting between poorly defined battle zones, worrying about sand in their laptops, a dodgy satellite connection that might make filing impossible, and driving over a landmine.

Nor do they face the daily pressure to "feed the beast" – the insatiable news beast – with not just articles but blogspots, audio and video footage for their employers' websites. Their pieces are probably written somewhere quieter, more attuned to reflection and analysis, and if they go into greater depth and subtlety, so they damn well should.

Academics enjoy word counts reporters can only dream about. Web-based news should in theory have loosened up space, but in practice it rarely does, because editors know there's a limit to how much information a general reader can absorb. Journalists use "reductive" definitions because they don't have the luxury of space. If you want to get any fresh information in your 600-word piece about modern-day Rwanda, then yes, you are going to summarise the 1994 genocide in one paragraph. You have to.

More fundamentally, the writers seem to have lost sight of the definition of news, which aims to convey distant events to a non-specialist audience as succinctly as possible. That's a lot easier to say than do.

My Reuters training editor, trying to drum the principle of the concise "intro" into pup reporters (it must answer six questions: Who, What, When, Where, Why, and How), told us to imagine we were standing on an old-fashioned Routemaster London bus, open at the rear. The bus is drawing away from the kerb and a friend on the pavement asks what's going on. You have seconds to shout a précis. It's a good exercise – try it. What you'll discover is how this form of obligatory shorthand strips away nuance. A screamed "It's a lot more complicated than that", won't really do.

Which brings me to back to the lost opportunity of that lecture on Darfur. A lot of academic writing excels at – even prides itself upon – a type of analysis either so intimately focused or carefully qualified that it confounds rather than clarifies. At the glimpse of a possible conclusion, this type of writer blushes and stammers, refusing on principle to answer the basic question put by the ordinary reader, as opposed to the diplomatic envoy or UN peace negotiator: "What's going on?" Cover every angle, and you end up with an Escher staircase leading nowhere.

In targeting reporters who spend much of their professional lives badgering their editors to make room for longer – and yes, more nuanced – articles, the academics are essentially misdirecting their fire. It should not have escaped their notice that the sources of reliable, independent foreign news are not expanding to keep pace with modern technology. Al Jazeera's arrival had a bracing impact, but foreign coverage of African hotspots remains dominated by a few international news agencies, with African newspapers and broadcasters making no real attempt to fill the space left by cash-strapped Western news outlets. That's not healthy. Novelist Chimamanda Adichie's warning about the dangers of "the single story" applies to reporting, too.

As it is, there's a strong element of self-congratulation to the academics' lament. "Why, oh why, aren't journalists just like us?" they wail. To which the answer would be: "We don't have time, we don't have space, and anyway, that's why you guys exist, remember?"

We're just not in the same line of business, so while carping about each other's performances certainly sheds interesting light on our respective industries' insecurities, it is unlikely to alter the way any of us write.

Note

1   A version of this article was published on the African Arguments website on 21 February 2014.

References

AFP (2013) "Witnesses recount massacre, murders and rape in South Sudan", *AFP*, 24 December.

Hovil, L. (2014) "Why do we continually misunderstand conflict in Africa?", *African Arguments*, 10 February.

Nyabola, N. (2014) "Why do the Western media get Africa wrong?", *Al Jazeera*, 2 January.

Chapter 3

Reporting and writing Africa in a world of unequal encounters

Francis B. Nyamnjoh

Both in journalism and in academia it is commonplace to seek to identify with the underdog. Journalists and academics may be pro-establishment in how they put reality together, but they are uncomfortable with perceptions of them as simply doing the master's bidding. They are more comfortable claiming to be voicing the voiceless and empowering the powerless.

Beyond this reality or fantasy of a commitment to the underdogs, what academics and journalists do have in common are traditions of thought and practice that privilege reproduction over creativity and innovation. This is because they are human and social beings. Their sociality derives from generalised relationships and practices that are internalised and reproduced in their particular contexts of practice over time, passed down from one generation to another of journalist or academic, and occasionally activated to new degrees of potency by technological innovations.

Their credentials as journalists or academics, and their disciplinary and professional practices, are not entirely inborn or just the result of training and education. They come from years of schooled repetitiveness and discipline to the point of synchrony between what we might call their first and second natures. When they speak, write, and think, they do so in particular ways that are shaped not only by their biological and psychological dispositions, but also, and often more importantly, by histories of their sociological and anthropological realities. Their thoughts and practices are the products of both nature and nurture over time. This is what links the journalist and the academic, beyond real or vacuous claims of siding with the underdog.

This commonality is there even when the journalist might envy the academic for enjoying "word counts reporters can only dream about", or seek to explain journalists' resort to reductionism with their lack of "the luxury of space" (from the chapter by Michela Wrong, in this book, originally on africanarguments.org). The commonality is there even when academics might seek to distinguish and distance themselves from journalists with claims of being more empirically grounded and theoretically sophisticated in how they go about making sense of social phenomena. Indeed, it is because of this commonality that technological advances, however potentially revolutionary, often end up thoroughly domesticated, harnessed, or appropriated to reproduce skewed economic, cultural, social, and political power relations among individuals and social categories, among states and citizens, and among states and regions of the world. Be it in journalism or in academia, nuance is not something that comes naturally to a world of binary oppositions, exclusionary logics of belonging, and zero-sum games.

Sociologically, given their social backgrounds (racial, class, ethnic, gender, generational, etc.), upbringing, and the cultural assumptions that have become second nature to journalists and academics from particular regions of the world, it is illusory or delusory to expect a journalist to cover a news story or an academic to write about a phenomenon or an issue in a manner that is objectively universally satisfactorily appealing to all and sundry. If the aim of news is "to convey distant events to a non-specialist audience as succinctly as possible" (Wrong, this volume), such an audience has got to share the same social background, cultural and value systems, worldviews, and basic assumptions about being human with the reporter for this report to be consumed without the need to resort to correctives such as salt, pepper, and sugar. The same could be said of any academic and what they write.

Indeed, a journalist accused of simplistic, reductionist reporting on Africa would be thrilled to know that he or she has many partners in crime in the academy (Nyamnjoh, 2004, 2012a, 2012b). Driven by political correctness, a sense of business as usual, or an age-old tradition of seeing and relating to others in terms of hierarchies, we academics are not that different from journalists whom we have the habit of accusing of a tendency to caricature and misrepresent reality. Recently, I found myself writing essays such as "Blinded by sight" (2012a) and "Beyond an evangelising public anthropology" (2015) to make exactly this point in relation to how we anthropologists, who loathe being likened to journalists, research and write about those we study in Africa. Journalist or academic, our problem in representation is the constant challenge posed by social reality to its chroniclers and students. How meaningfully does one chronicle or write about a complex world of intricate entanglements that is constantly on the move? How does one capture and cage sensibly and sensitively a world in which there is as much sense in people and their actions as there is madness? How does one recognise and provide for there being much more to people and things than meets the perceptive faculties of even the most sympathetic journalists and academics?

If journalism and scholarship are in general challenging, they are particularly challenging with regard to Africa and African realities. As a victim of stereotypical and evolutionary representations in the popular imagination, literature, and scholarship of the dominant West, and as a continent that continues to suffer negatively from unequal encounters with the West and other regions of the world, Africa and Africans are particularly vulnerable to being misrepresented and caricatured with impunity (Nyamnjoh 2004, 2012a, 2012b). A classic illustration of literature inspired by evolutionary racial theories in the form of a novel is Joseph Conrad's *Heart of Darkness*, first published in 1899. This seminal work has inspired writers right into the 21st century, including Nobel Prize-winning novelists such as V. S. Naipaul, whose *A Bend in the River* offers compelling reasons why Africans are condemned to be "nothing" unless they "trample" and "crush" the past – which "doesn't exist in real life" but in the "mind alone" (Naipaul 1979: 20) – by breaking "free from primitive ties to a doomed continent" with little more than "bush" to offer civilisation (Achebe 2000: 89–90). It is Joseph Conrad's reluctance to credit Africans with any humanity that seems to have appealed the most to writers seeking to justify the inequalities, contradictions, and inhumanities of their own societies. Whatever you do, however animalistic or immoral you get, you cannot fall lower than the abysmal freak creatures that inhabit the Dark Continent. Not even Hitler and his excesses are thought to have surpassed the gruesome capacities of the Heart of Darkness to surprise the world with repulsive novelties: *semper aliquid novi ex Africa* (there is always something [negatively] new out of Africa). And Conrad was at his cynical best when he denied Africans humanity: "Well, you know, that was the worst of it – this suspicion of their not being inhuman" (Conrad 1995: 91). To those who have retorted that *Heart of Darkness* is "just a work of fiction, and in any case, Conrad was highly critical of Western imperialism!", it is worth recalling that intended meanings do not foreclose unintended outcomes, as to some Conrad's "Heart of Darkness ... reproduces the imperialism which it overtly condemns" (Lyon 1995: xxxvii).

For journalists and academics groomed in institutions and societies in which these stereotypical representations of Africa are widespread or swept under the carpet in the name of political correctness, it is difficult to extricate oneself enough to cultivate the sensitivities and sensibilities necessary to report and write about Africa the way Africans would. No amount of evangelical commitment to saving souls in Africa can magically convert committed academics and journalists from Saul to Paul when we are dealing with the worlds we embody and not merely with our rationalisations or dreams of a better world for all. To own up to this beyond rhetoric is to acknowledge a challenge that requires careful thinking-through for lasting solutions.

As I argue in "Potted plants in greenhouses" (Nyamnjoh 2012b), to call for African perspectives is not synonymous with claiming that anyone who passes for an African would necessarily report or write about Africa and African issues in a manner free of stereotypes or misrepresentations. What it calls for, rather, is the imperative to recognise a plurality of voices and perspectives sensitive to the palates of social categories configured around factors such as race, place, class, gender, and generation, such that no single perspective enjoys an exclusive prerogative of (mis)representing Africa, consciously or inadvertently. This is only proper, since African identities, like identities elsewhere, are a permanent work in progress. Stereotypes and evolutionism aside, Africa and Africans are as complex and intricate as the West and Westerners, and their identities no less the result of processes of becoming, best understood as flexible, fluid, and full of ellipses – an unfinished and unfinishable story.

Many Africans who can read and write the languages of Western colonialism in Africa are uncomfortable with what they perceive as repeated indifference to their sensitivities and sensibilities in how they are chronicled and written about, especially by Western journalists and academics. This is a running theme among African writers, from whom one could learn more about the nuanced complexities of being African than one would from academics who often are either narrowly psychologistic and micro-sociological in their categories of binary oppositions, or are drowned in unsubstantiated macro-generalisations.

Chinua Achebe has contributed in challenging stereotypical and evolutionary representations of Africans in European literature (Okolo 2007). Achebe is renowned for declaring that, "until the lions [prey] produce their own historian, the story of the hunt will glorify only the hunter" (Achebe 2000: 73). It is Achebe's conviction that Africa, like Cecil the lion, could tell its own story about its encounters with the rest of the world in its own voice and style and not necessarily in the zero-sum manner of the hunter, if it were able to survive the hunt. To those overly eager to proliferate the world with their monologues and single stories, Achebe reminds them that "every community has enough firewood in its own forests for all the cooking it needs to do" (2000: 7) and "no man should enter his house through another man's gate" (2000: 17). As one of his best-known literary protégés, Chimamanda Ngozi Adichie, puts it, it is from reading Chinua Achebe's books that "I realised that people like me, girls with skin the colour of chocolate, whose kinky hair could not form ponytails, could also exist in literature" (*Economist* 2013). Adichie's creative and highly political literary works – especially her talk "Danger of a single story" (2009a), short story "The headstrong historian" (2009b), and novel *Americanah* (2013) – are excellent examples of the nuanced multivocality needed in representing the complexity of identities forged from the navigation and negotiation of myriad encounters by Africans in and out of the continent.

To report or write meaningfully on Africa is to recognise that being African is claimed and denied with expediency. While all claims and denials may be founded, not every claim is informed by the same considerations. If being and becoming African were compared with shopping at a supermarket, one could argue that some are flexible in what they put into their shopping baskets while others are picky. And some have products thrust down their consumer palates. I am particularly interested in how being African is claimed and denied in history, socio-anthropologically and politically, and, above all, represented by African journalists and writers conscious of the nuanced complexities of their own existence.

Those who report or write about Africa, may draw inspiration from the growing body of predicament-oriented literature sensitive to African humanity and to the nuanced complexities of being African as an open-ended pursuit. In this regard, Achebe invites chroniclers and scholars of Africa to bear in mind that, "The world is like a Mask dancing. If you want to see it well you do not stand in one place" (Achebe 1964: 46). If Africa is like a mask in motion, to report or write about it well, one must not be confined to one's practised ways. Improvisation and reaching out to the unfamiliar are in order and encouraged. This might require collaboration and co-production between outsider and insider, non-African and African journalists and academics. Journalists and academics interested in more representative reporting and scholarship on Africa would do well to enter into conversations and co-productions with African writers and storytellers.

References

Achebe, C. (1964) *Arrow of God*, Oxford: Heinemann (African Writers Series).

Achebe, C. (2000) *Home and Exile*, New York: Anchor Books.

Adichie, C. N. (2009a) "The danger of a single story", TED Talk, at www.ted.com/talks/lang/eng/chimamanda_adichie_the_danger_of_a_single_story.html [accessed 14/08/2015].

Adichie, C. N. (2009b) "The headstrong historian", in *The Thing Around Your Neck*, London: Fourth Estate.

Adichie, C. N. (2013) *Americanah*, London: Fourth Estate.

Conrad, J. (1995) "Heart of Darkness", in J. Lyon (ed.), *Joseph Conrad: Youth, Heart of Darkness, The End of the Tether*, London: Penguin.

Economist (2013) "Chinua Achebe", 30 March, at www.economist.com/news/obituary/21574453-chinua-achebe-africas-greatest-storyteller-died-march-21st-aged-82-chinua-achebe [accessed 28/08/2013].

Lyon, J. (1995) "Introduction", in *Joseph Conrad: Youth, Heart of Darkness, The End of the Tether*, London, Penguin.

Naipaul, V. S. (1979) *A Bend in the River*, Harmondsworth: Penguin Books.

Nyamnjoh, F. B. (2004) "From publish or perish to publish and perish: what 'Africa's 100 Best Books' tell us about publishing Africa", *Journal of Asian and African Studies*, 39(5): 331–355.

Nyamnjoh, F. B. (2012a) "Blinded by sight: diving the future of anthropology in Africa", *Africa Spectrum*, 47(2–3): 63–92.

Nyamnjoh, F. B. (2012b) "Potted plants in greenhouses: a critical reflection on the resilience of colonial education in Africa", *Journal of Asian and African Studies*, 47(2): 129–154.

Nyamnjoh, F. B. (2015) "Beyond an evangelising public anthropology: science, theory and commitment", *Journal of Contemporary African Studies*, 33(1): 48–63.

Okolo, M. S. C. (2007) *African Literature as Political Philosophy*, London/Dakar: CODESRIA/Zed Books.

Chapter 4

Media perspectives

How does Africa get reported? A letter of concern to *60 Minutes*

Howard W. French

Editors' note: In March 2015 veteran *New York Times* correspondent Howard French, their former bureau chief for West and Central Africa, reacted to coverage of Africa by the popular US television news programme *60 Minutes*, the flagship long-form news programme of CBS News. His letter, published on his blog, soon had well over two hundred signatories.[1] The open letter was addressed to then Executive Producer at *60 Minutes*, Jeff Fager. In a *Columbia Journalism Review* story about the letter in which French reflects further on the problem he identifies, *60 Minutes* responded that it "is proud of its coverage of Africa and has received considerable recognition for it."[2]

Dear Mr Fager,

We, the undersigned, are writing to express our grave concern about the frequent and recurring misrepresentation of the African continent by *60 Minutes*.

In a series of recent segments from the continent, *60 Minutes* has managed, quite extraordinarily, to render people of black African ancestry voiceless and all but invisible.

Two of these segments were remarkably similar in their basic subject matter, featuring white people who have made it their mission to rescue African wildlife. In one case these were lions, and in another, apes. People of black African descent make no substantial appearance in either of these reports, and no sense whatsoever is given of the countries visited, South Africa and Gabon.

The third notable recent segment was a visit by your correspondent Lara Logan to Liberia to cover the Ebola epidemic in that country. In that broadcast, Africans were reduced to the role of silent victims. They constituted what might be called a scenery of misery: people whose thoughts, experiences, and actions were treated as if totally without interest. Liberians were shown within easy speaking range of Logan, including some Liberians whom she spoke about, and yet not a single Liberian was quoted in any capacity.

Liberians not only died from Ebola, but many of them contributed bravely to the fight against the disease, including doctors, nurses, and other caregivers, some of whom gave their lives in this effort. Despite this, the only people heard from on the air were white foreigners who had come to Liberia to contribute to the fight against the disease.

Taken together, this anachronistic style of coverage reproduces, in condensed form, many of the worst habits of modern American journalism on the subject of Africa. To be clear, this means that Africa only warrants the public's attention when there is disaster or human tragedy on an immense scale, when Westerners can be elevated to the role of central characters, or when it is a matter of that perennial favourite, wildlife. As a corollary, Africans themselves are typically limited to the role of passive victims, or occasionally brutal or corrupt villains and incompetents; they are not otherwise shown to have any agency or even the normal range of human thoughts and emotions. Such a skewed perspective not only disserves Africa, it also badly disserves the news-viewing and news-reading public.

We have taken the initiative of writing to you because we are mindful of the reach of *60 Minutes*, and of the important role that your programme has long played in informing the public. We are equally mindful that American views of Africa, a continent of 1.1 billion people, which is experiencing rapid change on an immense scale, are badly misinformed by much of the mainstream media. The great diversity of African experience, the challenges and triumphs of African peoples, and above all, the voices and thoughts of Africans themselves, are chronically and woefully under-represented.

Over the coming decades, Africa will become the backdrop of some of the most significant developments on the planet, from unprecedented population growth, urbanisation and economic change to, potentially, the wholesale reconfiguration of states. We would like to see *60 Minutes* rethink its approach to Africa, and rise to the challenge of covering topics like these, and many more, that go well beyond the bailiwick of the staid and stereotypical recent examples cited above. In doing so, *60 Minutes* will have much to gain, as will the viewing public.

Howard W. French
Associate Professor, Columbia University Graduate School of Journalism

Notes

1   For the full list of signatories, see http://www.howardwfrench.com/2015/03/how-does-africa-get-reported-a-letter-of-concern-to-60-minutes/ [accessed 04/04/2016].
2   C. Ip (2015) "*60 Minutes'* Africa 'problem'", *Columbia Journalism Review*, 26 March, available at http://www.cjr.org/analysis/60_minutes.php [accessed 06/11/2015].

Chapter 5

How not to write about writing about Africa

Martin Scott

The aim of this chapter is to highlight a number of significant logical flaws and empirical gaps within the existing literature concerned with Africa's media image. I begin by drawing on the results of a comprehensive scoping review to show that, despite common assumptions, the existing evidence base in this area is insufficient for reaching firm conclusions about how Africa is represented in the US and UK news media. The irony is that a subject area focused on exposing taken-for-granted assumptions is in fact responsible for maintaining its own myth – that we know how Africa is represented in the news media.

I further argue that this myth about the comprehensiveness of existing research has persisted for so long, in part, because of certain citation practices and patterns of interpretation within the literature. Finally, I suggest that repeatedly emphasising only the anticipated and problematic aspects of representations of Africa may, inadvertently, end up serving to reinforce the very same ideas that these studies often seek to challenge. If nothing else, generalised critiques about the apparent limitations of all news coverage of Africa can inhibit constructive dialogue with those responsible for producing such coverage.

What do we really know about representations of Africa?

The assumption that we know how Africa is covered in the US and UK news media, and that we know it is consistently covered in predictable and problematic ways, has come to constitute common sense. It is central to numerous NGO campaigns encouraging us to "See Africa Differently", for example, and the premise of many articles and commentaries such as Binyavanga Wainaina's well-cited satirical essay "How to write about Africa" (see Introduction). As Lennart Wohlgemuth (2001: 5) put it, "it is indisputable that negative images of Africa increasingly dominate everyday reporting".

Academic literature has played a key role in both reproducing this assumption and producing research that appears to support it. Zerai (2007: 4), for example, states that, "study after study reveals, when Western media, including the U.S. media, do cover African countries and peoples, stories are often conceived in a very narrow focus. Stories are largely event-based and crisis-oriented. Most commonly, media coverage of Africa represents an Africa enmeshed in a series of imbroglios stemming from ethnic violence". But can such broad claims about all "Western media" coverage really be true? Is the quantity and nature of news coverage not likely to vary significantly over time, between different news outlets, and between representations of different events, regions, and countries within Africa? And is the evidence base really substantial enough to allow us to reach such sweeping conclusions?

In order to begin to address these questions and attempt to establish more firmly what we know and do not know about representations of Africa, I conducted a comprehensive scoping review of the existing research. Such a review entails the systematic selection, collection, and summarisation of existing knowledge in a broad thematic area. Included was all original empirical research into US and/or UK media representations of African countries (or Africa in general) published between 1 January 1990 and 1 April 2014. The constraints of time and resources meant that PhD theses, masters dissertations, and work not published in English were all excluded. The search strategy involved: (1) electronic key word searches of eleven different bibliographic databases, (2) hand searches of five key journals, and (3) searches of the websites and publications of relevant NGOs, government departments, broadcasters, academic associations, and book suppliers.[1] The full review included all studies of representations of Africa in film, television, magazines, newspapers, radio, the internet, and textbooks, published in both academic and grey literature (see Scott 2015). In this chapter, though, only studies of representations of Africa in news coverage published in peer-reviewed journal articles are discussed.

Figure 5.1 reveals that there has been a significant increase in research on this subject in recent years. A total of 44 of the 75 peer-reviewed studies of US and UK news coverage of Africa (59 per cent) were published since 2007, 19 of which were published in 2012 and 2013 alone. Figure 5.1 also shows that 41 studies analysed US news coverage, 21 analysed UK news coverage, and 13 included analysis of both. There was an almost even number of studies adopting a quantitative methodology (33 studies) as a qualitative methodology (32 studies). A further 10 studies combined both approaches. While 14 studies also included an original empirical analysis of news production, only two studies included any audience research.

Table 5.1 shows that news coverage of Africa (and sub-Saharan Africa) *in general* was the subject of analysis of 20 different studies (27 per cent). Out of these studies, three quarters adopted a content analysis methodology, typically analysing the quantity, distribution, and topic of news coverage

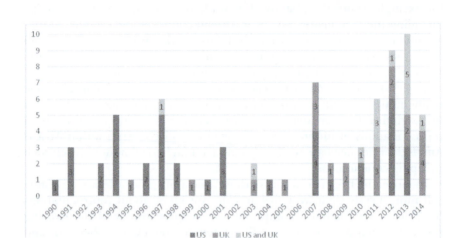

Figure 5.1 Number of studies of US and UK news coverage of Africa published annually
(January 1990 – April 2014)

of all African countries by a small number of media outlets, over multiple years. Beyond this, Table 5.1 shows that – aside from being included in such large-scale content analyses – 33 African countries were not the subject of any other study. This includes countries such as Botswana, Cameroon, Chad, Madagascar, Niger, Senegal, and Tanzania. Moreover, of the 21 countries whose representations have been analysed (outside of these content analyses), only 12 have appeared in more than one study. Studies of US and UK news coverage of North Africa are particularly rare.

Table 5.1 also shows that there have been far more studies of US and UK news coverage of South Africa than any other African country (15 studies). These analyses have focused largely on news coverage of the end of Apartheid (6 studies) and the 2010 FIFA World Cup (3 studies). While representations of Sudan, Rwanda, and Egypt have also been studied more than most, all except one of the analyses of these countries have focused on news coverage of just three events – the 1994 Rwandan genocide, the 2003–2009 Darfur crisis, and the 2011 Egyptian Revolution. Similarly, studies of Somalia have focused mostly on representations of either piracy (2 studies) or the famine in 1991 (2 studies). Although there were only 5 studies of news coverage of Nigeria, these did all focus on different events and time periods, including the 1993 Nigerian presidential election, the actions of Royal Dutch Shell in the 1990s, and a terrorist incident in 2009.

Figure 5.2 shows that existing research into US and UK news coverage of Africa is dominated by analyses of newspapers. Altogether, 45 of the

Table 5.1 Number of studies of US and UK news coverage to include an analysis of different countries or locations within Africa

	US media	UK media	US and UK media	Total
Africa (in general)	11	3	4	18
South Africa	9	4	2	15
Rwanda	5		1	6
Sudan	4	2		6
Egypt	3	1	1	5
Nigeria		4	1	5
Somalia	2	2	1	5
Ethiopia	2		1	3
Kenya	1	2		3
Zimbabwe	1	2		3
DRC	1		1	2
Liberia	2			2
Sierra Leone	2			2
Sub-Saharan Africa		2		2
Angola	1			1
Ghana	1			1
Ivory Coast			1	1
Libya	1			1
Mozambique	1			1
South Sudan			1	1
Tunisia	1			1
Uganda			1	1
Zambia	1			1

75 peer-reviewed studies (60 per cent) included a focus on newspapers and 41 of these focused exclusively on such coverage. By contrast, this scoping review identified only one peer-reviewed study of UK television news coverage of Africa and one study of news coverage on radio.

Studies of UK newspaper coverage were heavily dominated by analyses of *The Guardian* (included in 75 per cent of studies) and, to a lesser extent, *The Telegraph* (included in 54 per cent of studies). Analyses of coverage of Africa in *The New York Times* dominated studies of US newspapers, featuring in 27 of the 29 studies (93 per cent). On 12 occasions it was the only US newspaper to be analysed. *TIME* magazine was included in all but one of the 13 analyses of US news magazine coverage of Africa. Analysis of daily news bulletins on ABC, CBS, and NBC were the focus of every one of the 9 studies of US television news coverage – although two also included analysis of CNN coverage. The BBC News website was included in all five analyses

of UK online news. News bulletins and publications in the UK that were seldom studied include *The Daily Mail* (3 studies), *The Daily Mirror* (3 studies),
The Sun (1 study), *BBC Newsnight* (1 study), BBC Radio news bulletins
(1 study), *BBC Six O'Clock News* (1 study), *BBC Ten O'Clock News* (1 study),
ITN Early Evening News (1 study), *ITN News at Ten* (1 study), *Sky News* (1 study),
and *Channel 4 News* (0 studies).

In summary, existing peer-reviewed studies of news coverage of Africa
do allow us to be relatively well informed about how a small number of
news outlets (especially *The Guardian* and *The New York Times*) have covered
specific – often crisis-related – events in a small number of African countries (particularly South Africa, Rwanda, Sudan, and Egypt). Beyond this,
though, we know remarkably little about how most of Africa is represented
in much of the news media, most of the time. Studies of radio content,
UK television news, North Africa, and non-elite newspapers are particularly
scarce. It is also worth noting that only 7 out of the 75 studies (9 per cent)
compared US and/or UK news coverage of Africa directly with news coverage of a non-African location. Figure 5.3 helps illustrate some of the key
gaps in the available evidence.

As a result of this, it is difficult to see how any claims about how (all of)
Africa appears in the news media in general could be substantiated. To
be clear, I am not seeking to deny the existence of numerous studies that
have documented examples of stereotypical and selective news coverage of
Africa. Rather, I am pointing out that, given that these studies are generally
concentrated around a small number of countries and media, they provide

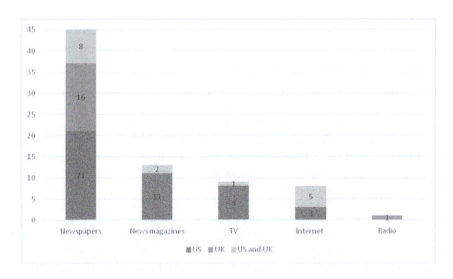

Figure 5.2 Number of peer-reviewed studies of US and UK news coverage of Africa that
include a focus on different media

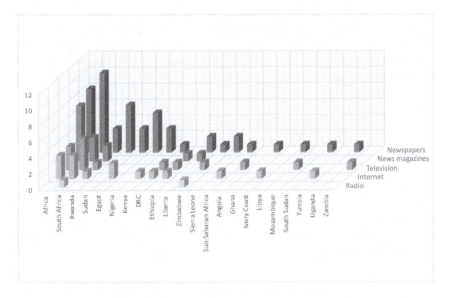

Figure 5.3 Number of studies examining representations of different African countries within different media

insufficient evidence to support any broad assertions about the nature of news coverage of Africa overall.

Maintaining the myth of representations of Africa

Interpreting evidence

An important way in which assumptions about what we know about news coverage of Africa have been maintained is through the ways in which evidence is often interpreted, both within and between empirical studies. For example, based on the results of a content analysis of coverage of Africa in four US television news bulletins between 2002 and 2004, Golan (2008: 53) concludes that, "American television newscasts do not view the African continent to be newsworthy". He states in the abstract that his results show that, "the African continent received limited coverage" (2008: 41). While Golan may have identified 878 stories about Africa in his sample period, he offers no comparison that we might use to judge the relative size of this figure. Instead, this conclusion is based on the finding that, "a dozen or so African nations account for the majority of US coverage, while the majority of African nations received limited to no coverage" (2008: 53). In this case, evidence of the distribution of coverage *within* Africa is used to support a claim about the *relative* quantity of coverage of Africa overall.

Thus, while Golan may well be right to assert that Africa receives less coverage than other continents, his study does not provide sufficient evidence to support this claim nor does he cite evidence from elsewhere to support it. This inconsistency between Golan's evidence and his conclusions may be explained by a number of factors, such as word limit or time constraints. Nevertheless, it also illustrates how evidence can be interpreted in a way that conceals gaps in our knowledge about how Africa is represented in US and UK news.

Another conclusion that Golan (2008: 53) claims his results support is that, "the majority of stories about African nations focused on negative and highly deviant issues such as conflict and disasters". He adds that, "this finding is consistent with previous studies that claim that the majority of news from the Third World usually focuses on negative news (Masmoudi 1979)". There are at least two issues with this particular conclusion. First, by his own admission, Golan's sample period does not provide a reliable basis for examining how "negative" or "deviant" coverage of Africa (or indeed the "Third World") is in general.

> The African continent was chosen because of the newsworthy events that took place in the continent during the sample period. These include an AIDS crisis in sub-Saharan Africa, famine in western Africa, disputed elections in Zambia and a terrible ethnic cleansing campaign in the Darfur region of the Sudan. (Golan 2008: 42)

The second major issue with this conclusion concerns Golan's use of the term "negative" to characterise both his results and the results of "previous studies". This is problematic because the term is used by Golan and many others as the basis for suggesting that there is consistency between the results of different studies, when they are often measuring entirely different things. In this case, Golan appears to define "negative" news as any coverage of "conflict and disasters". Yet in other studies examined for this scoping review the term "negative" was deployed in a much wider range of contexts. It was variously used to refer to narratives, frames, imagery, and neo-colonial discourses. There is even a lack of consensus about what topics might be defined as "negative". In the *Viewing the World* (DFID 2000) study, for example, news about "visits by Westerners" are included within its description of "negative coverage" of "developing countries". Thus, while many studies may conclude that news coverage of Africa is "negative", this does not necessarily mean that their findings are consistent with each other.

To be clear, the aim here is not to question the quality of Golan's research but to highlight how certain ways of presenting and interpreting evidence can contribute to the impression that we know more about coverage of Africa than we actually do. Golan's study is, however, an extreme example of this. In most cases, it was more subtle patterns in the way results were interpreted, rather than inaccuracies or inconsistencies, that contributed to this impression. For example, in her well-cited critical discourse analysis of the headlines of two UK newspapers (*The Guardian* and *The Telegraph*) over a one-month period (in 1990), Brookes (1995: 461) concludes that the UK press reproduces a dominant stereotypical discourse about Africa that helps to reproduce neo-colonial, racist perceptions of the continent and maintain Western hegemony. The apparent similarity between coverage of African countries within the headlines of these two newspapers is used as the basis of her conclusion that this discourse is "highly uniform" and "completely naturalized", with an "entrenched stability ... [that] holds little possibility for challenge or transformation".

There are two key issues with Brookes' conclusions. First, it is unclear how an analysis of the headlines of only two newspapers over a short period of time (one month) can support her conclusions about the nature of all UK press coverage, now and in the future. Second, little consideration is given to evidence that may contradict Brookes' overall conclusion. For example, from her study of the headlines of the 133 articles in her sample, Brookes identifies 15 different macro-propositions that they appeal to, including, "Africans are uncontrollably and excessively violent" and "Africans are helpless". All of these 15 macro-propositions reflect Afropessimist discourses. However, there *are* headlines within her sample (given in her appendix) that do offer possible counter-interpretations, including "Poachers caught", "Lesotho referendum", "Ceasefire progress", and "Peace talks start".

The point here is not to suggest that Brookes' analysis is flawed or inaccurate. Indeed, a discourse analysis methodology seeks to characterise overall trends within media texts, and does not deny exceptions. Rather, the aim is to draw attention to a tendency within Brookes' article – that was also apparent in many other studies – to interpret findings in ways that corresponded with dominant assumptions about what we already know about representations of Africa, even when the data also appear to offer a range of other, equally valid, interpretations. While it is not possible to quantify how often this occurred, it was, nevertheless, a notable feature of many articles studied and it reinforces the impression that academic research consistently supports what we think we know about Africa's media image.

Citation practices

Another way in which assumptions about the state of existing research were reproduced was through a tendency to take the conclusions of previous studies at face value. Tesfaye (2014: 17), for example, claims that Golan's study, "reveals that despite the presence of some negative stories focusing on wide-scale famine, civil conflict, disputed elections and AIDS epidemic, the African continent received limited coverage". Tesfaye does not question the extent to which these conclusions are supported by Golan's evidence.

It was also common for the results of studies conducted a significant period of time ago to be taken, uncritically, as evidence of the nature of contemporary news coverage. For example, in an article published in 2013, Cook cites El Zein and Cooper's (1992) analysis of *The New York Times* coverage of Africa between 1976 and 1990 as the sole evidence to support his claim that, "Africa rarely makes it to the front pages of the *LA Times* and the *New York Times*" (2013: 373). While this is a particularly extreme example of citing out-of-date evidence, Cook does at least specify which media outlets El Zein and Cooper studied. In many cases, analyses of specific news organisations are interpreted as offering reliable evidence of "media coverage" in general. Harrison (2013: 16), for example, describes Brookes' (1995) study as, "a rigorous discourse review of *the media*" (emphasis added). Reference here to "the media" conceals the fact that this study focused only on a one-month analysis of the headlines of two UK newspapers (in 1990).

Finally, there was a notable tendency for assertions about how Africa is covered in the news to be supported, not by empirical evidence, but by previous assertions. Wall (2007: 263), for example, cites Ebo's (1992) chapter on *American Media and African Culture* as evidence that, "historical background that might reveal the link between Western policies and tragic events ... [is] usually left out of reports about Africa". Yet Ebo (1992) only asserts this idea, providing no evidence to support it himself. Such citation practices are at least partly a consequence of the time pressures and word limits associated with producing academic work and are certainly not unique to research into representations of Africa. Nevertheless, they are also central to preserving the idea that we know far more than we actually do about how Africa is covered in the news.

Counter-productive claims

If our widely held assumptions about the nature of news coverage of Africa are indeed lacking in sufficient supportive evidence, why does it really matter? While it may be an exaggeration to say that *all* news coverage of Africa is stereotypical and focused on suffering, isn't this excusable, so long as this argument can be used to lobby for "improved" coverage? I want to suggest here that, for a number of reasons, sweeping assertions about the "negative" character of all news coverage of Africa may in fact be counter-productive for efforts aimed at reforming content.

There was an overwhelming tendency within the studies analysed to focus on, as Gruley and Duvall (2012: 31) put it, "the exposure of problematic discourse and imagery". Such a focus is of course important for pursuing the vital task of uncovering what V. Y. Mudimbe (1988) referred to as the "system of citations" from the "colonial library" of stock images and tropes around which Africa is often constructed. However, by seeking evidence only of aspects of the representation of Africa that are anticipated and problematic, this may inadvertently end up reinforcing the very same discourses that these studies seek to challenge.

Žižek (1989: 28–30) argues that the contemporary world increasingly functions in terms of "cynical reason". He describes this as, "a paradox of an enlightened false consciousness .... One knows the falsehood very well, one is well aware of a particular interest hidden behind an ideological universality, but still one does not renounce it". The workings of cynical reason were also alluded to by Horkheimer and Adorno (1998[1944]: 167), who wrote that, "the triumph of advertising in the culture industry is that consumers feel compelled to buy and use its products even though they see through them". The suggestion is that the practice of being critical of something may in fact be a constituent of its influence.

Applied here, this argument suggests that some of the literature critiquing media discourses of Africa may not necessarily work against the influence of these discourses. Instead, it may paradoxically enhance their authority because they do not negate the idea that, though limited, such discourses do reflect deeper truths about the continent. This possibility is perhaps most apparent in the titles of studies of representations of Africa that draw on the very same discourses they seek to critique. Examples include *The Hopeless Continent?* (Botes 2009), "A place on the edge" (Famuyiwa 2007), "In the heart of sickness" (Levin 2001), and my own previous work, entitled "Marginalised, negative and trivial?" (Scott 2009). In short, one way in which problematic discourses about Africa are reproduced is through efforts to critique them, even if the intention is to be ironic.

The point here is certainly not to question the value of critically interrogating representations of Africa. Rather, it is that if analyses and accounts of media representations focus exclusively on exposing anticipated and problematic discourses of Africa then there is, as Nothias (2014: 9) puts it, "a risk of reproducing an epistemological framework akin to the one being targeted in the first place". To avoid this, there is a need to focus also on unexpected, alternative, and contradictory aspects of Africa's representation. It is in this context that Garuba and Himmelman (2012: 17) suggest we read media texts about Africa not only for citations of the "colonial library" but also for the *un*cited, or the images and sequences "[that] do not fit into the structure of our expectations". If nothing else, more complex and qualified accounts of media representations may generate a more productive dialogue with media producers, who, as Harrison (2013: vii) has noted, tend to have a "palpable antagonism" towards "tendentially critical" researchers.

Conclusion

Drawing on the results of a comprehensive scoping review of the academic literature, this chapter has highlighted, (1) the myth about the comprehensiveness of existing research concerning US and UK news coverage of Africa, (2) a number of citation practices and patterns of interpretation that have helped to maintain this myth, and (3) some of the potential consequences of assuming that we know how (all of) Africa is represented in the news.

Two key implications for future work stem from this research. First, and perhaps most obviously, this scoping review has identified a number of areas in which the gaps in our understanding are most acute. These include a lack of research into representations of North Africa, radio content, popular newspapers, and UK television news coverage. Comparative research, longitudinal studies, and research that combines textual analysis with audience studies are also scarce.

However, while beginning to fill some of these empirical gaps may go some way towards improving our understanding of Africa's media image, it is not just the *focus* of research that requires attention. The second major set of implications of this study concerns the nature of analysis and argumentation within academic work. Previous literature must be reviewed critically and thoroughly. Future research should be sure to adopt clear and transparent procedures for data collection and analysis. Vague terminology, such as use of the terms "positive" and "negative", should be avoided. If research findings are inconclusive, contradictory, counter-intuitive, or open to multiple interpretations, this must be revealed. Finally, any conclusions reached about how (all of) Africa is represented in the media in general should be qualified and well evidenced. In summary, research in this area must be careful not to commit the same errors – of essentialisation, subjective interpretation, and naturalising assumptions – that it often accuses the media of making.

Note

1 I am indebted to Kristian Porter and especially Thomas Reid for their dedicated and thorough contributions to the review, selection, and coding procedures.

References

Botes, J. (2009) *The Hopeless Continent? 2007/2008 Local and International Media Representations of Africa*, Saarbrücken: VDM Publishing.

Brookes H. J. (1995) "Suit, tie and a touch of juju' – the ideological construction of Africa: a critical discourse analysis of news on Africa in the British press", *Discourse & Society*, 6(4): 461–494.

Cook, C. (2013) "Coverage of African conflicts in the American media: filtering out the logic of plunder", *African and Asian Studies*, 12(4): 373–390.

DFID (Department for International Development) (2000) *Viewing the World: A Study of British Television Coverage of Developing Countries*, London: DFID.

Ebo, B. (1992) "American media and African culture", in B. Hawk (ed.), *Africa's Media Image*, New York: Praeger.

El Zein, H. & Cooper, A. (1992) "*New York Times* coverage of Africa 1976–1990", in B. Hawk (ed.), *Africa's Media Image*, New York: Praeger.

Famuyiwa, O. A. (2007) "A place on the edge: textual analysis of online news about Africa", *Global Media Journal* (e-journal), 6(10), no. 8.

Garuba, H. & Himmelman, N. (2012) "The cited and the uncited: toward an emancipatory reading of representations of Africa," in M. E. Higgins (ed.), *Hollywood's Africa after 1994*, Athens, OH: Ohio University Press.

Golan, G. J. (2008) "Where in the world is Africa? Predicting coverage of Africa by US television networks", *International Communication Gazette*, 70(1): 41–57.

Gruley, J. & Duvall, C. (2012) "The evolving narrative of the Darfur conflict as represented in *The New York Times* and *The Washington Post*, 2003–2009", *GeoJournal*, 77(1): 29–46.

Harrison, G. (2013) *The African Presence: Representations of Africa in the Construction of Britishness*, Manchester: Manchester University Press.

Horkheimer, M. & Adorno, T. (1998[1944]) *Dialectic of Enlightenment*, New York: Continuum.

Levin, J. (2001) "In the heart of sickness: a 'LIFE' portrait of Dr Albert Schweitzer", in D. M. Mengara (ed.), *Images of Africa: Stereotypes and Realities*, Trenton, NJ: Africa World Press.

Mudimbe V. Y. (1988) *The Invention of Africa: Gnosis, Philosophy, and the Order of Knowledge*, Bloomington, IN: Indiana University Press.

Nothias, T. (2014) "How do French and British journalists actually write about Africa? The case of the celebrations of 50 years of African independence", conference paper, IAMCR, Hyderabad.

Scott, M. (2009) "Marginalized, negative or trivial? Coverage of Africa in the UK press", *Media, Culture and Society*, 31(4): 533–557.

Scott, M. (2015) "The myth of representations of Africa: a comprehensive scoping review of the literature", *Journalism Studies*, 11 August, at http://www.tandfonline.com/doi/abs/10.1080/1461670X.2015.1044557?journalCode=rjos20 [accessed 02/04/2016].

Tesfaye, A. M. (2014) "The coverage of Ethiopia in BBC and CNN news websites", *Online Journal of African Affairs*, 3(2): 15–25.

Wall, M. (2007) "An analysis of news magazine coverage of the Rwanda crisis in the United States", in A. Thompson (ed.), *The Media and the Rwanda Genocide*, London: Pluto Press.

Wohlgemuth, L. (2001) "Foreword", in M. Palmberg (ed.), *Encounter Images in the Meetings between Africa and Europe*, Uppsala: Nordic Africa Institute.

Zerai, A. (2007) "U.S. press and the Southern Sudanese conflict: missing elements in the narrative jigsaw", conference paper, International Communication Association.

Žižek S (1989) *The Sublime Object of Ideology*, London: Verso.

Chapter 6

Bringing Africa home

Reflections on discursive practices of domestication in international news reporting on Africa by Belgian television

Stijn Joye

In 2015, several news platforms of Belgian public broadcaster VRT featured a special series on Africa that would portray "the other face of Africa" during the entire month of March. By not dwelling upon the negative but explicitly focusing on positive developments, the news items were meant to qualify and adjust the dominant image of Africa for Belgian audiences. Looking at the several items being broadcast, it appears that the so-called "other face of Africa" is a very Western and neo-liberal one, as the overall theme of progress was depicted through a framework of economic growth and images portraying, among others, shopping malls, fashion designers, people playing golf, traffic jams, construction works, and exchange markets, hence resonating with Schmidt and Garrett's (2011) critique on discourses of Afro-optimism. Nonetheless, these images also serve the general objective of the series to bring modern-day Africa closer to home. This constructive journalism initiative, however, also raises questions about the portrayal of Africa during the rest of the year, as the special series can equally be interpreted as an implicit acknowledgement by the newsroom of their everyday news practices and reporting on Africa that tend to overlook the continent and/or favour the negative over the positive.

Previous studies (Joye & Biltereyst 2007; Joye 2010) have shown that Africa largely remains an unknown, "dark continent" for Belgian news media in terms of devoted attention, alongside findings that indicate a rather stereotypical and negative representation. However, there are a few notable exceptions to this persistently dominant way of reporting on Africa. For example, it is evident that the former Belgian colonies such as Congo, Rwanda, and Burundi receive more attention than other African countries. This is related to the emerging journalistic practice of domestication, which refers to the framing of a foreign news event within the perceived national or local context of the audience (Clausen 2004), in this particular case the shared colonial past. Integrating such a local or domestic perspective appears to thrive in contemporary news reporting (Chang et al. 2012), but it is nothing new. Peterson in 1979 stated that "the majority of foreign news is domestic news about foreign countries, not international news" (120). Such statements tend to position the notion of proximity as central in the different stages of the news production process, particularly as a news selection criterion and as a determinant for politics of representation. Here, proximity is defined in a very broad sense, by including not only the geographical distance, but also other relationships of involvement such as cultural affinity, tourism, historical links, and emotional proximity.

By focusing on the journalistic practice of domestication, this chapter addresses the issue of how domestic news media can discursively attribute a sense of relevance and proximity to events occurring in Africa. According to Gurevitch, Levy, and Roeh (1991), domesticating international events makes them comprehensible, appealing, and more relevant to local audiences. In recent years, a growing body of research has started to uncover different modes of domestication (e.g. Alasuutari et al. 2013; Olausson 2014). For instance, Alasuutari et al. (2013) observed the range of constructed interconnections between the domestic and the global in news reporting on the Arab Spring and identified four modes of domestication: appealing to emotions; focusing on compatriots involved in the events; reporting on statements and acts by domestic actors; and utilising the foreign event as a model that can be applied to local politics. This contribution explores the practice of domestication in news reporting on Africa and investigates how these representations can open up spaces of identification between the Belgian audience and the African other.

Methodology

As domestication is defined as "the discursive adaptation of news from 'outside' the nation-state so as to make it resonate with a national audience as it is perceived" (Olausson 2014: 711), the methodology of discourse analysis is very appropriate here. The understanding of discourse dwells upon Jørgensen and Phillips (2002: 1), who regard it as "a particular way of talking about and understanding the world". Discourses create representations of the world that reflect as well as actively construct reality by ascribing meanings to our world, identities, and social relations (Jørgensen & Phillips 2002). We build on social constructionist approaches to discourse, specifically Critical Discourse Analysis (CDA), as power in general and issues of power asymmetries, manipulation, and exploitation in particular are central to many investigations within this field (Blommaert & Bulcaen 2000). Furthermore, critical schools of discourse require that discourse should be empirically analysed within its broader social context (Jørgensen & Phillips 2002). According to Richardson (2007), CDA is mainly used to explore how discourses are realised linguistically in texts to constitute knowledge and social relations, such as a relationship of involvement, identification, or compassion with a distant other.

This study adapts Fairclough's (1995) model of CDA, which consists of three dimensions: text, discursive practice, and the wider social practice. Following a case-based methodology, it investigates how the two main (Dutch-speaking) Belgian television stations (the public broadcaster VRT and the commercial channel VTM) domesticated African current affairs in 2013. Cases were selected from the electronic news archive ENA, which is based at the University of Antwerp. The archive holds all news broadcasts on public and commercial television in Flanders (Belgium). News items are pre-coded in the archive by geographical criteria into domestic news, mixed international news, and foreign news. The pool of cases is drawn from the second category, as these items involve either the home country as an actor in the event or events in which journalists made a conscious effort to make Belgium part of the news narrative. Olausson (2014: 715) identifies this particular mode as "extroverted domestication, which interconnects the domestic and the global". In total, 241 news items that explicitly linked an African event to Belgium were analysed, 134 broadcast by VRT and 107 by VTM. These domesticated items echo a particular kind of enforced proximity (cf. the concept of cosmopolitanism as defined by Tomlinson (1999)) but also hint at Silverstone's (2007) notion of proper distance, which refers to a particular politics of the representation of otherness and our mediated relationship to the (African) other.

Findings

Text

From the perspective of the majority of Belgian spectators, the selected news items depict ethnic or cultural others. The journalistic practice of domestication can help to minimise the distance between the Belgian spectator and the African other. By selecting specific images or highlighting particular details of a story, journalists can thus construct a sense of (emotional) proximity. Fairclough's first dimension of text particularly looks at such (discursive) choices made by the text's author. As the study shows, rendering a foreign African event more relevant through domestication can be realised in several ways. Overall, three dominant modes of domestication were revealed in the analysis.

The most common strategy of domesticating distant suffering is by establishing an emotional bond or connection. For this purpose, the broadcasters focus on human-interest stories that (emotionally) appeal to the audience. Manifesting itself in diverse ways, the eyewitness account was the most prominent and visible technique applied. Accounts from Belgian tourists or expats who were affected by the particular event allow the spectator to get an inside look by someone who is like them. Several items featured testimonies from Belgians abroad who – via Skype or telephone – gave a personal and often emotional account of what happened and how they personally lived through the experience (e.g. "we were very frightened", "panic and chaos everywhere"). Remarkably, many of these reports established the Belgians abroad as authoritative sources, qualified to make (often overtly harsh) statements about the foreign governments' dealing with the event and assessing the potential risks. In some events (e.g. the hostage situation in a Kenyan mall, the military putsch in the Central African Republic), there were compatriots involved, which is generally considered to be a determining factor for a high level of news value and attention (Joye 2010). In these cases, the news reports were built around the fate of Belgian victims and/or their families, henceforth reducing the relevance of the non-Belgian victims despite the latter's omnipresence. In other words, the African other and his/her life are made inferior to the lives of compatriots.

Belgian journalists further constructed a sense of emotional proximity by selecting moving images (e.g. close-ups of children, images of fugitive pregnant women and elderly ladies), using expressive adjectives in the voice-over comments or highlighting emotional details of a story. This particular mode of domestication can foster a cosmopolitan outlook, as the audience is invited to relate to the other. The implied invitation to care or help can also be made very explicit when the news item covers relief aid, charity organisations, or military operations. Several items focused on initiatives from Belgians to raise money or act on the suffering, although the majority covered institutionalised forms of relief work by NGOs and the Belgian government. A recurrent narrative shows compatriots involved in humanitarian assistance. For instance, Belgian soldiers were followed from their departure to the ground work in the conflict area. The main protagonist, however, was the iconic C-130 airplane of the Belgian air force, as practically all reports on the Mali conflict showed or mentioned it. Constructing a narrative around the C-130 is also beneficial to practices of domestication: it is instantly recognisable to Belgian spectators, since it is one of our army's most successful and deployed assets. News media thus introduce a kind of "soap" element that allows them to continue their daily reports on the African event. By contrast, the local population and/or army were portrayed as less relevant, also in terms of screen time.

A second dominant mode of domestication relates to the attention paid to the implications or repercussions of the African event for the home country. This strategy brings the distant event to the doorstep of the Belgian spectator, but simultaneously manages fears of the dangers it could represent to life in Belgium. A standard pattern that was identified starts with an enumeration of potential risks that establishes a sense of urgency, followed by a discussion of domestic safety measures alongside a prominent stress on the skills and expertise of the Belgian authorities involved, hence articulating a dominant discourse of control and safety. Furthermore, this journalistic formula draws on credible Belgian experts or authorities, who were interviewed on location or invited to the studio to interpret a distant event and its (anticipated) consequences for Belgium. News items, for instance, discussed the potential consequences of Belgium joining a French military operation in Mali against terrorist organisation Al Shabaab. The latter was introduced as "an extremist Muslim group", "clashing with the Western model of society", and "a danger to global safety", thus justifying military action. An important subcategory concerns tourism. A large number of the news reports on the Egyptian turmoil in 2013, for instance, exclusively dealt with travel alerts and updates from the Belgian ministry of foreign affairs while also focusing on the Belgian tourists abroad. Spokesmen of the two main travel agencies regularly commented on the developing situation regarding holiday flights to Egypt and journalists also visited the popular seaside resorts. Similar reports were found in the aftermath of the terroristic attacks in Tunisia and Kenya, also two popular holiday destinations. Another subcategory focuses more on the long-term consequences, particularly the issue of (im)migration. The overall majority of these items are rather negative in tone, emphasising problems, cultural differences, and failing migration policies of Belgium and Europe.

A third and often overlooked mode of domestication is related to the format of the news broadcast and to a series of subtle stylistic, narrative, and technical practices that appear unremarkable by virtue of their ubiquity. These (routine) practices are less concerned with establishing involvement, as they mainly act to create a sense of familiarity and recognition. For instance, frequently used footage from foreign broadcasters and global news agencies is expounded by well-known voices of Belgian expert journalists. Other examples include the use of metaphors or short illustrations that directly relate the foreign event to the spectators' daily life. Journalists are thus looking for some common ground to make the African event accessible and comprehensible. Furthermore, many news items started with an animation of the globe that starts in Belgium and then spins to the African country. Such items implicitly establish Belgium as the news item's absolute – though latent – point of reference. Finally, the most common way to make the unknown more familiar was by means of journalistic narrative and foreign correspondents. Explicit voice-over references to Belgium (e.g. "our country", "also in Belgium") and live interventions of correspondents are textbook examples of linking the African event with the home country.

On a textual dimension, the image we receive of Africa is quite dual. On the one hand, Africa is regularly presented as a vast continent and as one entity, hence its immense diversity is largely ignored. This thrives on discursive strategies that are similar to collectivisation and include different levels of abstraction or generalisation (Machin & Mayr 2012). For instance, one report on the Mali conflict started with enumerating one by one all Western countries involved, while assistance from neighbouring countries was classified as "African forces". Another example was the attribution of one climate type to the entire continent ("In Africa, it is very hot").

On the other hand, our encounters with Africa are equally very individualised. Domestication through eyewitness accounts, for example, allows us to see Africa through the eyes of individual Belgian compatriots and/or journalists. When Africans are portrayed, they are "exceptional and courageous" individuals who stand up for justice and make a difference. The most notable instance is, of course, Nelson Mandela, who died in 2013. Other less-known figures are the Congolese Doctor Mukwege, the Rwandan political prisoner Victoire Ingabire, and Bogaletch Gebre, who received an important Belgian prize for her work on human rights in Ethiopia. The strategy of personalisation, alongside the personal and often emotional accounts, ascribes Africa – as an abstract and unknown entity – with more concrete characteristics to make it comprehensible and tangible.

Discursive practice

A key characteristic of CDA is to analyse text in its context (Richardson 2007), whereby news is the outcome of a broad range of professional and institutional practices that limit the choice of journalists (Fairclough 1995). Of interest to our study are a number of contextual dimensions that concern the editorial policy. Although the public broadcaster VRT and the commercial channel VTM both enjoy a good reputation regarding the quality and amount of their foreign news, they tend to adhere to a Eurocentric or Western vision of the world in their news reporting (Joye & Biltereyst 2007). Since 2010, domesticated international news is steadily rising and accounted for 26.3 per cent of the total news output in 2013, slightly more than pure foreign news (25.7 per cent) (Steunpunt Media 2014). Remarkably, some journalists of the public broadcaster were explicitly critical of Africa's status as being neglected by the rest of the world and its lack of newsworthiness. Concluding an item on the uprisings in the Central African Republic, the journalist stated that the country "barely seems to receive any attention, as was the case for the last decades". Likewise, there were two items on the commemoration of Moroccan soldiers who died during the First World War, which tempted the journalist to point out that throughout the years non-Western casualties were all too easily forgotten.

The corporate mission of a television network is another significant element of this editorial context. Despite a high level of similarity in the events selected and the footage shown, some subtle discursive differences in the applied modes of domestication between VRT and VTM are noticeable. For instance, commercial channel VTM domesticates fewer items but performs the task in a more intensive way than its publicly funded counterpart. VTM journalists made more frequent use of testimonies via Skype and telephone alongside more live interventions and stand-ups. In the past, several editors of the VTM news have repeatedly started to focus more on the news that matters to the Belgian audience, resulting in a higher intensity of domestication. Notable in this respect is VTM's choice to use the story of a young compatriot fleeing from rebels as the channel's main angle to cover the March uprisings in the Central African Republic. VRT did not even mention this particular story, while VTM followed it for three days up until the compatriot's reunion with family and friends at Brussels airport. Other differences deal with tendencies to stress the negative and to personalise the news events. Public broadcaster VRT made less use of these practices.

Social practice

News discourse is also permeated by institutions and values from outside the newsroom, such as the economy, politics, and ideology (Richardson 2007). This dimension of Fairclough's model essentially refers to ideological processes (Blommaert & Bulcaen 2000). Although van Dijk (2009: 199) admits that it is theoretically and empirically impossible to provide a complete "account of the ideologies involved and the structures of news that are controlled by them", he states that a polarisation between the in-group (the self) and the out-group (the other) is characteristic of many such ideological structures. In terms of the presented study, the practice of domestication itself already refers to such a socio-cultural polarisation. News items about the other first need to be domesticated in order to gain some relevance or importance. An additional element in the news coverage is the fact that Belgium – and by extension the West – is mainly represented in a positive way, either stepping in to help Africa as a caring community or being firmly in control of the situation by demonstrating agency and effective crisis management skills, such as was very prominent in the coverage of the Mali conflict where French and Belgian forces were represented as leading the operation while the "unstructured" Malian army was in need of training. This resonates with the Orientalist (Saïd 1987) discourse of the civilised West (identified as superior) versus the barbarian other (categorised as inferior and represented in a negative way, e.g. the labelling of African countries as "regimes"). International news is permeated by such power relations of inequality, while Olausson (2014: 719) claims that these "polarized discursive constructions of Us and Them in the construction of power" are clearly manifested in the mode of extroverted domestication.

Exemplary for this are the numerous items on Belgium's – apparently quintessential – involvement in relief aid and military operations as well as the coverage of Belgian trade missions. Although the latter depicted local (economic and educational) success stories in Angola, Kenya, and South Africa, the reports tend to imply that these successes could not be achieved or preserved without the Belgian contribution and assistance – hence articulating the traditional discourse of Afro-pessimism. Simultaneously, the trade mission can be seen as a civilised modern-age equivalent of colonial trade as the head of one mission, Princess Astrid, stated in the news report that, "by stimulating development and growth in South Africa, our own companies and people in Belgium will benefit." Therefore, it is not difficult to connect the findings of our study with a discourse of latent neo-imperialism that is heir to older processes of colonisation. Regarding the latter, there is a strong impact of Belgium's colonial past that is recurrent in the news selection and reporting. For instance, in an item on the visit to an Angolan oil company as part of the trade mission, one local manager was quoted as saying that, "[y]ou also have a history of colonization in Africa. I believe that expertise is most welcome here." However, Belgium has a troubled past with Africa as well, as was clearly demonstrated in the discourse surrounding the military operations in Mali and the Central African Republic. The role of Belgium in the Rwanda genocide (1994) and the death of ten Belgian soldiers during that conflict is part of the collective memory. News reports regularly evoke this traumatic past, explicitly by referring to the events themselves, but mostly in an implicit way by discursively stressing the logistic nature of the involvement in Mali; this explains the central focus on the C-130 airplane in these reports, as it articulates a very technical and clean image of the war. Additionally, high-ranked military and political leaders consistently stated and repeated that it was a safe operation and that "our boys" would not have to engage in combat or be close to the front line.

Concluding remarks

In their seminal work on domestication, Gurevitch et al. identified the practice of domestication as a "countervailing force to the pull of globalization" (1991: 207), by which they refer to the persistence of a domestic perspective in international news reporting, despite tendencies of homogenisation following the increasingly global exchange and production of news copy. Several years later, Olausson (2014: 711) confirmed the potential of domesticated foreign news discourse to counteract "discursive constructions of the global, reinforcing instead nation-state discourse and identity". What we may have witnessed in recent years, however, is a somewhat excessive use of domestication that can eventually produce "a rather Eurocentric if not ethnocentric picture of global affairs" (Manning 2001: 62). Acknowledging that audiences do not easily relate to foreign events and/or have limited knowledge of the far away, domestication can help to overcome that threshold, but it simultaneously holds the risk of establishing a new threshold as distant events, such as those developing in African countries, are increasingly assessed on their potential to be domesticated.

In this context, our study on African reporting in Belgian news broadcasts recognises the potential of domestication to foster identification and to bring the distant and unknown African other (discursively) closer, by means of establishing emotional bonds or familiarising the unfamiliar in various ways. At the same time, the findings also demonstrate that domestication practices tend to reiterate known discourses of Orientalism and neo-imperialism, ultimately reinforcing the socio-cultural binary of "us" and "them". Despite notable exceptions, it appears that traditional discourses of Afro-pessimism still prevail in everyday (domesticated) foreign news reporting on Africa.

References

Alasuutari, P., Qadir, A., Creutz, K. (2013) "The domestication of foreign news", *Media, Culture & Society*, 35(6): 692–707.

Blommaert, J. & Bulcaen, C. (2000) "Critical discourse analysis", *Annual Review of Anthropology*, 29: 447–466.

Chang, T., Southwell, B., Lee, H., Hong, Y. (2012) "A changing world, unchanging perspectives", *International Communication Gazette*, 74(4): 367–384.

Clausen, L. (2004) "Localizing the global", *Media, Culture & Society*, 26(1): 25–44.

Fairclough, N. (1995) *Media Discourse*, London: Edward Arnold.

Gurevitch, M., Levy, M, Roeh, I. (1991) "The global newsroom", in P. Dahlgren & C. Sparks (eds.), *Communication and Citizenship*, London: Routledge.

Jørgensen, M. & Phillips, L. (2002) *Discourse Analysis as Theory and Method*, London: Sage.

Joye, S. & Biltereyst, D. (2007) "All quiet on the ...? Een analyse van het buitenland-aanbod van VRT en VTM [An analysis of international news coverage on VRT and VTM]", in M. Hooghe, K. de Swert, and S. Walgrave (eds), *De kwaliteit van het nieuws* [The quality of news], Leuven: Acco.

Joye, S. (2010) *De media(de)constructie van rampen* [The media (de)construction of disasters], PhD thesis, Ghent University, Ghent.

Machin, D. & Mayr, A. (2012) *How to Do Critical Discourse Analysis*, London: Sage.

Manning, P. (2001) *News and News Sources*, London: Sage.

Olausson, U. (2014) "The diversified nature of "domesticated" news discourse", *Journalism Studies*, 15(6): 711–725.

Peterson, S. (1979) "Foreign news gatekeepers and criteria of newsworthiness", *Journalism Quarterly*, 56(1): 116–125.

Richardson, J. E. (2007) *Analysing Newspapers*, New York: Palgrave Macmillan.

Saïd, E. (1987) *Orientalism*, New York: Penguin.

Schmidt, S. J. & Garrett, H. J. (2011) "Reconstituting pessimistic discourses", *Critical Arts*, 25(3): 423–440.

Silverstone, R. (2007) *Media and Morality*, Cambridge: Polity.

Steunpunt Media (2014) *Het binnenlandse en buitenlandse nieuws verweven* [Domestic and foreign news interwoven], Antwerp, Steunpunt Media, at http://www.steunpuntmedia.be/wp-content/uploads/2014/02/Nieuwsmonitor-Flash_buitenlandberichtgeving.pdf [09/04/2015].

Tomlinson, J. (1999) *Globalization and Culture*, Cambridge: Polity.

van Dijk, T. (2009) "News, discourse, and ideology", in K. Wahl-Jorgensen and T. Hanitzsch (eds.), *The Handbook of Journalism Studies*, New York: Routledge.

Chapter 7

The image of Africa from the perspectives of the African diasporic press in the UK

Olatunji Ogunyemi

Introduction

The representation of Africa in the Western media remains relatively marginalised compared with other continents in the world. The significance of this should not be underestimated because "as globalization and migration continue to encourage the interaction of different peoples and cultures, so the media portrayal of different parts of the world plays an increasingly important role in either discouraging or promoting respect for other cultures" (Scott 2009: 535). In relation to Africa, scholars have noted that the Western media distort Africa's image by over-emphasising negative events and employing stereotypes to add colour to the stories. Hence, they urge that "recognising voices that challenge stereotypical portrayals is necessary to developing place images that are geographically more accurate" (Gruley & Duvall 2012: 29).

While there is a wealth of literature on the portrayal of Africa in the Western media, there is a paucity of research on the image of Africa from the perspectives of the African diasporic press. This is a notable gap because African diasporas have, in the past two decades, appropriated the new information technology to counter the negative and stereotypical portrayal of Africa in the Western media and to portray another view of Africa to "friends of Africa" and to the diasporas themselves, some of whom are second and third generations who have never visited Africa, and for whom the media are their main "window" on Africa.

Mainstream media coverage of Africa

The mainstream media are often criticised for reinforcing a stereotypical image of Africa. Critics blame Western media for prioritising stories about diseases, political ineptitude, conflict, economic woes, and social upheaval. For example, the London-based *New African Magazine* published two special editions in July/August 2000 and June 2008 to depict how the Western media use "hyperbolic reporting of the Kenyan and Zimbabwean elections" (Ankomah 2008: 9) and diminutive phrases to dehumanise Africans (see Duodu 2008: 18). The negative approach is further evident in Ibelema's (2014) analysis of *The New York Times* and the Associated Press, which found references to "tribal fixation", that is, a "tendency to focus on ethnic differences and rivalries in press coverage and interpretation of Africa's contemporary conflicts" (164); references to "peripheral coverage", that is, "the minimal attention to African affairs outside of wars and conflicts" (165); and references to "diminutive portrayal", that is, "the tendency to lump African nations into a whole, which is another indication of perceptual distance" (165). The shallow approach is evident in Gruley and Duvall's (2012) study, which found the "news coverage of Darfur in *The New York Times* and *The Washington Post* remained historically and geographically shallow" (42). Regarding the marginal approach, Hawkin's (2012) study concludes that, "for *The New York Times*, the events of 9/11 did not appear to trigger a renewed focus on Africa. While the total number of articles referencing Africa increased in the five years following 9/11, the number of substantive articles focusing specifically on issues within Africa actually decreased in the year following 9/11" (22).

The mainstream media have responded by arguing that "most of the countries that were unfavourably covered either had serious domestic problems or persistent international troubles in 'reality'" (Kim 1993; Ibelema 2014: 171). This "mirror image" defence seems to have been imbibed by some African media as research found that "images of Africa projected on official country websites may still reinforce certain aspects of otherness" (Ibelema 2014: 205). Therefore, Poncian (2015) argues that the slant in the framing of Africa "may have more to do with what Africans do and how they perceive themselves against the Westerners" (76).

However, Norman Mudibo, Kenyan freelance journalist, has refuted the mirror image defence, stating that,

> whereas I subscribe to the doctrine of telling it as it is, still it has to be done in a responsible and balanced way. But the slant of the Western media coverage has been appalling. They have put a spin on events, negating the very principles of a fair and just practice of the trade. They have disproportionately made everyone to think that the whole country is aflame. (Norman Mudibo, quoted in Kabukuru 2008: 33)

But the representation of Africa in the Western media is shifting towards a mixed approach, as Scott (2009) found that the "coverage of Africa, in the UK press at least, is not as negative as is often assumed" (548) and that the "UK press does not contain a significantly higher percentage of negative news stories, the percentage of articles covering civil war and civil conflict [is] approximately the same as in the *AllAfrica* sample, and the UK press even contains a far higher percentage of articles on culture, religion and tourism" (550).

Nevertheless, the implications of dominant negative image are that they create "a stereotypical view of the continent as a place where life is nasty, brutish and short" (Pawson 2007: 51); they "had a toll on business, scaring away tourists and prospective investors, messing up business deals, and job losses across sectors" (Kabukuru 2008: 33); they made Africans to "loathe themselves and their heritage" (Ankomah 2008: 14); and they entrench a negative perception of Africa in the minds of Western audiences.

Frames in African coverage

Media frames assign and convey meaning by defining problems, diagnosing causes, making judgements, and suggesting solutions in socially or culturally subjective ways (Kuypers 2009).

Generally speaking, frames can be negative, positive, or neutral/mixed. The negative frames describe "negative properties or actions in more specific detail, the use of propositions that have (many) negative implications about Africa, the attribution of negative properties about Africans as inherent, and special focus on any participant, property or action" (see van Dijk 2011: 397–398). The use of these negative frames in the Western media leads to the representation of "Africa primarily as a blighted receptacle for their charity and benevolence" (Goodwin 2008: 28). But the positive frames encompass "any reduction in the use of simplistic tropes about Africa and Africans" (Gruley & Duvall 2012: 43). This means avoiding the use of tropes such as "tribal" or "genocide" because they discourage "actions that could prevent or reduce violent conflict" (Gruley & Duvall 2012: 29). Moreover, the positive frames focus on good governance, peaceful transition of power, economic progress, and sustainable development. For instance, "Ethiopia is well placed to meet the UN's Millennium Development Goals (MDGs) at the end of 2015" (*New African* 2008: 57). As the name suggests, neutral/mixed frames promote a mixed focus on positive news about individuals or elite people and also about negative, violent, or dramatic happenings.

In the process of news selection, journalists are expected to uphold professional standards and avoid bias and ethnocentrism. But some African leaders seem to be urging African journalists to negate these expectations by prioritising national interest in order to redress the dominant negative frame surrounding reports of Africa in the Western media. One such leader is Thabo Mbeki, the former president of South Africa, who told African journalists, "the time has come that we, as Africans, take responsibility for how our continent is portrayed" (2008: 25). He referred to a communiqué produced by former African heads of state at a Presidential Routable hosted by Boston University in May 2005 that states, "African countries, and institutions ... need to develop a set of strategies to counter the negative media portrayal of Africa, including developing alternative media through which to tell Africa's story; a multimedia campaign to counter Africa's negative image in the Western press; and a strategy for engaging major media outlets in order to encourage more fair and balanced coverage of the continent" (2008: 27).

While this exhortation was not directed at the African diasporic media, a commitment to contribute to the redefinition of African narrative is conspicuous in their editorial philosophy. For example, *New African Magazine* aims to cover Africa in a context that does not deny that "corruption is endemic and must be confronted head on ... that recognises that Africa is a continent that is diverse and complex as it has a lot in common ... that celebrates enduring peace after decades of conflicts in places such as Mozambique ... and that celebrates entrenchment of democracy in countries such as Namibia and Ghana, economic successes in Mauritius, Botswana, Tunisia and others" (Jere-Malanda 2008: 39–40). However, a few scholarly studies have been conducted on how this commitment impacts on the process of news selection.

Research design

Brixton, London, is regarded as the spiritual home of black press because *The Voice* newspaper, which appeals predominantly to the African Caribbean, was launched there in 1981. This chapter draws on a case study of *African Voice*, a weekly newspaper published in Brixton. The aim is to discover whether *African Voice* reproduces the dominant negative stereotypes of Africa or subverts these by employing positive, negative, or neutral/mixed frames in their news stories. The researcher conducted a textual analysis of the online content of the *African Voice* website, comprising current and archive stories. The online edition has a database of 28,000 subscribers.

Articles were selected from a range of standard journalism genres – political news, education, conflict, business/economy, crime/legal, health, lifestyle (tourism/fashion/property), environment, human interest (entertainment, culture, religion, personal tragedy), and sports (see Project for Excellence in Journalism 2005). Twenty articles were chosen per genre using a progressive sampling method: "the selection of materials based on emerging understanding of the topic under investigation" (Altheide 1996: 33). The word count for each genre was about 4,000, with a total of 49,154 words across all genres. The textual analysis was applied to the headline, "lead", and paragraphs to capture "the journalist's overall perception and 'construction' of the event" (Ploughman 1995: 312) through the use of semantic categories and sources.

In this study, semantic categories are regarded as an integral part of framing devices including "vocabulary, catchphrases, and depictions" (see van Gorp & Vercruysse 2012: 1275) that are used to project negative presentation, positive presentation, or both viewpoints to the story. However, scholars caution that "frame analysts must take account that their own mental constructs may interfere with the identification of a frame" (see van Gorp & Vercruyssee 2012: 1275; van Gorp 2010). Nevertheless, the frame "provides a way to tie news content to larger structures and develops new ways of capturing the power of media to define issues visually and verbally, thereby shaping audience perceptions" (Reese & Lee 2012: 255). And this method "remains a useful technique for examining the ways in which African affairs are presented and made comprehensible to the public" (Scott 2009: 551).

Articles were analysed for evidence of three semantic categories: negative frames including references to victims, corruption, disease, poverty, famine, AIDS, debt relief, war, terrorism, and kidnapping; positive frames including references to peaceful transition, economic growth, peacekeeping, conflict resolution, human rights, and personal achievements; and neutral/mixed frames, that is, references to both viewpoints to the story, as shown in Table 7.1. Moreover, the articles were analysed for source diversity to identify "the number of sources quoted and their frequency of mention" (Haas 2007: 86), that is, African officials, non-African officials, African non-officials, and non-African non-official sources. The coding schedule or approach for these two broad source types is official sources (politicians, public institutions, private institutions, international organisation sources (UN, African Union), institutional intellectuals, media organisations) and non-official sources (citizens, religious leaders, campaigns/activists, voluntary organisations, others, i.e. terrorist organisations), as shown in Table 7.2.

Finally, the researcher interviewed the editor, Mike Abiola, via email and telephone to gain a deep insight into the newspaper's agenda about Africa and how newsroom resources are deployed to cover African news. The email interview enabled the collection of a considered and accurate response to a set of questions and the follow-up telephone interview was conducted on 24 March 2015, to enable the editor to comment on some of the research data.

Frequency of frames and diversity of sources in *African Voice*

The *African Voice* newspaper was established in 2001 and has a circulation of 75,000 copies and a readership of approximately 500,000, according to the editor. In terms of readership profile, the editor suggests that the newspaper's readership is split into first-generation migrants to Britain (45 per cent), British-born second generation Africans (40 per cent), short- and medium-stay visitors and holidaymakers from the African continent (5 per cent), and British-based non-Africans with an interest in African affairs (10 per cent). Their age profile indicates that 65 per cent of the newspaper's readers are between 30 and 55 years, which suggests that the newspaper appeals to the young, educated, and employed. However, there is a regional divide in terms of their location in the UK, as over 40 per cent of the newspaper's readers have lived in England for more than twenty years: 70 per cent in Greater London, 10 per cent in the Midlands, 12 per cent in Yorkshire, and 8 per cent in the North West. This pattern in regional division is also evident in relation to their country of origin, as 50 per cent are West Africans, 30 per cent are Southern Africans, 10 per cent are East and Central Africans, and 10 per cent are North Africans.

The editor, Mike Abiola, is aware of this readership profile and has catered to readers' interests in terms of presentation, layout features, and multimedia approach. The features cover a range of genres including interview, business, entertainment, politics, sport, tourism, African news, World news, and UK news. This layout is consistent with the editorial policy to "breathe a fresh perspective into the headlines by promoting the positive contribution British Africans make to the UK economy" (interview with the editor, 24 March 2015).

The findings of the textual analysis presented in Table 7.1 suggest that the newspaper presents a range of topics, as well as positive, negative, and mixed frames, across its news genres. This could be attributed to the readership profile, which indicates that readers are open minded and are exposed to different viewpoints because they also read the mainstream and other alternative media to complement their understanding of social reality. Therefore, the newspaper is mindful of alienating some users when trying to "provide a window to the continent for those interested in looking past the sensationalist and often unrepresentative headlines" (interview with the editor, 2015). As such, the high frequency of positive frames at 45.68 per cent could be regarded as consistent with its

Table 7.1 Frequency of frames in the African Voice

News genres	Negative frames	Positive frames	Neutral/mixed frames
Political news	3.34%	3.34%	1.60%
Education	2.67%	3.07%	0.26%
Conflict news	2.27%	7.48%	3.74%
Business/economy	3.34%	7.62%	3.34%
Crime/legal	4.41%	5.61%	2.67%
Health	6.01%	2.27%	3.87%
Lifestyle (tourism/ fashion/property)	2%	6.55%	2.54%
Environment	2.13%	2.40%	2.13%
Human interest (entertainment, religion, personal tragedy)	2.40%	5.74%	2.54%
Sports	1.73%	1.60%	1.20%
Total	**30.3%**	**45.68%**	**23.89%**

editorial policy. An example of a headline containing this frame, published on 18 May 2014, is "Africa's natural resources could improve the lives of millions". The three top genres in the positive frames are conflict news at 7.48 per cent, business/economy news at 7.62 per cent, and lifestyle at 6.55 per cent. The high percentage of the conflict news could be attributed to the inclusion of stories about peacebuilding in the unit of analysis. Other examples of semantic phrases within this frame from the articles analysed include: "new options to control the threat"; "striking a balance between fighting terrorism and respecting human rights"; "assist and rehabilitate the victims"; "build solar power plants and wind energy facilities"; and "plan to develop the tourism sector to generate more earnings and create more jobs".

The newspaper contains a medium frequency of negative frames at 30.3 per cent. An example of a headline containing this frame, published on 27 September 2014, is "3.2 million in need as Central African Republic health service collapses". The three top genres in the negative frames are health news at 6.01 per cent, crime/legal news at 4.41 per cent, and political news and business/economy news jointly at 3.34 per cent. Other examples of semantic phrases within this frame from the articles analysed include: "growing numbers of girls are running away from home to escape genital mutilation"; "there were 1800 confirmed and suspected cases of Ebola and more than 1000 deaths as of 9 August"; "at one clinic, vaccines are not kept in cold storage (as there is no fridge or electricity), yet the vaccines are given to unsuspecting mothers and children"; and "homosexuality is illegal in 37 of 54 African countries, according to Amnesty International".

The newspaper contains a low frequency of mixed/neutral frames at 23.89 per cent. An example of a headline containing this frame, published on 11 July 2014, is "Tunisia Minister peers through terrorism threat and sees tourism targets". The three top genres in the neutral/mixed frames are health at 3.87 per cent, conflict news at 3.74 per cent, and business/economy news at 3.34 per cent. Other examples of semantic phrases within this frame from articles analysed include: "another opinion proffered that the 'political craze' for power and wealth at all costs has drastically watered down the ethics of our culture such that nobody advocates the integrity of our culture anymore"; "in the present case of Angola, despite the achievements, there is the awareness that the Angolan women still continue to face numerous problems for their full emancipation"; and "they can either invest their natural resource revenue in people to generate jobs and opportunities for millions in present and future generations. Or they can squander this opportunity, allowing jobless growth and inequality to take root". The editor attributed the differences in the frequency of frames to the need to "conform to the ethics of the profession by having a balanced view but conscious of the newspaper's objective" (interview with the editor, 2015).

The findings in Table 7.2 are consistent with previous studies (see Lewis & Brookes 2004; Atton & Wickenden 2005; Ogunyemi 2012) that find news content prioritises the voices of officials over those of non-official sources. The top African official sources are the politicians at 30.80 per cent, while the top non-African official sources are members of the international institutions at 7.60 per cent. The editor attributed the high level of African official sources at 56.60 per cent to their goal: "to stand out and not pretend to be a UK national title" (interview with the editor, 2015).

The top African non-official sources are citizens at 5.90 per cent; the top non-African non-official sources are members of the voluntary organisations at 3.79 per cent. The editor argues that the low total percentage of non-official sources at 13.75 was not deliberate. Redressing this is challenging for the newspaper because it is based in the UK and relies on news filed by correspondents based in urban cities. However, Mike Abiola is optimistic that the newspaper will change this ratio in the near future by partnering with non-governmental organisations to reach the remote places in Africa. This is not to say that the newspaper should ignore non-official sources in the urban centres, but rather it should recognise the need to give a greater voice to people in the rural communities.

The low diversity of sources suggests that the newspaper encounters challenges in deploying newsroom resources to gather news from sources in urban and remote areas of Africa. However, such challenges are minimised in the UK because, according to the editor, "the London office benefits from its close proximity to the capital's African embassies, as well as the headquarters of several African organisations and the Foreign and Commonwealth Office. This enables us to deploy newsroom staff to cover news/press conferences and respond to invitations to interview key figures". Moreover, he argues that, while the coverage of Africa in the

Table 7.2 Diversity of sources in the *African Voice*[a]

African official sources	Non-African official sources	African non-official sources	Non-African non-official sources
Politicians – 30.80%	2.40%	Citizens – 5.90%	0%
Public institutions – 14.90%	2.80%	Religious organisations – 0.75%	0%
Institutional intellectuals – 8.30%	6.40%	Campaigns and activists – 3.1%	1.40%
Private institutions – 0.50%	0%	Voluntary organisations – 1.40%	3.79%
International institutions – 0%	7.60%	Others – 2.60%	0%
Media organisations – 2.10%	5.20%		
56.60%	**24.40%**	**13.75%**	**5.19%**

Note

a   The final row displays the total of each column.

Western media is improving, it has not reached the level expected. He said it is in the best interest of the mainstream media to report news about Africa that will influence development and encourage investors to go to Africa because of the cultural ties Britain has to some African countries. However, he acknowledged that changing the portrayal of Africa is not the prerogative of the Western media alone, but that the African diasporic press has a major role to play. He also recognised that changing Africa's image is a gradual process requiring all African diasporic media to forge a "better, stronger and more influential synergy in respect of effective news gathering and dissemination".

Conclusion

This study established that the African diasporic press subverts the dominant negative stereotypes of Africa in the Western media in some notable ways. First, the newspaper shuns the use of simplistic tropes such as tribalism in reporting conflict or political issues. Second, it provides a range of positive, negative, and mixed frames to give readers different viewpoints on the political and socio-economic realities in Africa. This means that the newspaper is not just giving facts about problems but also providing additional information on diagnoses, judgements, and solutions from socio-cultural standpoints.

Third, the newspaper covers Africa widely to show its political, economic, and geographic diversity. By doing this, it provides alternative perspectives that are outside of wars and conflicts reporting. Fourth, it gives prominence to African news through page placement, bold headlines, and quantity of news reports. Such increase in the number of substantive articles focusing specifically on African issues may trigger a renewed interest in Africa among readers. And fifth, the newspaper brings cultural knowledge to the process of news selection and to the treatment of stories by putting them in the appropriate historical and cultural contexts. But whether these are adequate to challenge Africa's negative image in the global public sphere will depend on how African governments and people construct African narratives.

References

African Voice newspaper, at http://www.africanvoiceonline.co.uk/ [accessed 16/03/2015].

Altheide, D. (1996) *Qualitative Media Analysis*, Thousand Oaks, CA: Sage.

Ankomah, B. (2008) "Reporting Africa", *New African Magazine*, 474 (June): 9–14.

Atton, C. & Wickenden, E. (2005) "Sourcing routines and representation in alternative journalism: a case study approach", *Journalism Studies*, 6(3): 347–359.

Duodu, C. (2008) "Beware the propaganda", *New African Magazine*, 474 (June): 16–20.

Goodwin, C. (2008) "Bad reporting on fertile soil", *New African Magazine*, 474 (June): 28–31.

Gruley, J. & Duvall, C. S. (2012) "The evolving narrative of the Dafur conflict as represented in *The New York Times* and *The Washington Post*, 2003–2009", *GeoJournal*, 77: 29–46.

Haas, T. (2007) *The Pursuit of Public Journalism: Theory, Practice and Criticism*, New York: Routledge.

Hawkins, V. (2012) "Terrorism and news of Africa post-9/11 coverage in *The New York Times*", *Journal of African Media Studies*, 4(1): 13–25.

Ibelema, M. (2014) "'Tribal fixation' and Africa's otherness: changes and resilience in news coverage", *Journalism and Communication Monographs*, 16(3): 162–217.

Jere-Malanda, R. (2008) "And now ... Positive Africa", *New African Magazine*, 474 (June): 36–40.

Kabukuru, W. (2008) "Kenya: spare us the agony and bias", *New African Magazine*, 474 (June): 32–33.

Kim, T. (1993) "The effect of foreign news on readers' attitudes toward foreign countries", paper presented at the annual meeting of the AEJMC, Kansas City, MO.

Kuypers, J. A. (2009) "Framing analysis", in J. A. Kuypers (ed.), *Rhetorical Criticism: Perspectives in Action*, Lanham, MD: Scarecrow Press.

Lewis, J. & Brookes, R. (2004) "How British television news represented the case for the war in Iraq", in S. Allan and B. Zelizer (eds), *Reporting War: Journalism in Wartime*, London: Routledge.

Mbeki, T. (2008) "Who will define Africa?", *New African Magazine*, 474 (June): 25–27.

New African Magazine (2008) "Country report: Ethiopia at the threshold of a renaissance", 474 (June): 55–58.

Ogunyemi, O. (2012) "Sourcing and representation routines in the black African press in the United Kingdom", in I. Rigoni and E. Saitta (eds), *Mediating Cultural Diversity in a Globalized Public Space*, Basingstoke: Palgrave.

Pawson, L. (2007) "Reporting Africa's unknown wars", in S. Maltby and R. Keeble (eds), *Communicating War: Memory, Media and Military*, Bury St Edmunds: Arima Publishing.

Ploughman, P. (1995) "The American print news media 'construction' of five natural disasters", *Disasters*, 19(4/December): 308–326.

Poncian, J. (2015) "The persistence of Western negative perceptions about Africa: factoring in the role of Africans", *Journal of African Studies and Development*, 7(3): 72–80.

Project for Excellence in Journalism (2005) "The state of the news media", at www.stateofthemedia.com/2005/ [accessed 17/03/2015].

Reese, S. D. & Lee, J. K. (2012) "Understanding the content of news media", in H. A. Sometko and M. Scammell (eds), *The Sage Handbook of Political Communication*, Los Angeles, CA: Sage.

Scott, M. (2009) "Marginalized, negative or trivial? Coverage of Africa in the UK press", *Media, Culture and Society*, 31(4): 533–557.

van Dijk, T. A. (ed.) (2011) *Discourse Studies*, 2nd edn, London: Sage.

van Gorp, B. (2010) "Strategies to take subjectivity out of framing analysis", in P. D'Angelo and J. Kuyper (eds), *Doing News Framing Analysis: Empirical and Theoretical Perspectives*, New York: Routledge.

van Gorp, B. & Vercruysse, T. (2012) "Frames and counter-frames giving meaning to dementia: a framing analysis of media content", *Social Science & Medicine*, 74: 1274–1281.

Part II

The image makers

Part II

The image makers

Mediating the distant Other for the distant audience

How do Western correspondents in East and Southern Africa perceive their audience?

Toussaint Nothias

The representation of foreign correspondents in popular culture and public debates generally oscillates between heroes and villains (Hannerz 2002: 60; Ehrlich & Saltzman 2015). In the case of Western correspondents based in Africa, this representation is polarised between, on the one hand, the intrepid, cosmopolitan, and human rights defender portrayed by Jennifer Connelly in the Hollywood blockbuster *Blood Diamond,* and on the other hand the self-righteous, hypocritical, prejudice-ridden agent of media imperialism as depicted, for instance, by Kenyan writer Binyavanga Wainaina (2012).

In fact, much has been said about foreign correspondents in the academic literature on Africa's media image. They come to embody the set of professional values associated with the industry at large and, as a result, they end up on the receiving end of the criticism of Western media coverage of Africa. One of the most public faces of this criticism, academic Laura Seay, also known as @TexasinAfrica on Twitter, notably wrote in a famous column: "many Africa correspondents file stories that fall prey to pernicious stereotypes and tropes that dehumanize Africans" (Seay 2012).

In spite of these numerous references to Western foreign correspondents in the debate on Africa's media image, there is surprisingly very little research that informs the experiences and views of these individuals (Bunce 2010, 2015; Vicente 2013). Instead, the literature focuses on the textual and discursive features of media coverage, and generally assumes the role of correspondents to be that of non-reflexive reproducers of colonial stereotypes who apply different journalistic standards when reporting from the continent, and actively contribute to representing Africans as distant Others. But since correspondents are at the heart of the journalistic production of Africa's image, engaging with their account provides a way to deconstruct the manufacturing of this image from within, and an opportunity, as Zelizer puts it, to read journalism "against its own grain" (Zelizer 2013: 145). Correspondents are located at a key nexus of the production process where they act as mediating agents between the ground and the demands of editors back home: a nexus where the politics of representation – central to the literature on Africa's media image – and the constraints of news production meet.

This chapter therefore fills this gap by providing a critical appraisal of the accounts of Western correspondents based in the two hubs of international news on the continent: South Africa and Kenya. I conducted 24 in-depth semi-structured interviews with a range of journalists working for international Western media organisations in Cape Town, Johannesburg, and Nairobi between September 2013 and May 2014. These individuals are either permanent staff or freelance journalists who have a regular working relationship with several Western media outlets, primarily British and French, but also German, Belgian, and US American. The majority of my interviewees (13) are foreign correspondents working for the British and French print media outlets analysed as part of a broader doctoral project, and I therefore draw the majority of my observations here from this core poll of interviewees.

I focus specifically on the way foreign correspondents imagine and talk about their audience. The idea of the audience is a sort of blind spot in the production of foreign news production. On the one hand, "what the audience wants" is naturalised within the newsroom (Paterson 1996: 375); as such, the audience is a representation in itself. On the other hand, because perceptions of the audience by journalists significantly influence news choices and shape news products (Ngomba 2011: 13), they ultimately impact media representations. Thus, I approach the audience as a discursive construct that dialectically links issues of news production and of media representation. How, then, do Western correspondents imagine and talk about their audience? What do these perceptions of the audience reveal about the production of African news? And what's the impact of these perceptions on the representation of Africa produced by correspondents?

The grandma, the tourist, the businessman, the political elite...

When asked who they think their audience is, or when talking spontaneously about their audience, correspondents most commonly referred to four categories: (1) the family member/the common person, (2) the tourist, (3) the businessman, (4) the politician/the decision maker. Not all foreign correspondents mentioned all these profiles. And depending on the editorial line of the paper, the emphasis would be put on different types of audience. Newspapers like the *Financial Times* or *Les Echos* emphasise their business readership (3), while papers like *Le Monde* and *The Times* emphasise their political readership (4). But looking across all interviews, these four categories constitute the main and recurring profiles used by foreign correspondents to describe their audience. What does this typology of audiences tell us about the production of African news?

The first observation is that foreign correspondents write primarily for an audience "back home". This is hardly surprising since this constitutes, historically, the primary reason behind the idea of foreign correspondence. Not unlike anthropologists, foreign correspondents are translators between cultures (Hannerz 1996: 118). Their job is to report on a part of the world and a culture, and to make sense of it to another. They share with anthropologists, "the condition of being in a transnational contact zone, engaged in reporting, representing, interpreting – generally, managing meaning across distances, although in part at least with different interests, under other constraints" (Hannerz 2002: 58).

The correlative of this audience being "back home" is that they are all perceived to belong to a national culture. As a result, for correspondents, the involvement of fellow national citizens in an event becomes a key indicator that a story will be relevant to their audience. This contributes, for instance, to the ongoing production of what British foreign correspondents call "Brits in shit" stories or to the framing of major disasters or conflict situations around the fate of fellow national citizens.

Embedded within the national belonging is also the racial identification of the audience as white. This was perfectly exemplified during the Westgate attack in Nairobi that claimed some 67 lives, including four British citizens, and where over 175 people were wounded. On 22 September 2013, as the siege was still taking place, *The Telegraph* was running on its website the headline, "Britons caught in Nairobi shopping mall attacks". At the time, no British victims had been reported yet and the title relied on a statement from William Hague, then Foreign Secretary, claiming British nationals were "undoubtedly caught up in the attack". Without confirmation of British citizens killed in the attack, the article frontloaded the fate of victims from other Western countries (US, France, and Canada).

A correspondent explained that there is a phenomenon of racial identification on the side of the audience whereby, "the images of the little white girl running alone in the mall had an impact." Conversely, we also see that the audience is envisioned by correspondents as a group collectively defined by its whiteness. For many correspondents, this phenomenon is neither new nor is it specific to the coverage of Africa. As one of them put it: "it is the famous joke about the Aberdeen newspaper headline: 'Titanic sinks; Aberdeen man drowns'." Yet, through this naturalised process driven by perception of the audience, the media actively contribute to the sense that certain lives, Western and white, are worth more than others.

The correspondents sometimes defined relevance as, "what will interest a given national readership", without necessarily involving fellow citizens in the story or appealing to racial identification. A French journalist gave the example of a story on shale gas in South Africa that would talk to the interest of the French readership, as a national debate about shale gas was raging at the time in France. He recognised, however, that finding the relevant angle was "not always obvious" and sometimes "problematic", as with the coverage of rhino poaching:

> We have done a lot of stories on this. But clearly this is part of the post-materialist values of the Western reader who will be interested in what happens to rhinos but much less about what happens in a township. ... I think the media coverage is a bit excessive on that story. And at the same time, we are all part of this system, and we feed this trend because there is a demand.

A significant consequence of the way the audience is imagined is simplification. The audience is assumed to have little to no prior knowledge or interest, especially when it comes to the first two categories (the common person/the tourist). This significantly impacts what background and contextual information journalists deem important in any given story. Talking about Zimbabwe, David Smith, the Africa correspondent for *The Guardian*, explains that he rarely talks about how the Movement for Democratic Change (the main opposition party to Mugabe between 1999 and 2005) had broken down into different factions:

> If you are in Zimbabwe or you are a Zimbabwe aficionado, you want to know that stuff. ... Frankly, I think the average British reader is still about Mugabe vs MDC. You don't want to muddy the water too much.

The way correspondents imagine their audience drives what they see as "relevant" news and often confines media coverage of Africa to specific, stereotypical boxes:

> Brits in shit. Shark attacks. Or "Pilot kidnapped by CAR rebels". Or "Foreign oil worker found with his pants down in a Lagos hotel". Those are all things that I know will pique their [the audience's] interest. ... Congo mineral stuff? No. Nigeria kidnapping? Yeah. Boko Haram? Yep. AQMI? Yep. Because it just fits with this plastic narrative: all the brown people want to kill the white people.

This echoes the claims by an Africa correspondent that most of the British press tends, "to presume that our readers are only interested in major calamities, countries with which we have a historical colonial relationship, Brits in troubles, wildlife and white mischief".

In sum, the four types of audiences and how correspondents talk about them embody a cluster of news values that significantly drive media coverage of Africa. These notably include: negativity; the involvement of Western nations or people; the focus on countries or people more familiar to a given audience; economic relevance; the unambiguity of the story. In addition, the way they talk about their audience suggests that their work is "less shaped by an appreciation of the diversity of things actually there on the beat, and more by the attitudes and ideas brought from home" (Hannerz 2007: 307). Dialectically, then, this imagined audience contributes to the covert process through which African news becomes simplified and stereotyped.

The audience also plays an important role in the defensive rhetoric used by correspondents when faced with criticisms of Western media coverage of Africa. The audience becomes a way to divert the responsibility away from journalists. This was made clear by a correspondent who argued that, "the audience plays a huge role in agenda setting and I don't want to let them get away without having at least 50 per cent of the responsibility!" This rhetorical use of the audience as part of a defensive strategy relied on two cornerstones. On the one hand, correspondents would argue that the media deliver what the audience wants, and that unfortunately stereotypes sell. In the commercial environment of news production, then, the reproduction of stereotypes can be explained by the need to cater to demands from the audience. On the other hand, correspondents would argue that they are not responsible for how people interpret media content – two strategies that van Dijk (1992: 92) found to be regularly used in racism denial by the press.

At best, correspondents would recognise that they rely on assumptions about the audience, with one claiming that journalists have been playing a "guessing game for centuries", while another argues that, "there are a lot of unpleasant, unspoken truths within knowing what the readers are interested in". But very rarely would they recognise the media's responsibility in shaping the audience preferences that then feed back journalists' perceptions of the audience. Perhaps it takes stepping back from the professional socialisation in the journalistic field to question this? Commenting on his public letter criticising the quality of CNN's reporting on Africa in its flagship programme *60 Minutes*, Howard W. French, a former foreign correspondent now turned writer and academic, wrote:

> The media pretends that it's only serving up what people are interested in. ... What the media is doing, in fact, is training the public's sensibilities by its own approaches to a variety of topics. Africa has traditionally been accorded very little space in the media ... [except for] immense tragedy, interest in a white person playing a starring role, or wildlife. Over time, these become accepted as the only reasons most people would want to pay any attention to Africa. (Adegoke 2015; see also French chapter in this volume)

Foreign correspondents report for a distant audience. On the one hand, there is a distance between what they perceive interests their audience, and what interests them personally and professionally as correspondents. Talking about the Pistorius case, a freelance correspondent explained that this was of "zero interest, journalistically speaking" for him, but that since this is the type of story the audience is fascinated by, he keeps on reporting it. On the other hand, the distance is the geographic one between the field and "home". Except for one, all my interviewees have been living in Africa for at least four years. In their daily lives, they don't encounter their audience back home. The geographic distance translates into assumptions about what the audience is interested in; these assumptions, in turn, influence story selections and writing. This way, the journalistic eye is on "the lookout for scenes that carry an already established interest for a Western audience, thus investing perception itself with the mediating power of cultural difference" (Spurr 1993: 21). How foreign correspondents imagine their audience is therefore a key discursive feature in the mediation of the distant Other, and partly explains why this reporting makes "a kind of return trip, catering to ideas, even stereotypes, which are in fact already well-established at home" (Hannerz 2007: 307). In that sense, representations of the distant audience – upstream – and of distant Others – downstream – are in a dialectic relation whereby assumptions about the former feed stereotypes about the latter.

...and the digitally connected Other

However, the story of how foreign correspondents perceive their audience would not be complete without looking at the role played by local audiences. From the coverage of the 2010 World Cup to the 2013 Kenyan elections or the death of Mandela, South African and Kenyan audiences in particular increasingly use social media to discuss, comment on, and question the Western media coverage of Africa news. In fact, these constitute the audience that foreign correspondents engage with the most, both through social media and in their daily lives. Seven foreign correspondents shared the statistics of their Twitter followers. In the majority (four out of seven cases), most of their followers were from the African country where they are based, before followers in their home country. On average, this amounts to 32.5 per cent of local followers versus 19.5 per cent of home followers. In other words, local populations who have long held only the status of distant Others to be represented, are now increasingly becoming readers and viewers.

Through this local involvement, African voices are increasingly heard and take part in shaping the narratives about Africa. And this impacts how foreign correspondents write and work. For one correspondent, the involvement of local audiences through social media in fact contributes to raising journalistic standards: "Nowadays, especially in Kenya, you get picked up on very quickly by the Twitterati if there is anything that looks like it could be slightly dodgy; which is good!" He recalled being in assignment in 2005 with a seasoned correspondent who was surprised to see him take so many notes when interviewing a woman:

> He said: "If you have a 'the' instead of an 'a', or a 'with' instead of a 'from', what is she gonna care about?" That's changed now. You can be anywhere and some guy is like, "Hey" – on his phone – "I saw what you wrote about me in a refugee camp or whatever!"

As this story suggests, the role of local audiences in the digital age is primarily a reactive one. A perfect example of this reactive role was the international reporting of *Kony 2012* (Nothias 2013). *Kony 2012* was a 30-minute video created by the Christian American NGO Invisible Children, Inc. It aimed at raising awareness about the crimes committed by the Lord's Resistance Army and its leader Joseph Kony. In April 2012, the video went viral, eventually reaching 110 million hits in a few days (Chalk 2012: 3). This success was as surprising as the online reactions it spurred were numerous. Observers in Uganda and elsewhere raised questions about its accuracy (Kony was portrayed as still in Uganda, whereas he had left the country six years ago), the policy it advocated (US military intervention), and its reliance on dehumanising stereotypes and colonial tropes that disempower Africans and present them as voiceless distant Others (Nothias 2013). The backlash grew in parallel to the video spreading on the web, and a blog compiling the different criticism "Visible Children" also went viral (it attracted at least 2.3 million views in a few days) (Tutton 2012).

While the international media initially focused on the "buzz" created by the video – thereby giving it further publicity – it then incorporated this backlash in its coverage. Two Ugandan journalists who had been at the forefront of the online backlash, Rosebell Kagumire and Angelo Izama, were interviewed on most international news organisations, including CNN, CNTV, the BBC, France 24, *The New York Times*, *The Guardian*, and Al Jazeera English (Chalk 2012: 8). Social media thus enabled these voices to be granted a space in mainstream media platforms that have, historically, silenced such voices. This local engagement through social media became part of the international coverage, and played a role in shaping the mainstream news narrative. Looking at the 2013 Kenyan elections, Bunce observed a similar phenomenon where Kenyan tweets using the hashtag #SomeonetellCNN managed to make CNN amend its coverage and "were not restricted to the 'twittersphere' – they entered into, and became stories in mainstream international news coverage" (2015: 57).

The engagement with local audiences via social media is not a panacea. On the one hand, internet penetration within and across African countries vary greatly, which means that there are strong communicative inequalities among local audiences. On the other hand, there is a risk to fetishise authentic "African" voices as able to "provide some kind of unchallengeable African truth" (Jacobs 2013). Talking about Kony 2012, Jacobs reminds us that Invisible Children "has 'African voices' on its staff" and that "this was part of the filmmakers' defense when they responded to criticisms." However, I would argue that there is one area where this engagement from local audiences certainly heralds a strongly disruptive potential. It is the fact that foreign correspondents increasingly envision the local population as either actual or possible audience members.

I will illustrate this point with a story shared by a correspondent. This young journalist was embarking on a yearlong radio project that followed the lives of kids in a school in one of the poorest townships of the Cape Town region. After having spent a couple of months in the school in preparation for the programme, the journalist prepared a video that would accompany the launch of the programme online. He chose the title "Learning in poverty" and shared his choice with his editor. Upon hearing the title, the editor told him that he couldn't use this title. Perplexed, the journalist asked, "Why?" The editor then told him that, before putting the video online and choosing a title for the programme, he should go to the classroom and show the video to the schoolkids. As he looked at them watching the video, the journalist recalled thinking: "Thank God I didn't use this title!" When I asked him to unpack what was wrong with this title, he explained that it reduced these kid's lives and learning experience, their present and their future, to the experience of "poverty"; that it equated them exclusively with "poverty"; and that it completely failed to communicate the complexity, nuances, and basic sense of common humanity that they were in fact trying to show in the programme. Ultimately, they settled on the title "School Year", with the subtitle, "Learning, Poverty, and Success in a South African Township".

This story illustrates what can happen when foreign correspondents envision the local population as potential audience members. It was not until he considered the subjects of his reporting as potential viewers that this foreign correspondent realised that his title could be considered dehumanising and reductive. For now, local populations have mainly played a reactive or interpretative role in the news production process (à la Kony 2012 or #SomeonetellCNN). But the fact that all correspondents I interviewed talked instinctively about the local engagement via social media heralds some potential for a stronger impact on the production process. More than ever before, foreign correspondents can't afford not to envision local population as potential readers (Franks 2010). Whether or not they welcome the local backlash, whether or not their media decide to become "more nationalistic in the face of global exposure" (Sambrook 2010: 57), foreign correspondents are all impacted by the fact that there is a local audience that may read their content. In that sense, the primarily reactive role of local audiences via social media contributes to cultivate journalistic sensitivities over time that will impact the news production process upstream, not only downstream. My argument is not that foreign correspondents will or should write primarily with local audiences in mind. But it's likely that, faced with growing local feedback, correspondents will come to integrate more systematically the "local citizen" as a category alongside "the tourist", "the grandma", "the businessman", and "the politician".

Conclusion

My analysis draws a more nuanced portrait of foreign correspondents than the polarised representation that often dominates these debates. How they think about their audience is a vector of both continuities and changes in the reporting of Africa. Naturalised perceptions of the audience embody news values that simultaneously contribute to simplification and to the reproduction of stereotypes. But correspondents also increasingly envision local populations as potential audience members. In the age of digital and social media, local populations are impacting the reporting of Africa downstream – by being reactive and keeping Western media coverage in check. But they also have an impact on reporting upstream: as correspondents integrate the local population as a potential audience, this increases the accuracy and accountability of their reporting. In fact, these findings are linked to my focus on a subgroup of foreign correspondents working for nation-based outlets. But the majority of international correspondents in Africa work for media outlets such as AFP, AP, Reuters, Al Jazeera, and the BBC, which have adopted a more global agenda. By virtues of this globalising media market, it is possible that the majority of foreign correspondents in Africa have already started to operate a significant evolution in their perceptions of their audience, something that future research should help illuminate. Along with the increasingly important role played by local journalists in international news reporting (Bunce 2013, 2015), this emergent trend heralds some potential to delivering higher levels of accountability in the reporting of Africa in international news, and is likely to become more salient in the future as the continent itself is increasingly seen as a media market.

References

Adegoke, Y. (2015) "An open letter to '60 Minutes' criticizes America's most-watched news show over its Africa coverage", *Quartz*, at http://qz.com/370791/an-open-letter-to-60-minutes-criticizes-americas-most-watched-news-show-over-its-africa-coverage/ [accessed 11/04/2015].

Bunce, M. (2010) "'This place used to be a white British boys' club': reporting dynamics and cultural clash at an international news bureau in Nairobi", *The Round Table*, 99(410): 515–528.

Bunce, M. (2013) "Reporting from 'the field': foreign correspondents and the international news coverage of East Africa", unpublished PhD thesis, University of Oxford, Oxford.

Bunce, M. (2015) "International news and the image of Africa: new storytellers, new narratives?", in J. Gallagher (ed.), *The Image of Africa*, Manchester: Manchester University Press.

Chalk, S. (2012) "Kony 2012: success or failure?", International Broadcasting Trust, London, at http://www.ibt.org.uk/reports/kony-2012-success-or-failure/ (accessed 11/03/2016).

Ehrlich, M. C. & Saltzman, J. (2015) *Heroes and Scoundrels: The Image of the Journalist in Popular Culture*, Champaign, IL: University of Illinois Press.

Franks, S. (2010) "Globalising consciousness: the end of 'foreign' reporting and no more foreign secrets", *Ethical Space: The International Journal of Communication Ethics*, 7(4): 39–47.

Hannerz, U. (1996) *Transnational Connections: Culture, People, Places*, London: Routledge.

Hannerz, U. (2002) "Among the foreign correspondents: reflections on anthropological styles and audiences", *Ethnos*, 67(1): 57–74.

Hannerz, U. (2007) "Foreign correspondents and the varieties of cosmopolitanism", *Journal of Ethnic and Migration Studies*, 33(2): 299–311.

Jacobs, S. (2013) "New media in Africa and the global public sphere", *African Futures*, at http://forums.ssrc.org/african-futures/2013/02/21/new-media-in-africa-and-the-global-public-sphere/ [accessed 11/04/2015].

Ngomba, T. (2011) "Journalists' perceptions of 'the audience' and the logics of participatory development/communication: a contributory note", *Ecquid Novi: African Journalism Studies*, 32(1): 4–24.

Nothias, T. (2013) "'It's struck a chord we have never managed to strike': frames, perspectives and remediation strategies in the international news coverage of Kony2012", *Ecquid Novi: African Journalism Studies*, 34(1): 123–129.

Paterson, C. (1996) "News production at worldwide television news", unpublished PhD thesis, University of Texas, Austin, TX.

Sambrook, R. (2010) *Are Foreign Correspondents Redundant? The Changing Face of International News*, Oxford: Reuters Institute for the Study of Journalism – Challenges.

Seay, L. (2012) "How not to write about Africa", *Foreign Policy*, at http://foreignpolicy.com/2012/04/25/how-not-to-write-about-africa/ [accessed 11/04/2015].

Spurr, D. (1993) *The Rhetoric of Empire: Colonial Discourse in Journalism, Travel Writing, and Imperial Administration*, Durham, NC: Duke University Press.

Tutton, M. (2012) "Nova Scotia blogger leads the online charge against Kony 2012 campaign", *The Globe and Mail*, at http://www.theglobeandmail.com/news/world/nova-scotia-blogger-leads-the-online-charge-against-kony-2012-campaign/article534811/ [accessed 11/04/2015].

van Dijk, T. (1992) "Discourse and the denial of racism", *Discourse & Society*, 3(1): 87–118.

Vicente, P. N. (2013) "Foreign correspondence from Sub-Saharan Africa: an evolving communicational paradigm shift", at https://www.academia.edu/4488615/Foreign_correspondence_from_Sub-Saharan_Africa_An_evolving_communicational_paradigm_shift [accessed 30/06/2014].

Wainaina, B. (2012) "How not to write about Africa in 2012: a beginner's guide", *The Guardian*, 3 June, at http://www.theguardian.com/commentisfree/2012/jun/03/how-not-to-write-about-africa [accessed 11/04/2015].

Zelizer, B. (2013) "Tools for the future of journalism", *Ecquid Novi: African Journalism Studies*, 34(2): 142–152.

Chapter 9

Media perspectives

Television reporting of Africa: 30 years on

Zeinab Badawi

Editors' note: Zeinab Badawi is a BBC television journalist and since 2014 has been the Chair of the (UK) Royal African Society. Badawi was born in Sudan and raised in the UK. She was for many years a co-presenter of *Channel 4 News*, and subsequently became a presenter of *BBC World News Today* and the show *HARDtalk*, an interview programme produced for the BBC World News channel.

In 1986 Badawi contributed a book chapter entitled "Reflections on recent TV coverage of Africa" to an edited volume *The Black and White Media Book* (Twitchin 1986). Badawi had spent some months making a film in her native Sudan that prompted her reflections upon the way that Africa was being reported in the international media at that time. Anticipating Hawk's introductory essay to *Africa's Media Image* (Hawk 1992), Badawi wrote about how she felt that, despite superficial changes in the post-colonial period, international television coverage of Africa still had serious deficiencies and could be so much better. She said in 1986 that she found it "disturbing that in recent TV coverage of Africa ... an apparently enlightened approach gives rise to some unpalatable side effects; cultural superiority is still presupposed, only now it is more subtle." Some thirty years after that was published, we invited Badawi to reflect on what has changed and also what has stayed the same in the way that international TV covered stories in Africa.

Cultural chauvinism and imperial stereotypes

Suzanne Franks (SF): In 1986 you wrote that TV deals in imperialist stereotypes, leaving the impression that "Africans starve to death ... and it is the West, this time in the guise of Bob Geldof ... which comes to their rescue. They are portrayed as passive helpless, spectators to their own destiny whilst the West is the superior partner." Is that still a valid criticism of the coverage today?

Zeinab Badawi (ZB): Today we see a great deal more use of local African reporters on television, instead of always flying someone in from outside to "explain" what is going on. This use of "indigenous reporting" is certainly an improvement. All over the continent from Egypt to Nigeria, the BBC is using talented local reporters.

Similarly NGOs will very often put up local representatives as interviewees, which is a positive change, rather than the old trope of the "white helper". But sometimes if you scratch beneath the surface we still see the coverage reverting to type and offering the same old distortions. One particular example here was the reporting of the West African Ebola outbreak in 2015. The relentless focus in much of the reporting upon a small handful of Western health workers, some of whom became ill, was out of all proportion. What about the hundreds of local nurses and doctors who were facing risks daily and doing the really awful work like clearing up bodies for salaries of only $300 per month? The role of these people who were the mainstays in coping with the disease rarely featured in the coverage. Once again the story we saw was all about the international community and what it was doing to "help"; the same old idea that one has to look to outside agents to fix the problem.

Changing news agendas

SF: You wrote about the problem that viewers lacked "alternative information and first hand experience of Africa. They cannot put things into context and will always be viewing in a vacuum ... into which any pre-existing stereotypes and prejudices are left uncorrected." To what extent does that remain a problem in the way that the news is reported today?

ZB: Well, the agenda of how Africa is reported has improved somewhat. Nevertheless there is still a danger of kneejerk reactions; approaching African stories in a uni-dimensional way. For example there is too often an assumption that a rich African must therefore also be corrupt. Look at the way that Western billionaires like Bill Gates or Steve Jobs are venerated by comparison. We still need a more multidimensional approach to stories about Africa.

The approach of domestic news programmes is particularly to blame here and I feel on these channels there has been far less change over the years. If they do cover African news there is more of a tendency to sensationalise stories, because they would claim that is necessary in order to engage the domestic UK audience. By comparison the international outlets, like BBC World or Al Jazeera, take a more nuanced approach because they are speaking directly also to international audiences including many viewers who are of course in Africa. Personally that is why I much prefer to report for an international channel.

International reporting and local sensitivities

SF: When you wrote your original chapter on reporting Africa, you were critical of the notion of an "electronic village" because it was still the West peering voyeuristically at Africa rather than a reciprocal relationship. However, you were concerned about the impact of stereotypical portrayals of Africa on the domestic racial agenda. "If blacks abroad are for example seen as starving, helpless and in need of Western assistance, it can reinforce in *some* British people's minds the idea that black immigrants *here* are flee- ing economic hardship from their own poverty stricken countries." And you warned about the danger that stereotypical reporting of Africans would translate into a view of black immigrants in Europe as "needy outsiders who take up jobs and scrounge off social security." Given the recent crisis in migration and refugees, do you still feel that the news of Africa affects how audiences in Europe see other people around them?

ZB: When I was writing about this in 1986, it was still in a pre-globalised world. Given the huge changes brought about through the internet and digi- tal media, we do now live in a global village where as journalists we have to be far more responsive to audiences. And today we also have a much more diverse audience here in the UK, for example a big African diaspora which did not really exist when I wrote the original chapter, and so we need to take all of this into account in the way that we report.

Whatever I wrote earlier, it is more important than ever nowadays when we are covering Africa (and elsewhere) to portray people with sensitivity. We have seen in the recent past many more outsiders arrive on our shores and this highly topical issue of how we relate to immigrants is still crucially affected by the way that we report on international stories.

References

Hawk, B. (ed.) (1992) *Africa's Media Image*, New York: Praeger.
Twitchin, J. (ed.) (1986) *The Black and White Media Book: Handbook for the Study of Racism and Television*, Stoke-on-Trent: Trentham Books.

Chapter 10

Foreign correspondents in sub-Saharan Africa

Their socio-demographics and professional culture

Paulo Nuno Vicente

A sizeable portion of our everyday knowledge about sub-Saharan Africa comes from the work of international news reporters stationed on the continent. Even though they play a critical role in communicating about the distant Other (communication frequently criticised for its representational deficits), scholarly empirical research on the work of foreign correspondents has been neglected: it is now decades old and lacks a systematic examination of the on-the-ground realities of journalism in Africa.

This chapter is about the socio-demographics, the professional cultures, and the news work of these individuals. It examines long-term trajectories in international journalism combined with short-term developments resulting from transformations in microelectronics and digitisation. Three main lines of inquiry are outlined: who is actually reporting across the continent, what are the main characteristics of the occupational cultures in place, and what are the constraints that limit the range of news workers' production routines?

Professional international news reporters are repositioning themselves in a transforming communicative environment. Thus, it is crucial to know how they interpret their own occupation and the role of rising actors in the transnational media sphere. To do so, a pan-African online survey[1] was conducted between January and February 2013, collecting answers from 124 participants in 41 countries.[2] These findings were complemented by *in loco* semi-structured interviews with 43 professionals based in three hubs that have historically been the main centres for international correspondents in Africa: Nairobi (Kenya), Dakar (Senegal), and Johannesburg (South Africa). Both the online survey and the interviews focused on staff journalists and freelancers working for news organisations based outside the continent.

Who is reporting across sub-Saharan Africa?

The geographical locations of foreign correspondence have received little academic attention (Farish 2001). Studies of the geographic distribution of foreign press corps show not only that they are mostly concentrated in the US and Western Europe, but also that elitism and proximity are two major determinants in the deployment of journalists around the world. Given "their small numbers and the importance of their jobs, correspondents began to be seen as a professional elite, who operated fairly autonomously from the home office" (Hamilton & Cozma 2009: 605).

Previous studies resorted to surveys in order to reveal the socio-demographic constitution of foreign press corps (Hess 1996, 2005; Nosaka 1992; Maxwell 1956). These studies have mainly addressed US reporters working overseas and, alternatively, international reporters based in the US. They are now as much as decades old and do not consider the emerging and crucial questions brought about by media convergence. Previously, no systematic and updated study was available of the socio-demographics of international news reporters working across sub-Saharan Africa.

Currently, the most common contemporary professional correspondent working across sub-Saharan Africa is a male (68.55 per cent) between 23 and 42 years old (72.51 per cent); he has 6 to 17 years of experience in news work (49.19 per cent), but is a beginner in international news reporting (52.42 per cent) with recent experience in the current post (69.35 per cent). He has a higher education degree (77.41 per cent) in the field of Humanities and Social Sciences (68.55 per cent) and works for three or

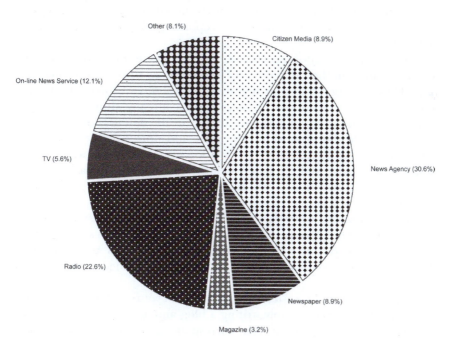

Figure 10.1 Type of news media organisation

more news organisations (50.81 per cent), and most frequently for a news agency (30.65 per cent). He is a freelancer (50.81 per cent), often working alone (48.39 per cent), and perceiving himself as a general assignment reporter (75.81 per cent).

This socio-demographic characterisation of international news reporters working across sub-Saharan Africa is consistent with previous research implemented in other geographies of foreign correspondence (Hess 1996, 2005; Nosaka 1992), confirming a male-oriented occupational field composed of an educated elite: the combined values of completed higher education degrees (Bachelor, Master, and Doctorate: N = 96; 77.41 per cent) suggest that formal education is a very significant factor in the access to a foreign correspondence career path.

How is international news reporters' culture defined?

Journalists' culture has been theorised as the interaction of their ideas, practices, and artefacts. In this sense, journalists are not detached from cultural considerations: "They belong to a specific culture and to specific professional subcultures" (van Ginneken 1998: 65). Professional international news reporters working across sub-Saharan Africa highly value empirical research (92.74 per cent), that is, evidence based on observation and direct experience. Objectivity (as detachment) is the guiding principle ensuring that information collected during field reporting conforms to professional standards.

How they gather information and how they make themselves accountable are central to their definition of journalism as a professional occupation. These practices not only delineate the validity of the cultural rules and norms that regulate practitioners who are already within the occupational boundaries, but, in addition, they critically define those who shall be kept outside the profession. The rules and norms define contemporary journalism as a professional occupation rather than an informal communication activity, and ultimately delineate its societal role as a task for professionals: citizen media workers shall be kept outside professional journalism boundaries.

"People know that when they turn to us, they can have a certain kind of trust in what we do, because we are careful, we do it ourselves, we do insist on being on the ground ourselves when we can," suggests Adam Nossiter, *The New York Times*' correspondent based in Dakar, adding,

> I know that now it is easier for you to publish yourself, but there's a vast difference between simply writing a blog and actually doing the business of journalism and foreign correspondence. The two worlds have nothing to do with each other.

From this perspective of occupational protectionism, "what citizen journalism also highlights is that journalism is a proper job and it shouldn't be forgotten," stressed Thomas Fessy, a BBC correspondent based in Dakar. "I think we need to ensure that proper journalists are on the ground, because it's a proper job and it needs to be taken seriously. Especially in these times of fast-paced information, it goes so quickly that people need professionals to give them guidance and to sort this information," he said.

Practitioners who can be described as news innovators (Lewis 2010) promoted a more inclusive interpretation of the journalistic field, interpreting it as one that should be, ideally, kept open to functional reconfigurations. "Citizen journalism? I think it's good in terms of information circulation," believes Stéphanie Braquehais, RFI and France 24 correspondent, based in Nairobi. Guy Henderson, CCTV's correspondent in Johannesburg, agrees: "As long as there is more information out there, the better for us. And I think that there will always be professional institutions that will channel information, whether it's a news channel or a newspaper."

International news reporters are aware of their role as translators of otherness and most clearly recognise representational deficits regarding Africa's media image (61.29 per cent). Journalists like Ilona Eveleens, correspondent for TROUW, TAZ, and N-24 based in Nairobi, observed that, "Africa has a problem: it is not very popular with the established journalist. They all want to go to Washington, London, Paris, Beijing. Those are the places where your career is going," she says, explaining, "You don't stay in Africa. You just don't. So, when you get here there are a lot of young people who start their career here. They start and then go to some place, you know, more glamorous than Africa."

Eveleens' words describe sub-Saharan Africa as a less desirable assignment within the career path for professional news reporters. This perception of location is reinforced, believes Alan Boswell, by the importance given to news content. This McClatchy Newspapers correspondent based in Nairobi declared that, "US editors don't consider stories out here in Africa as must-haves – the few exceptions only highlight how little the rest of the continent is consistently covered."

Two distinct levels of restriction for this translation of otherness exist. First, this happens at a cross-cultural level, with correspondents having to frequently cross their cultural comfort zone. Second, it occurs at a cognitive level, with reporters having to balance context-rich information obtained via cultural immersion and the rules of objectivity and detachment. "In order to explain something that has a human nature you have to be there, it's necessary," states Xavier Aldekoa, a freelance correspondent for *La Vanguardia*, based in Johannesburg. "Living here and being able to travel allows you to open your eyes and to understand better the continent," he adds.

Contemporary correspondents often find themselves far away from this prescribed ideal. In part, that is due to the use of digital technologies in

piece, temporary employment contracts, social insecurity, and extremely flexible production routines. "The expectation is that you'll do all this stuff without necessarily any extra pay. Yet it takes a huge amount of time and there's the recognition amongst us that what we are producing is not that good," says Ilona Eveleens (quoted earlier). So, "gone are the days where all that a journalist needed to do in order to earn his money was to tell his story by telephone to the newsroom," according to Anthony Morland, a journalist working for IRIN News, based in Nairobi, who adds, "Now you have many more demands, updates, web-based channels, 24 hour news, Twitter feeds, Facebook updates, video blogs, blogs. There's also a tremendous pressure for a convergence of skills: take photos, write the story, update the story."

Further, citizen participation emerges also as a renewed core issue within networked international journalism and news reporters are actively connected via online social networks (94.45 per cent). Online social network use is already among the most common newsgathering activities for international news reporters, being perceived as a relevant platform (54.84 per cent). Social networks notoriously emerge in practitioners' self-narratives as important monitoring tools for news-uptake and story ideation, platforms for community-building and interaction with the audience, barometers for competition awareness, and as reporting/recording tools.

As shown in Figure 10.3, a considerable portion of international news reporters now have to manage direct audience feedback in their news work: 41.13 per cent of the respondents to the survey receive it at least once per week.

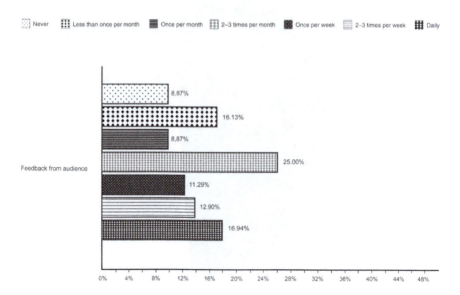

Figure 10.3 Audience feedback frequency among foreign correspondents

This level of direct interaction represents a profound transformation in professional journalism, clearly demanding a reorganisation of its functions and production routines. This comes as an additional burden in an already considerably competitive field of work, where most (81.81 per cent) feel that they are competing with other international news reporters. Interviews with international news reporters reveal six emerging forms of competition. These are the rise of local African media as direct competition, the rise of non-professional ('pro-am') news production, the rise of social media platforms, competition resulting from increasing monetisation of content, competition with freelancers, and finally growing competition among newcomers to international news reporting.

Discussion

Contemporary international news reporting from sub-Saharan Africa is not detached from the global transformations in journalism and is being affected by a number of important disruptive developments. These transformations, directly linked to digitisation and networked media, are reworking the meaning of foreign correspondence and suggest renewed challenges for Africa's media image. A profound reconfiguration of the set of practices that previously defined journalism as a discipline during a particular period of time suggests a systemic reorganisation of international news reporting as a field of knowledge production.

Concerning the contemporary socio-demographics of foreign correspondence from sub-Saharan Africa, empirical findings show how tradition and innovation coexist: modern international news agencies retain a central role within contemporary journalism. It is noteworthy that no significant transformation has occurred with reference to gender (in)equality, which has been an important research topic on foreign correspondence (Beeson 2004; Born 1987; Fennel 2005; Hess 1996; Hudson 1999; Morrison & Tumber 1985; Nosaka 1992; Utley 1997). Likewise, international news reporting is still an occupational field for a cognitive elite with high levels of formal education (Fennel 2005; Hess 1996; Maxwell 1956).

However, despite these localised continuities, basic conditions for a perfect storm have been gathering in recent decades. An occupational paradigm shift is occurring that stems from the ample criticism of modern professional foreign correspondents' work, the emergence of new players supported by networked digital media technologies, and, more recently, international economic and financial crisis. The last is clearly demonstrated by the considerable role assigned to freelance workers, with their unstable ties to news organisations, as well as by the pressure towards multiskilling and multitasking.

The fact that audiences are now able to directly and in a self-organised way hold international news reporting practices to account is no small transformation, particularly in the case of sub-Saharan Africa. News innovators under study here also show awareness that a need for occupational repositioning comes not just from outside its boundaries, but from inside the journalism profession. Contemporary international news reporting in Africa is no longer an exclusive territory of empiricism and objectivity.

Pressure towards a repositioning comes from the articulation between the traditional physicality and empiricism of foreign correspondence and the emerging information flows of online networks. Criticism of international news narratives about Africa has often stressed the lack of historical and contextual depth and the reporters' frequent ethnocentric standpoint. This chapter has addressed how international news is made from the perspective of its practitioners. Findings suggest that a considerable part of reporters' behaviour can be understood in the context of deeply uncertain times, as the autonomy of journalists is more limited than is generally admitted.

Notes

1   The survey was based on a mix of purposive/judgemental and theoretical non-probability sample: while not requiring a list of all possible elements in a full population, it requires an effort to create a kind of quasi-random sample and a clear idea about what group the sample may reflect. We purposely generated an effect towards snowball sampling. Correspondents were asked for the names and contacts of other people with similar attributes ("Do you know any other foreign correspondent in the region and/or the continent?"). The hyperlink to the survey platform and the associated unique password were always sent to the personal email address of the participant. This way we were able to collect answers from a total of 124 respondents, with a completion rate of 100 per cent.
2   Angola, Benin, Burkina Faso, Burundi, Cameroon, Cape Verde, Central African Republic, Chad, Democratic Republic of Congo, Ethiopia, Gambia, Ghana, Guinea, Guinea-Bissau, Ivory Coast, Kenya, Lesotho, Liberia, Madagascar, Malawi, Mali, Mauritania, Mauritius, Mozambique, Namibia, Niger, Nigeria, Rwanda, São Tomé and Príncipe, Senegal, Seychelles, Sierra Leone, South Africa, South Sudan, Swaziland, Tanzania, Togo, Uganda, Zambia, Zanzibar, and Zimbabwe.

References

Beeson, D. E. (2004) "In search of women's history: conflicting narratives in the autobiographies of two women foreign correspondents", PhD thesis, The University of Iowa, Iowa City, Iowa.

Born, D. J. (1987) "The reporting of American women foreign correspondents from the Vietnam War", PhD thesis, Michigan State University, East Lansing, Michigan.

Campbell, V. (2004) *Information Age Journalism: Journalism in an International Context*, New York: Arnold.

Farish, M. (2001) "Foreign correspondents, geopolitical vision, and the First World War", *Transactions of the Institute of British Geographers, New Series*, 26(3): 273–287.

Fennel, M. (2005) "Women war correspondents: three generations on the front-lines or the sidelines? A content analysis of the newspaper coverage written by leading American women correspondents in Vietnam, the Persian Gulf, and Iraq Wars", MA thesis, Carleton University, Ottawa, Ontario.

Hamilton, J. M. & Cozma, R. (2009) "Foreign correspondents, print", in C. H. Sterling (ed.), *Encyclopedia of Journalism*, Thousand Oaks, CA: Sage.

Hess, S. (1996) *International News & Foreign Correspondents*, Washington, DC: The Brookings Institution.

Hess, S. (2005) *Through Their Eyes: Foreign Correspondents in the United States*, Washington, DC: Brooking Institution Press.

Hudson, L. S. (1999) "Jane McManus Storm Cazneau (1807–1878): a biography", PhD thesis, University of North Texas, Denton, Texas.

Lewis, S. (2010) "Journalism innovation and the ethic of participation: a case study of the Knight Foundation and its news challenge", PhD thesis, University of Texas, Austin, Texas.

Maxwell, J. W. (1956) "The foreign correspondents: a social and functional analysis", PhD thesis, State University of Iowa, Iowa City, Iowa.

Morrison, D. E. & Tumber, H. (1985) "The foreign correspondents: date-line London", *Media, Culture & Society*, 7(4): 445–470.

Nosaka, T. (1992) "American foreign correspondents in Japan: profile and problems in coverage", MA thesis, California State University, California.

Shoemaker, P. J. & Reese, S. D. (1996) *Mediating the Message: Theories of Influences on Mass Media Content*, New York: Longman.

Sreberny, A. & Paterson, C. (2004) "Shouting from the rooftops: reflections on international news in the 21st century", in C. Paterson and A. Sreberny (eds), *International News in the 21st Century*, Luton: University of Luton Press.

Utley, G. (1997) "The shrinking of foreign news: from broadcast to narrowcast", *Foreign Affairs*, 76(2): 2–10.

Chapter 11

Media perspectives

Reflecting on my father's legacy in reporting Africa

Salim Amin

In 1984 my father Mohamed Amin filmed images in Ethiopia that changed the world. They prompted the greatest act of giving in the 20th century and changed the way governments and NGOs operated in Africa and elsewhere.

My father plied his trade in Africa for more than four decades. He loved Africa and its people, but most of the stories he did while working for Western broadcasters or agencies only highlighted the very worst the continent had to offer. It did not make him happy or proud to win awards for successfully showing how people died, and he spent a large part of his life trying to balance the picture of the continent through the photography of Africa's beauty – her people, her cultures, her nature, landscapes, flora, fauna, wildlife. He published over seventy-five books on the continent that have nothing to do with what he covered for the news.

As the TV industry changes and is run more and more by the "bottom line", Africa has again drawn the short end of the stick. Budget cuts have affected staffing and bureaus around the continent and now only a handful of broadcasters have bureaus in Africa. Of those that do, even the major broadcasters cannot afford more than two or three offices. Africa cannot be covered by three offices!

With the beast that we know as 24-hour news, correspondents have to file stories constantly, allowing themselves little or no time to get to the root of often complex stories, especially in Africa, and thus we continue to get sensational headline-making news of a genocidal, starving, disease-ravaged continent.

When Al Jazeera English (AJE) launched a few years ago, I hoped that this situation would be slightly corrected. AJE launched with multiple bureaus around Africa and more than doubled any other broadcaster's capacity on the continent. Additionally, they attempted to hire local talent to a greater degree than other broadcasters, and this has meant more in-depth and insightful pieces on Africa on AJE.

However, this is still NOT ENOUGH. AJE, like other broadcasters, has their editorial headquarters outside Africa; decisions on what should be covered are largely made by people that have little or no knowledge of the continent. This has to change.

I will cite an example that I have often used. One of my producers did a feature on female circumcision in southwestern Kenya. He was a Kenyan graduate of my training institute in Nairobi, The Mohamed Amin Foundation, and worked with a team of fellow students.

That feature won the overall CNN African Journalist of the Year Award in 2007. However, CNN never actually ran the 7-minute feature, in its entirety, on their channel. I was shocked and surprised, and I did not receive an explanation. It was not a financial issue, as we waived any broadcast fee. Eventually I was told that they had done a story on female circumcision in Mali a couple of years before, which is why this piece was not run.

The story was well produced, shot, and edited – far better than many features I have seen on CNN; it was, after all, good enough to win their award. But this is where I find the basic problem with international broadcasters – I am sure that if the piece had been more "sensational" and had included elements such as corruption, it would have had a better chance of being aired. I am also sure that if it had been done by the network's correspondent, it would have appeared.

There are plenty of good, actually great, stories in Africa: stories of success and human achievement, of sport, fashion, music and business and art. But despite all the talk about an "Africa Rising" narrative, these stories are only rarely explored in the depth they deserve. At conferences and industry events I will often ask why, and I receive one of two answers: the cost of working in Africa is too high, and there is not enough good local talent to produce stories.

Let me tackle these points separately. I agree that Africa is the most expensive continent in the world to cover, but that's because most of the crews that come here expect and get five-star treatment – hotels, meals, and so on. They are also overcharged because they are foreigners. African crews can get around much easier and cheaper than international crews. They also have the vast added advantage of knowing the terrain, speaking the local languages, and understanding how Africa works. So an easy answer to this argument is: USE LOCAL CREWS!

On the point of talent and ability – RUBBISH. I have worked with crews from all over the world and I would have to say that the Africans we work with are as good, if not better. The level of talent and training on the continent has progressed in leaps and bounds over the last ten years; this should no longer be given as a reason not to hire local crews.

What my father taught me was that Africa can only be covered by Africans. And he proved it, time and time again. He knew this continent like no other journalist, and far better than any visiting foreign correspondent. He had an unmatched contacts book and he went where no other journalist could.

Through our work with The Mohamed Amin Broadcast Training Centre, Camerapix (the company my father established), and Africa24 Media, we are trying to empower Africans with the most powerful tool in the world – knowledge. And we hope our presence and reporting will continue to create an impetus for better governance both in public life and in commerce, something that is sorely needed.

We are trying to provide a balance against the more negative images of the continent that are presented as "real life" for all Africans by the international media. By showing the real Africa as a place of good and bad, honesty and corruption, economic vibrancy and poverty, eager entrepreneurs as well as those who still rely on foreign aid, we present to Africans the truth about their world.

This, for me, is the greatest social purpose the media can achieve. Information is power and, for too long, the power has not been in the hands of the people of Africa.

Chapter 12

Media perspectives

We're missing the story: The media's retreat from foreign reporting[1]

Anjan Sundaram

The Western news media are in crisis and are turning their back on the world. We hardly ever notice. Where correspondents were once assigned to a place for years or months, reporters now handle 20 countries each. Bureaus are in hub cities, far from many of the countries they cover. And journalists are often lodged in expensive bungalows or five-star hotels. As the news has receded, so have our minds.

To the consumer, the news can seem authoritative. But the 24-hour news cycles we watch rarely give us the stories essential to understanding the major events of our time. The news machine, confused about its mandate, has faltered. Big stories are often missed. Huge swaths of the world are forgotten or shrouded in myth. The news both creates these myths and dispels them, in a pretence of providing us with truth.

I worked in the Democratic Republic of Congo as a stringer, a freelance journalist paid by the word, for a year and a half, in 2005–2006. There, on the bottom rung of the news ladder, I grasped the role of the imaginary in the production of world news. Congo is the scene of one of the greatest manmade disasters of our lifetimes. Two successive wars have killed more than five million people since 1996.

Yet this great event in human history has produced no sustained reporting. No journalist is stationed consistently on the front lines of the war telling us its stories. As a student in America, where I was considering a PhD in mathematics and a job in finance, I would read 200-word stories buried in the back pages of newspapers. With so few words, speaking of events so large, there was a powerful sense of dissonance. I travelled to Congo, at age 22, on a one-way ticket, without a job or any promise of publication, with only a little money in my pocket and a conviction that what I would witness should-be news.

When I arrived, there were only three other foreign reporters in Congo. We were all based in the capital, Kinshasa, while the war raged more than 600 miles to the east. My colleagues lived well: one in a luxury hotel suite, another in an immense colonial home with servants and guards. I envied them. To make matters worse, shortly after arriving I was robbed at gunpoint.

I found work as a stringer for the Associated Press, and rented a room from a family in a rundown home in one of Kinshasa's poorest but liveliest areas. The house frequently lacked water and electricity, and neighbourhood children would run through it after playing in sewage. It became the AP's headquarters in Congo.

I shared with my host family the only meal they ate each day. I helped draw the curtains and hide with them when a band of street boys pillaged our neighbourhood. I was present when their baby first crawled.

My proximity to people was essential to my reporting. They were as surprised as I was by news of a rape or a political killing – especially if it wasn't in the war-torn east of the country.

But the world outside is rarely surprised by a Congolese death. Those same rapes and killings were not deemed important enough to make news. Ignored, they were soon forgotten. The world saw Congo as a violent place, but not worth reporting on, unless the story was spectacular and gruesome.

Joy was often ignored.

Few Congolese, even in the war, see themselves as victims. The idea of their victimhood is imagined, and the news in these moments seems to be speaking to itself.

Our stories about others tell us more about ourselves.

The telltale sign of such mythical, distant reporting is a distinct assuredness. Confusion and vulnerability are stripped away, as are the subtleties and contradictions of life. People and places are reduced to simple narratives – good and evil, victim and killer. Such narratives can be easy to digest. But they tell us only a portion of the story.

A few months ago I travelled to a remote town in the Central African Republic that had just been burned and destroyed by the government. The town, now empty, was believed to have sheltered anti-government militiamen during a battle. Bodies were strewn across the bush, quickly decomposing, beside baby clothes dropped by fleeing mothers. On my way back from the town I saw groups of outraged militiamen who wanted to fight back. There was little reporting from there at that time; the government had been demonised and the militiamen portrayed as victims. African Union and French peacekeepers tried to curb the fighting by disarming government forces. But the militiamen, unchecked, began widespread massacres.

News from a distance worsens these problems. Living among Congolese, I was continually held accountable for what I wrote, whether about killings and rapes, election politics, or Pygmy tribes who had given away sections of forest to foreign logging companies for some sacks of salt.

A warlord once told me that war crimes were more comprehensible than crimes in times of peace; the world didn't realise, he said, that such atrocities were committed in times of confusion. He didn't deny that war crimes should be punished, but merely asked to be understood. He had become a warlord when armed men had stormed into his home and killed his daughter. Unable to protect his family, he had formed a militia. His subsequent brutality, whose targets included other fathers and daughters, was criminal. It would be easy to dismiss him as evil. His story tells us that his context produced evil.

Such immersive reporting is essential if news is to serve its purpose and help us construct any real sense of the world.

News systems are not designed for this. Reporters move like herds of sheep, flocking to the same places at the same times to tell us, more or less, the same stories. Foreign bureaus are closing. We are moving farther away.

News organisations tell us that immersive reporting is prohibitively expensive. But the money is there; it's just often misallocated on expensive trips for correspondents. Even as I was struggling to justify costs for a new round of reporting in Congo, I watched teams of correspondents stay in $300-per-night hotels, spending in one night what I would in two months. And they missed the story.

Parachuting in with little context, and with a dozen other countries to cover, they stayed for the vote but left before the results were announced. A battle broke out in Kinshasa after they left, and I found myself hiding in an old margarine factory, relaying news to the world, including reports to this newspaper.

News organisations need to work more closely with stringers. Make no mistake: life as a stringer, even for those eager to report from abroad, is daunting. It's dangerous, the pay is low, and there is little support. For years after I left Congo, my position with the AP remained – as it is now – vacant. The news from Congo suffers as a result, as does our understanding of that country, and ultimately ourselves. Stories from there, and from places like the killing fields of the Central African Republic, are still distant, and they are growing smaller.

Note

1 'We're Missing The Story' reprinted New York Times op-ed by Anjan Sundaram. Copyright © Anjan Sundaram 2014, used by permission of The Wylie Agency (UK) Limited.

Chapter 13

Instagram as a potential platform for alternative Visual Culture in South Africa

Danielle Becker

In this chapter I discuss the potential for the social media platform Instagram to broaden the sphere of individuals who can call themselves "image makers" and so are able to position themselves within South African Visual Culture. With Instagram as a specific case study, I discuss the nature of the image making within new media, and use examples of specific South African Instagrammers (or IGers) to illustrate the potential for such a platform to impact global media perceptions of Africa.

National identity and access to Visual Culture

It has been 21 years since South Africa's first democratic elections. While this is something to celebrate, there is still undeniable inequality and a seeming difficulty in imagining a national identity that moves beyond the rhetoric of the "Rainbow Nation". For many the ideology of the "rainbow", famously articulated by Nelson Mandela, *instructs* the nation on how to see the real and historically entrenched diversity that exists in South Africa (Sontag 2003). In this sense the metaphor provides a form for how the nation can be *imagined* (Anderson 1983) rather than necessarily describing a lived reality.

South Africa purports to encourage local perspectives within cultural production, rather than simply supporting the mimicry of international standards. This appears to stem from an acknowledgement of the crucial role that the arts have played in the transformation from an apartheid state to a democratic nation officially championing diversity, freedom of speech, and cultural expression. Yet, for the majority of South Africans, the ability to access the institutions that govern art and visual culture is prevented by a lack of arts education in schools and limited institutional support.

In order to realise the already entrenched metaphorical dream of a national identity supported by cultural and artistic production, South African institutions seek to remedy a very explicit imbalance in the demographics of the visual arts sector. A study commissioned by the South African Department of Arts and Culture (DAC) in 2008 – and undertaken by the

Human Sciences Research Council (HSRC) – produced a report in 2011 detailing the status quo of the visual arts sector. The report showed that, while "black artists play an increasingly prominent role in the contemporary art market, the ownership of mechanisms for distribution and presentation continue[s] to be dominated by white South Africans" (2011: 26).

An acknowledgement of the inequality in the arts sector in South Africa is by no means a new observation. A video produced in 2003 by Vuyile Voyiya and Julie McGee entitled *The Luggage Is Still Labeled: Blackness in South African Art* sought to open up the debate around the nature of the inequality in the "art world". In 2015, despite many positive changes, there is still a lack of diversity among academics, creative practitioners, institutional heads, and those involved in visual culture production.

Such statistics and perceptions depict a visual arts sector that has, to a certain extent, maintained the "exclusions, marginalisations and hierarchies" entrenched by a colonial and apartheid legacy (Carman et al. 2011: 7). It also hints at the notion that, despite the ease with which we can declare a non-racist or non-discriminatory constitution and a commitment to transformation in South Africa, it is in fact entrenched discourses, economic systems, and market forces that perpetuate imbalances rather than or despite progressive ethical philosophies.

Access to visual culture allows subjects to assist in constructing a particular view of the post-apartheid nation and a visual prototype for the imaginary. In this way image making becomes a powerful act. Here we are reminded of the well-known notion of "Afro-pessimism", which, in relation to photography, speaks of how images create discursive frameworks determined by those who have control of the global media industry – *the global North* (Enwezor 2006: 11).

Digital divide

Much has been written about the potential of the internet, Web 2.0, and social media to counter Afro-pessimism and decentre the effects of "Northern" media dominance over the global South. For Enwezor, such an imbalance is largely due to those in the global North having "the broadest access to distribution systems" (Enwezor 2006: 14). The question becomes, therefore, what change can be registered in image production when internet access theoretically allows far greater access to social distribution systems? Does access to distribution on social media allow for a diversification of those who are included in discourses about visual culture in South Africa?

Many commentators warn against this kind of enthusiasm in the potential for social media and internet access to create real change, both in the perceptions of Africa and access for Africans. Writing in 2011 Marion Walton points out that "[e]nthusiasts for 'Facebook revolutions' seldom ask who is excluded from the networked publics of Web 2.0" and questions whether "the Internet [can] really be counted as a 'commons' on a continent where only 10% of the population access online media" (Walton 2011: 48).

The difficulty in assessing the impact of internet access and social media participation is that the statistics change incredibly fast. The United Nations International Telecommunication Union (ITU) noted that by 2014 the percentage of users in Africa doubled to almost 20 (2014: 5), with the media agency "We Are Social" reporting a 26 per cent penetration in January 2015 (2015: 10). While that still makes Africa the continent with the lowest internet penetration, the rapid *increase* in accessibility is greater than in any other region and the primary means to access the internet on the African continent remains mobile broadband. Any notions about access to the internet must take into account how quickly the statistics change. In South Africa, for example, we see an increase from 2 million users in 2000 to 24.9 million in 2015, with much of that increase occurring in the previous 5 years (We Are Social 2015: 271). Internet access is primarily gained through the mobile phone (in South Africa, as in Africa as a whole) and the use of social media accounts for a large portion of usage (PRC 2014 reports over 60 per cent).

The point is that while internet usage may still be limited – in both Africa and South Africa – the landscape is changing fast. If we theorise the potential for social media to democratise, we must take into account that internet use has both the potential to increase inequality between the global North and the global South (what is referred to as an increase in the digital divide) *as well as* broaden access to global discourse and change global ideologies.

Instagram: multiple narratives

For those in the global South, the impetus to disseminate cultural production has a social and political importance. Visual texts are increasingly able to structure ideologies and as such the ability to circulate images online allows one access to a global discourse and the opportunity to insert one's own view within it. In this sense the dominance of personal photographs on social media platforms can be seen as *potentially* contributing to multiple narratives and countering hegemony.

It is unsurprising, then, that Instagram is the fastest-growing social media application; this is a platform launched in 2010 that allows users to take, edit, and upload photographs onto an individual or group-affiliated profile. While the number of Instagram users still puts the application behind the likes of Facebook, Instagram reported 300 million active users globally in 2015, a substantial increase in 5 years. In South Africa, Instagram use has also seen a rapid increase from 100,000 active users in 2012 to 680,000 by 2013 and 1.1 million in 2014 (World Wide Worx 2015). As access to smartphone technology and internet connections increases, so too does the desire to take, share, and view images.

Instagram can be positioned within "popular culture" and is predominantly used to create personal accounts that provide a visual document of the photographer's life. Yet, for a growing community of Instagram users, the platform is seen as something of an online gallery and personal marketing tool. In an essay for *Art South Africa* online Christine Lundy writes, "the rise of digital photography and social media has democratized the art of image making" (Lundy 2014). This statement affirms the possibility that platforms like Instagram may provide the tools to broaden access to Visual Culture in South Africa. Other media sources such as *Mail & Guardian* have contributed to a growing sense that the visual focus of Instagram as a social media platform allows users to challenge perceptions of "globalisation as sameness" through specific and personal narratives that reveal "traces of a city's individuality on street corners, plates of food or on the garments that its people wear" (Jason 2014).

This potential to "democratise" and create agency is something typically attributed to social media and particularly, as a form of photography or image making, to Instagram (Champion 2012: 83). The potentially "democratic" nature of social media and of human experience in general is something that, according to Sontag, lies at the heart of photography itself: "to democratise all experiences by translating them into images" (Sontag 1977: 176). The visual experiences documented by Instagrammers (IGers) positions them easily within the category of popular culture for it is this ritualistic social function that most often enlists remark. As Champion puts it, "The Instagram functions as a register of social ritual without 'specialness'" (Champion 2012: 85).

It is this very "everyday" quality that governs the use of Instagram by many Africans as a counter to images of "Afro-pessimism": death, war, disease, famine, and wild animals. Valérie Gorin has made reference to what is known as citizen journalism and the potential for social media to create user-generated content that is read as more authentic and trustworthy (2015: 3). The Instagram community known as "Everyday Africa", for example, claims to be a group of "photographers living and working in Africa, finding the extreme not nearly as prevalent as the familiar, the everyday". Everyday Africa shows images by both amateurs and professionals in an attempt to counter mainstream perspectives with images of the ordinary (Gorin 2015: 5). While there is still a large amount of stereotypical imagery, the platform and many others like it on the continent, such as Lagos Photo Festival, provide a catalyst for alternative narratives that create followers, provide easy marketing, and allow for identification that is social, collective, and not exclusively governed by the global North.

Aesthetics and the social

Before delving into the nature of Instagram as a platform, let me begin with a note on research methods. In order to gain a greater insight into the use of Instagram by South African IGers I created an online survey that was advertised on Instagram through images, a hashtag (#africasmediaimage) and a Facebook page. Users were encouraged to complete the survey and upload images to the hashtag. The process of collecting information emphasised the image-based nature of Instagram and its collective, social function: while only 29 people completed the survey, the hashtag has collected over 100 images. I asked IGers about the kind of equipment they use, whether their profile is set to private or public, and how they see the nature and purpose of their Instagram profile. Their written views informed my perspective, but their images, captions, and networks provide greater clarity and insight.

As social ritual we may read the Instagram image as something of a performance or a disembodied act of communication. The images are intended to be viewed and disseminated to the extent that the prospect of sharing photographic documentation of an event can take on a greater importance than the event itself (Weilenmann et al. 2013: 1844). For users who are perpetually online there is something of an altered temporality in the expectation of photographic documentation, while the effect for the audience is "anticipatory" (Champion 2012: 87). As Champion puts it, Instagram "precedes 'real-time' pleasures" (2012: 87). The South African Instagram user known as "InstaCPTguy" states that his experience of Cape Town as a city has been rekindled by his use of Instagram (InstaCPTguy 2015). As he puts it: "weekends are no longer spent lazing on the couch but it becomes, 'What's our next adventure?'" (InstaCPTguy 2015). His change in perception gives us some indication of the extent to which users imagine their experiences existing as photographs on Instagram and how this catalyses action.

While the temporality of the singular image is expected to be immediate (with the hashtag "latergram" used to denote an image that occurred in the past), the images are often read in series. The typically frequent uploading of images means that they occur in rapid sequence and so must be read in this way (Champion 2012: 86). The notion of the series is highlighted by the work of various South African Instagram users. The collective known as "I See A Different You", for example, has a profile that reads very much like a virtual gallery. The trio collective is made up of twin brothers Redani and Fhatuwani Mukheli and their friend Vuyo Mpantsha. The collective have created very successful photographic careers based, in part, on their social media profiles. Their Instagram profile depicts images shot on a professional camera that are then edited and uploaded onto the platform. Visual themes include portraits of themselves in contemporary fashion clothing, images from commercial advertising shoots, shots from their travels on the African continent, and (most predominantly) images of their hometown of Soweto on the outskirts of Johannesburg. The trio explicitly aims to counter the pessimistic images that proliferate about Soweto as a historically poor, black township with images that depict a "different" side of the place and its people.

Figure 13.1 ISEEADIFFERENTYOU brings you SA KINGS. SA Kings is a Photographic and Filmic journey profiling the Kings from the various cultures in South Africa. It is a journey of celebration and rediscovery of our culture. #Iamnikonsa #DeptArtsCulture #Glowhire #JeepSA #MeetSouthAfrica

The Instagrammer can, in this sense, be seen as a virtual curator who frequently expects images to be read as part of a larger narrative, which often means using one image as a cover shot to frame those that follow (Weilenmann et al. 2013: 1848). The curatorial possibilities of Instagram were emphasised in two recent exhibitions of Instagram photography in Cape Town, South Africa. The "YeBook Instagram" exhibition (March 2015 at Skinny Legs & All) and the "Instagenic #sontagged" exhibition (March 2015 at Chandler House) that took place in central Cape Town displayed Instagram images as a series in a format that mimicked the virtual Instagram profile view rather than a conventional photographic exhibition. Images were displayed in a grid of nine with the Instagrammer's name, profile name, and profile picture above. This indicates the perspective both that Instagram images function as an alternative to "traditional" photography and that the images must be seen in sequence rather than in isolation. For the Instagram user known as "Tashlapics" the square format of the Instagram images provides the possibility for democratising and cata-lysing image production: "Everyone frames images using the same formats and presets so the conversation is a visual one in which the basic language of engagement has been set" (Tashlapics 2015).

The initial impetus for the creation of Instagram was to allow for users to choose what images they share and to have a certain level of control over the aesthetic manner in which they appear, with very little expertise or cost. The filters on the application, which borrow from a range of "looks" referencing film photography, allow users who may or may not be amateur photographers to make their images aesthetically pleasing in a world where it has been assumed that cell phone photography was simply about preserv-ing memories rather than creating beautiful images (Verdina 2013: 6). In

Figure 13.2 Instagenic exhibition, March 2015 at Chandler House, Cape Town, South Africa. Photographer: Danielle Becker

interviews, South African Instagrammers had wide-ranging opinions on the importance of Instagram filters. The use of filters is also linked to the distinction between users who shoot images using a phone camera and upload directly and those who shoot using more professional equipment and post-production programmes.

As far as artistic status and aesthetics are concerned, many Instagrammers with a large following are in fact creatives in other disciplines too. Among the 19 people listed by *Mail & Guardian* in 2014 as some of South Africa's top Instagrammers, we find photographers, designers, stylists, journalists, editors, and bloggers. There is a sense that the careers of many of these Instagrammers have been enhanced by the platform and that there are those who simply take pleasure in taking images and viewing the images of others. Instagram allows for a blurring of the distinction between the personal or company profile, since individual users tend to allow their profiles to be public and companies tend to post personal images as subtle advertising. In this vein Patricia Sánchez Abril and others (2012) point to virtual space and its ability to undermine the "fixed barriers" associated with social spaces of the past such as those established by Erving Goffman in *The Presentation of Self in Everyday Life* (1959). Engaging in social media does not allow one to segregate one's audience when *presenting the self* and as such the boundaries between social audiences are increasingly blurred (Sánchez Abril et al. 2012: 63).

Collective culture

In using the Instagram application, users often adopt a postmodern attitude to originality by referencing images and other media in what Lessig termed a "remix culture" (Lessig 2008). Many Instagram users see their images as being part of a collective and the use of hashtags to situate images within communities and categories further emphasises this. Various global Instagram communities exist and in South Africa the Instagram group "Instagram_SA", which has 33,000 followers (April, 2015), and "IgersSouthAfrica" organise meetings known as Instameets or Instawalks that allow for virtual communities to spill over into physical spaces. These communities connect to global Instagram communities through events such as the annual World Wide Instameet. The eleventh version of this global event was celebrated by various South African Instagram communities who met at locations established through the platform to meet, take photographs, and share and categorise them through hashtags. The public nature of Instagram means that users are more likely to connect both virtually and physically with others who they do not know outside of Instagram. The South African Instagrammer "millalorraine" sees the Instameets as potentially democratising: "When attending the instawalks you realise that it extends beyond just the creative [sphere of] art, design and photographers and includes many amateur or hobby photographers ranging from different industries and class or race groups" (millalorraine 2015).

The collective nature of the Instagram further emphasises its primary role as communication – a message transferred in visual form that creates a potentially non-hierarchical community (Murray 2008). In this sense the process of Instagramming is highly dynamic and allows for reposting, liking, and commentary both on the application itself and on other social media platforms (Weilenmann et al. 2013). The freedom and ability to control the visual signs that dominate the global media landscape means participating in the creation of narratives – a function vitally important for those on the African continent, where photographic image-making has historically been dominated by outsiders.

Potential versus reality

The kinds of images that thrive on Instagram profiles remind the viewer that despite the seeming ubiquity of smartphones and the internet one does tend to need access to both middle-class resources and middle-class discourse in order to participate fully in such a sphere. The reminder that we cannot extrapolate middle- and upper-class use of social media to the majority within South Africa is emphasised by a study in 2010 and 2011 of cellphone use in Khayelitsha, Cape Town by Marion Walton and Jonathan Donner. The study showed that cellphones were primarily perceived and used as shared devices rather than individual property, with memory card swapping rather than access via the internet being primary because of the high cost of airtime and data (Walton & Donner 2012). Such a study emphasises the importance of acknowledging that social media platforms are not easily accessible for many within South Africa and Africa. However, the study also showed that the participants used and shared the cameras on their phones more than any other feature – and with the rapidly changing landscape of affordable internet access, we are already finding that the existing fascination with image making is translating into a greater use of image-sharing platforms like Instagram (Walton & Donner 2012: 405). Instagram has a potential appeal for those who otherwise do not find themselves in positions of power, since authority as an image maker can be established regardless of one's identity in the outside world (Verdina 2013: 24).

Despite the still limited access to smartphone technology and affordable internet, the use of Instagram as a device for the dissemination of images has the potential to broaden access to Visual Culture in South Africa as it is positioned outside of dominant discourses that privilege media from the global North. The nature of Instagram and other social media platforms as being without geographical boundaries also means that otherwise disenfranchised practitioners have the capacity to insert counter-hegemonic narratives into global discourse.

References

Anderson, B. (1983) *Imagined Communities: Reflections on the Origin and Spread of Nationalism*, London: Verso.

Carman, J., Robbroeck, L. van, Pissarra, M., Goniwe, T., & Majavu, M. (2011) *Visual Century: South African Art in Context*, Johannesburg: Wits University Press; Oslo: Visual Century Project.

Champion, C. (2012) "Instagram: je-suis-là?", *Philosophy of Photography*, 3(1): 83–88.

Department of Arts and Culture South Africa & Human Sciences Research Council (2011) *An Assessment of the Visual Art in South Africa*, DAC and HSRC.

Enwezor, O. (2006) *Snap Judgements: New Positions in Contemporary African Photography*, Göttingen: Steidl.

Goffman, E. (1959) *The Presentation of Self in Everyday Life*, New York: Anchor Books.

Gorin, V. (2015) "A path into alternative models? The role of citizen journalism in global representation of humanitarianism", presentation, Global Humanitarianism and Media Culture Conference, Sussex.

InstaCPTguy (2015) Interview by D. Becker, online survey, South Africa.

International Telecommunications Union (ITU) (2014) "Connect Africa. Transforming Africa: the promise of broadband", at http://www.itu.int/en/ITU-D/Conferences/connect/Documents/Post%20Connect%20Africa%20Summit%20Report%20%28English%29.pdf [accessed 02/09/2014].

Jason, S. (2014) "Nineteen of SA's top Instagrammers", *Mail & Guardian*, 13 August, at http://mg.co.za/article/2014-08-13-20-of-sas-top-instagrammers [accessed 15/08/2014].

Lessig, L. (2008) *Remix: Making Art and Commerce Thrive in the Hybrid Economy*, New York: Penguin Books.

Lundy, C. (2014) "Ama Culture: #Artagram on Instagram", Art South Africa, 20 August, at http://art-south-africa.com/component/content/article/220-news-articles-2013/2272-ama-culture-artagram-on-instagram.html [accessed 25/08/2014].

Millalorraine (2015) Interview by D. Becker, online survey, South Africa.

Murray, S. (2008) "Digital images, photo-sharing, and our shifting notions of everyday aesthetics", *Journal of Visual Culture*, 7(2): 147–163.

Sánchez Abril, P., Levin, A., & Del Riego, A. (2012) "Blurred boundaries: social media privacy and the twenty-first-century employee", *American Business Law Journal*, 49(1): 63–124.

Sontag, S. (1977) *On Photography*, New York: Picador.

Sontag, S. (2003) *Regarding the Pain of Others*, London: Penguin.

Tashlapics (2015) Interview by D. Becker, online survey, South Africa.

The Luggage Is Still Labeled: Blackness in South African Art, South Africa (2003) V. Voyiya & J. McGee [video: DVD], South Africa.

Verdina, Z. (2013) "A picture is worth a thousand words: storytelling with Instagram", master's thesis, University of Antwerp, Antwerp.

Walton, M. (2011) "Mobilizing African publics (book review)", *Information Technologies & International Development*, 7(2): 47–50.

Walton, M. & Donner, J. (2012) "Public access, private mobile: the interplay of shared access and the mobile Internet for teenagers in Cape Town", Global Impact Study Research Report Series, Cape Town, South Africa: University of Cape Town.

We Are Social (2015) "Digital, social and mobile in 2015 report", at http://
wearesocial.com/uk/special-reports/digital-social-mobile-worldwide-2015
[accessed 10/04/2015].

Weilenmann, A., Hillman, T., & Jungselius, B. (2013) "Instagram at the museum:
communicating the museum experience through social photo sharing", in
Proceedings of the SIGCHI Conference on Human Factors in Computing Systems. New
York: SIGCHI.

World Wide Worx (2015) "South African media landscape 2014: executive summary",
at http://www.worldwideworx.com/wp-content/uploads/2014/11/Exec-Summary-
Social-Media-2015.pdf [accessed 10/04/2015].

Chapter 14

Media perspectives

Social media and new narratives: Kenyans tweet back[1]

H. Nanjala Nyabola

Tracking the build up and reaction to the 2013 Kenyan election on Twitter was a timely lesson in how important social media have become in helping Africans rewrite narratives about their lives. Facebook is an echo chamber: it allows you to measure support for your ideas among people you already know. Twitter takes the concept to the next level – letting you share 140 characters with millions of strangers – and it provides an important space for critical engagement, rebuttal, and parody.

Foreign journalists learned this the hard way in the build up to the Kenyan election in 2013. First they discovered that there are several thousand Kenyans on Twitter, using and shaping the space, and second they found that these several thousand Kenyans are not afraid to disagree with journalists and the representations they see within mainstream media.

Six years earlier, in December 2007, Kenyans were paralysed and helpless as alarmist reports often inaccurately depicted our country as another in the litany of African failed states. No one denied that there was violence in Kenya – there was more violence than had been seen since 1967. But even in the haze of violence, watching a CNN journalist completely mistranslate the cries of a protester waving a white flag in the streets of Nairobi in 2007 (he was crying for peace, but the journalist translated this as a cry for support for his ethnic group) was degrading and offensive, and dimmed any esteem I had for international media houses. I wrote emails to CNN and they were ignored. That experience of voicelessness over the construction and dissemination of my national narrative is partly what prompted me to start blogging and writing op-eds.

Technology and storytelling in Kenya

By 2013, Kenyan presence on the internet had expanded dramatically and it was harder for a media outlet to get away with this kind of overstatement and sensationalism. Once again, CNN was a culprit: in one notable report, a journalist commented on potential ethnic violence in Rift Valley Province – and was given a firm lesson in the extent to which Kenyans were determined to take control of their narrative. Three assumptions seemed to underpin the creation and dissemination of the journalist's alarmist report. One: that Kenyans wouldn't see it. Two: that Kenyans wouldn't react to it. Three: that any reactions couldn't be disseminated. All of these assumptions were roundly confounded.

It is possible that the journalist was right, and some people were preparing for violence. Absolutely; that wasn't the point of contention. Rather, it was the presumption that these individuals were the norm rather than the exception – and a failure to acknowledge the great lengths that people had gone to try to prevent violence during and after the election.

The backlash on Twitter under the hashtag #SomeonetellCNN is exemplary of the creation of an African-driven counter-narrative. This backlash reflected a number of phenomena. Unlike more complex platforms like blogs or even Facebook that require significant bandwidth, Twitter lends itself to quick adoption over an easily available mobile phone. This malleability, combined with the fact that even basic phones now often have cameras, makes it easier to rebut unfounded claims with evidence – including pictures of peaceful political candidates and citizens.

The second revelation is that a lot of Kenyans are determined to play a more active role in writing and shaping the story of the nation. Kenya has one of the highest literacy rates in the global South – UNICEF estimates it is as high as 87 per cent. In Kenya, poverty and illiteracy are not always linked. And while the former may create disempowered citizens, literacy skills allow them to enter any communication space (with a low cost to entry) and attempt to repossess their power.

What Twitter does successfully is allow those who may not be able to claim power in the context of traditional media (with higher economic barriers to entry and with more entrenched power dynamics) to claim that power in 140 characters or less. Twitter allows them to broadcast these ideas to a wide audience, to court support for these ideas, and to form networks with like-minded individuals.

The importance of national narratives

Narratives shape the way we interact and interpret the world. The recent emergence of the "Rising Africa" narrative is a case in point. Africa hasn't done much to court this kind of attention, but, facing stalled economies in their home countries, European and North American firms need to garner support for expanded investment abroad in "virgin" markets.

In Kenya at least, this "Rising Africa" meta-narrative is being approached with a great deal of cynicism and trepidation. There is no longer a blind belief in whatever non-Africans are selling. We welcome the investment, but we challenge investors to do so on our own terms. We welcome international aid, but we want it delivered through a different framework. Kenyans have always been deeply suspicious (and with good reason) of the motives of foreigners in this way; platforms like Twitter make it possible to express these suspicions in the language of the System.

As I've written in another context (Nyabola 2011), I don't necessarily believe that Twitter "causes social change" or "drives revolutions". What it does successfully is allow ideas to gain traction, while also allowing critics to challenge them. Twitter is like a large in-ear translator: it allows the powerful and the disempowered to communicate to each other, to articulate their concerns via a mutually intelligible language (technology). The powerless are able to speak out with less fear of repercussion; the powerful are forced to react and respond to maintain the appearance of egalitarianism and approachability.

It is into this minefield that CNN stomped with its report. Colloquial US lingo has a wonderful term to express the response this triggered from Kenyans: "the side-eye", which Urban Dictionary defines as, "a facial expression expressing one's criticism, disapproval, animosity or scorn of varying levels of intensity ... often an invitation of a fight or confrontation of some sort".

CNN was at the receiving end of a collective, national side-eye from Kenyans on Twitter at the idea that we would allow the national narrative to be hijacked again, either by criminals looking for trouble or by foreign journalists determined to portray us as a nations of criminals itching for a fight. This is a tremendously positive development. It is creating space that will hopefully lead to imagining a new politics for Kenya, one in which Kenyans themselves write the story rather than meekly accept what is dictated from outside.

Note

1 An earlier version of this article appeared under the title, "Kenya tweets back: #SomeonetellCNN", *Al Jazeera*, 8 March 2013.

Reference

Nyabola, N. (2011) "Twittering on the edge", *Pambazuka News*, 513, 20 January.

Chapter 15

A "New Ghana" in "Rising Africa"?

Rachel Flamenbaum

As the "Africa Rising" narrative has regained strength over the last several years, competing discourses have emerged that claim to represent or contest narratives of the continent's transformation (e.g., *Economist* 2011; Perry 2012; UNCTAD 2012; Wadongo 2014). Across the continent, Africans are participating in transnational media production in increasingly visible ways (e.g., Gratz 2011; Shipley 2013; Tsambu 2015), and are constructing alternative publics across social media (e.g., Bing 2015; de Bruijn et al. 2015; Manganga 2012; Tufekci & Wilson 2012). Yet scholarly attention to "Rising Africa" narratives in global media has not addressed Africans' own engagement with this discourse. Instead, research has tended to focus on shifting external representations of the continent from "hopeless" to "hopeful" (Nothias 2014; Ojo 2014), or on the abstractions of economic indicators (Mahajan 2009; Taylor 2014) and mobile penetration (Komunte 2015) as evidence of change.

In this chapter, I present a case study drawn from my extensive ethnographic research into Ghanaian digital literacies[1] to address the question of how "Rising Africa" tropes are taken up by Africans themselves, in what contexts, and to what ends. I examine how students at an elite Ghanaian university at the heart of the country's "New Ghana" zeitgeist are socialised into on- and offline practices and logics of neo-liberal self-branding. In an effort to reject the Afro-pessimism and rigid age-graded hierarchies of the Ghanaian status quo, students erase negativity and enduring challenges from their self-representations on social media in ways that map onto Rising Africa tropes of optimism and hopefulness. Yet in doing so, they inadvertently ratify the enduring hierarchies of African inadequacy (Pierre 2013) built into the moral logic of African Rising discourses (Ochs & Capps 2001; Nothias 2014). I argue that complementary attention to Africans' situated social practices can deepen scholarly understanding of Africa's media image by clarifying social actors' motivations in constructing that image – illuminating how and why such perspectives are excluded in framing the African media image from within.

Who/what is New Ghana?

The combination of Ghana's discovery of offshore oil reserves in 2007, its rapid rollout of mobile and internet technologies from the mid-aughts onwards, and the global economic downturn of 2008, helped to spur a reinterpretation of the value of African locality and Ghanaian identity in a fiercely positive light among youth and young professionals. These contemporary patterns echo past efforts of youth across the continent to forge cosmopolitan, millennial selves to push against their exclusion from avenues of power and participation (e.g., Newell 2012; Cole & Durham 2008; Comaroff & Comaroff 1999; Meyer 1998). Yet such attempts were often sustained by youth doubly marginalised by age *and* class. The New Ghana and its counterparts elsewhere in sub-Saharan Africa (cf. Poggiali 2013) are unique in their intensive alignment with technology as a tool of transformation, enabling an overlapping network of on- and offline spheres, and in the proportion of highly mobile and educated core participants. The youth – in practical terms, anyone younger than 40 – of the New Ghana might be thought of as a permutation of the media-producing new cultural elite that Avle (2011) identifies as emerging out of the convergence of structural adjustment and economic liberalisation in the early 1990s.

When I began research in the context of "Africa Rising" claims about the continent's viability as a site of tech entrepreneurship in 2012, Ghanaian social media and everyday conversations overflowed with exhortations to represent Ghana and Africa positively, *and* to actively reinterpret one's own experience optimistically. My research participants described these efforts – to me and to each other – as a necessary corrective to centuries of derogatory external characterisations of the continent. As Wainaina (2005) viciously satirised in "How to write about Africa", longstanding Western stereotypes narrowly represent the continent as a primitive site of moral turpitude, disease, poverty, and war. Though much literature focuses on the role of such imagery in colonial domination (e.g., Gordon 1997; Mitchell 1991) and its persistence in contemporary representations (e.g., Ferguson 2006; Lutz & Collins 1993; Mbembe 2001), the notion of the African Other can be traced back as far as Ancient Greece (Feinberg & Sodolow 2002). The New Ghana is both an outward-facing challenge to the violence of these ancient and enduring stereotypes, and an inward-directed rejection of the Afro-pessimism, or "fatalistic attitude toward economic and social crises" (Diawara 1998: 39), that pervades the West African post-colonial experience (Mbembe 2001).

Consider an image repeatedly shared on Facebook, Twitter, and Instagram from 2012 to 2013. On the left, under the heading "They Say", words in stark black fonts make up the shape of the African continent. This word art image is full of stereotypical associations of Africa with foreign aid, disease, and war. On the right, this negative image is juxtaposed against

a profusion of colours and fonts, also making up the shape of the continent, under the heading "We Say" – statements proclaiming entrepreneurship, creativity, and talent as characteristic of the continent. I documented
Facebook statuses from Ghana's most prolific bloggers, all of whom repeatedly highlighted the value of Africa's *human* resources, rather than its raw
exports, for both local and possible foreign audiences. Many of these status
updates almost took the form of public service announcements, spreading
the reach of statistics on African GDP growth, infographics demonstrating
Ghana's superior internet bandwidth speeds compared with neighbouring countries, and news articles about up-and-coming African start-ups and
tech entrepreneurs from international outlets such as Forbes and Business
Insider.

While New Ghana perspectives share much with the Africa Rising tropes
of positivity, "Africanness", optimism, entrepreneurship (cf. Nothias 2014),
my research participants repeatedly framed the values and politics that
animated such self-representations online as *directly opposed* to what they
characterised as the stagnant, overly stratified status quo. The age-graded
respect hierarchies of contemporary Ghanaian social and political life
consolidate knowledge production, access, authority, and status at the top
(cf. Coe 2005; Nugent 1995; Nukunya 2003). Mainstream Ghanaian
institutions – the civil service, schools – are characterised by titles, bureau-
cratic formality, and conservatism. The good Ghanaian student/child
respects elders, knows their place, and does not seek to improve upon tradition. In classrooms, the British colonial legacy of rote learning supports
the cultural value placed on youthful deference, allowing knowledge to be
reproduced and circulated in a closed circuit that "renders the knowledge
safe and appropriate for young people, without posing a threat to the more
deeply respected knowledge of chiefs and elders" (Coe 2005: 152). In and
beyond the classroom, adults often put impertinent young people in their
place by calling them "too known" – a label New Ghana author Sumprim
(2006) sardonically defines as someone who has "the audacity to tell someone to do the right thing" (26).

Many Ghanaians who are locked out of opportunities by virtue of their
youth see the Ghanaian preference for deference to elder authority figures as holding back not only their own material advancement, but, in discouraging potential innovations from below, that of the country as a whole.
In interviews, and across social media platforms, my research participants
repeatedly framed the perceived dichotomies between the failures of the
"old" Ghana and the promise of the new: the "old" Ghana is slow, corrupt,
responsible for failing infrastructure and stalled development, all talk and
no action; the New Ghana is future oriented and ready for change, rejects
foreign solutions to Ghanaian problems, refuses to give or take bribes, and
believes in the transformative power of technology and positive thinking.
Indicative of this trend, a popular Facebook group called, aptly, "The New

Ghana", broadcasts such sentiments with daily status updates such as, "We are the New Ghana. We respect any young Ghanaian trying to start a business on his own more than that state official robbing the country of her national wealth", and, "I am the NEW Ghana. I am positive and daring. I am not afraid to speak my mind."

The considerable appeal of online platforms for participants in New Ghana practices lies in the ostensibly horizontalising potential of mediated spaces, where, as my research participants claimed, "anyone" can participate and be heard. Sites of the New Ghana that extend out into the physical world – including the Blogging Ghana consortium, the electoral advocacy project Ghana Decides, GhanaThink's development-driven public workshops, innumerable TEDx events – are similarly communally organised, informally run, inclusive spaces built around individual creative expression, the imperative to "Tell the African Story" along positive lines, and the promise of technological transformation. The carefully worded letters of introduction required by the bureaucracies of the "Old Ghana" are laughably out of place in such contexts; instead, the ultimate right to participate is framed as the *willingness* to participate. I often heard analogies made to "good" software engineers, who are judged on the basis of the efficacy of what they produce, rather than their stated credentials – an implicit indictment of the Old Ghana as too status oriented to be effective. By participating in the mutually embedded physical and mediated sites driven by such participatory ideals, denizens of the New Ghana consciously pose a moral challenge to the hierarchies of the status quo.

Branding the self, rebranding the continent

The New Ghana site par excellence is Ashesi University, founded in 2005 by a Ghanaian software engineer with the mission to "cultivate a new generation of ethical entrepreneurial leaders for Africa".[2] Ashesi's faculty, students, and alumni are prominent participants in nearly every instantiation of the New Ghana. While other New Ghana spaces implicitly model alternative possibilities for Ghanaian personhood by virtue of their horizontal organisational structures, Ashesi's curriculum, and especially its Honour Code, is explicitly designed to socialise students into branded modes of digitally mediated, ethical self-representation as a means of transforming the continent (Ashesi 2010).

The university is built on a US liberal arts model emphasising critical thinking and self-expression rather than the rote learning that pervades mainstream Ghanaian education. While faculty at most institutions expect students to address them with honorifics and penalise students if they cannot reproduce the content of their lectures in their assignments (a practice often satirised as "chew and pour"), Ashesi faculty encourage students to address them by their first names and penalise students for failing to incorporate resources from beyond the classroom. Students are taught to use multiple forms of social media in their coursework, expected to engage in class discussions online, and actively encouraged to be "too known" when blogging or tweeting their opinions.

These curricular objectives are more than just pedagogical. Faculty exhort students to exhibit "reliability" by cultivating their perspectives as a coherent personal "brand" across face-to-face and digitally mediated interactions. Such moral expectations mirror the cohesive, mobile, and flexible neo-liberal personae that Gershon (2014) argues have become central to the hiring practices of US corporations. Students are also held accountable to the *school's* brand. At one all-school meeting in 2013, the founder warned students about using inappropriate language or behaviours when referencing the university in their Twitter posts, reminding them that their ability to leverage the prestige of the Ashesi reputation in their own futures depended on their individual participation in the brand in the present.

The heart of Ashesi's transformational efforts is its Honour Code. Students vow not to cheat during Ashesi's infamously proctor-less exams (Ashesi 2010), and to actively report other students who do. When the Honour Code is discussed, however, it is always embedded in a broader future-oriented narrative hinging on notions of trust, reputation, and branding located *beyond* the classroom. Students are repeatedly told by older students, faculty, and alumni that to join the Honour Code is to take part in the legacy of the established Ashesi "brand" of intensive trustworthiness. If they embody the brand in their actions *and* mediated self-representations, they will be capable of transforming their future (presumed corrupt) Ghanaian colleagues by example. The central aim of the university, after all, is to create ethical individual leaders who can be plugged into a corrupt system and transform it from the inside out. Students are told that the Ashesi brand will be their calling card to employment with prestigious transnational corporate entities who would not, it is implied, ordinarily trust the scruples of an African employee.

Ezra, an alumnus, expressed such ideas while addressing the sophomore class about the Honour Code in 2013:

> Without even me saying a word, all [an employer] has to know is I'm from Ashesi, and I have trust. Because if they knew the Ashesi brand, or the Ashesi alum, or the Ashesi student, is one they could trust. And for me that's a big big thing about the honor code. It's just trust. The idea that anybody anywhere can just automatically see me and say, I trust these guys. ... Right? That's where we need to start.

Ezra extends the argument made by the university's founder elsewhere that students have the ethical obligation to take responsibility for their actions in service of the larger collectivity. In Ezra's moral logic, if the students reinforce the Ashesi brand (e.g., through positive self-representations in the New Ghana mode), they ensure continued prestige for all the other students, staff, and alumni that rely on the brand's exchange value in their own lives and careers.

This is a recursive mode of market-oriented nation branding (Aronczyk 2013) on an intimate scale: positive, trustworthy, and "reliable" self-branding as a means of identifying with and maintaining a corporate brand. This is a not-so-implicit analogy for the possibility of such self-branding as the means of rebranding Africa itself as a corporate body worthy of trust and praise. Ezra explicitly highlights a connection between students participating in the Ashesi brand and their ability to perform as unmarked, mobile labour: individuals that "anyone anywhere" can trust purely on the basis of their branded associations. To take on the moral obligations of the Honour Code within the hyper-competent, tech-savvy Ashesi context, in other words, is to perform an exclusive, personal branded identity of The-Africans-You-Can-Trust for the benefit of audiences beyond Ghana and the continent.

Yet in locating the moral gaze outside of Ghana in global corporations and asking students to internalise this gaze to police themselves and their peers within and beyond the classroom, Ezra (and the university more broadly) also ratifies problematic foreign stereotypes of Africans as corrupt fraudsters, thus re-entrenching the racialised colonial hierarchies that Pierre (2013) argues were never fully dismantled at Ghana's independence in 1957. This double bind is hardly limited to Ghana: writing of his experiences in returning to Guinea in the mid-1990s, Manthia Diawara incisively captures the false choice between staying trapped in Afro-pessimism on the continent, or guiltily orienting outside for opportunity. "One also tends to feel," he writes of the latter, "that success in life depends on working with the same devil which thrives on racial superiority and which excludes the majority of one's brothers and sisters from participating in history" (Diawara 1998: 42).

Who and what can be heard in the New Ghana?

For all the framing of inclusive positivity, Ashesi and other New Ghana spaces are no less prescriptive than the rigid status quo they push against. In the New Ghana claim that the only obstacle to participation lies in individuals' own *willingness*, for instance, there is a moral imperative to take up the values of positivity, action, and inclusion; failure to do so is then a moral, rather than structural, failing. Participants often cite Ghana's remarkable recent mobile and broadband penetration and relatively low data costs as "proof" of emerging technologies' democratisation. This emphasis ignores enduring inequalities in access to technologies: access to devices themselves, to the necessary supporting infrastructure such as stable electricity, and crucially, to the print and digital literacies needed to participate in digitally mediated spaces (cf. Warschauer 2003).

Indeed, the New Ghana harbours little space for negativity or critique. My own questions about potential obstacles to the pervasive claims of transformation through technology were often interpreted as obstructionist, overly negative, or as a damning lack of faith in Ghana's future possibilities – certainly not the spirit in which the questions were posed. This was hardly an experience restricted to outsiders, allies or otherwise. The majority of the Ashesi students I worked with, many of them quite affluent and all of them committed to New Ghana futures, described feelings of frustration, even despair, at being "trapped" by their circumstances, yet were uncomfortable making such claims publicly in mediated settings. While they constructed the sort of sophisticated "branded" personae that could render them legible beyond the local context (Blommaert 2008) across their social media profiles, students' frustrations were limited to private, offline (and thus in some ways "off record") conversations. While the visible material culture of the New Ghana effusively lays claim to Africa Rising-style optimism, many young Ghanaians' continued experience of the built environment of the internet and the design of computer hardware – all operating on the presumption of reliable electricity, high bandwidth, and so on – is that of exclusion from the global conversation (Burrell 2012).

Implications

In traversing the numerous sites of the New Ghana in the course of my research, I came to see its core denizens as occupying a dual missionary role: on the one hand, they project positive images abroad, as a long-overdue corrective to centuries of deeply problematic narratives of the "Dark Continent"; on the other hand, they insist that fellow Ghanaians take on the mantle of digitally mediated, participatory positivity as a moral imperative. Following Bourdieu's (1985) characterisation of the political field, participants in the New Ghana constitute a class of "cultural intermediaries" whose "actions are shaped by a professional marketing habitus" (Surowiec 2011: 127). As intermediaries, they have the mobility, born of their class positions and attainment of particular digital skills and globally legible modes of self-representation (cf. Blommaert 2008; Gershon 2014), to traverse the hyperlocal and the hyperglobal. They can speak to all of these audiences, at different scales, in a way that only a select few in Ghana can. And yet in collectively producing narrowly optimistic self-representations, New Ghana participants inadvertently undermine their bids for inclusion in global conversations about Africa: because such discourses appear transposable with Rising Africa narratives of Afro-optimism, they do not visibly disrupt the logic that contends Africa was lower to begin with.

I have argued that the media practices of the New Ghana represent an unprecedented bid for "horizontalising" social and political change within Ghana, and it is these efforts that motivate youthful engagement with Africa Rising tropes. However, an examination of the uneven ways in which these mediated images are produced and circulated also demonstrates that autochthonous critiques are rendered invisible or locally policed out of globally visible social media platforms. In mapping Africa's media image in the 21st century, we must account for the revelatory potential of media produced by Africans for Africans, taking seriously the means by which young Africans are reimagining their collective trajectories and possibilities. At the same time, it is just as critical to account for the dynamics of enduring gaps and erasures in these self-representations in the shifting landscapes of who can and cannot be heard.

Notes

1 Between 2012 and 2014, I conducted 400 hours of participant observation and video of classroom interactions, recorded 80 hours of ethnographic interviews, and collected several thousand screenshots of social media posts. I obtained participant consent via UCLA IRB#13-000933, Ashesi IRB#001. This project was supported by the Wenner-Gren Foundation and the UCLA Anthropology Department.
2 This mission is printed on all the school's promotional materials and is mentioned repeatedly on their website: www.Ashesi.edu.gh [accessed 03/04/2016].

References

Aronczyk, M. (2013) *Branding the Nation: The Global Business of National Identity*, Oxford: Oxford University Press.

Ashesi (2010) "Ashesi University College Honour Code White Paper", at http://archives.ashesi.edu.gh/V3_2004_2010/HOME/The%20Honour%20System%20at%20Ashesi%20University%20College%20-%20White%20Paper.pdf [accessed 06/09/2012].

Avle, S. (2011) "Global flows, media and developing democracies: the Ghanaian case", *Journal of African Media Studies*, 3(1): 7–23.

Bing, N. (2015) "Kenya Decides: Kiswahili, social media and politics in Kenyas 2013 general elections", *Journal of African Media Studies*, 7(2): 165–183.

Blommaert, J. (2008) *Grassroots Literacy: Writing, Identity and Voice in Central Africa*, London: Routledge.

Bourdieu, P. (1985) *Distinction: A Social Critique of the Judgment of Taste*, Cambridge, MA: Harvard University Press.

Burrell, J. (2012) *Invisible Users: Youth in the Internet Cafes of Urban Ghana*, Cambridge, MA: MIT Press.

Coe, C. (2005) *Dilemmas of Culture in African Schools: Youth, Nationalism, and the Transformation of Knowledge*, Chicago, IL: University of Chicago Press.

Cole, J. & Durham, D. L. (2008) *Figuring the Future: Globalization and the Temporalities of Children and Youth*, Santa Fe, NM: School for Advanced Research Press.

Comaroff, J. & Comaroff, J. L. (1999) "Occult economies and the violence of abstraction: notes from the South African postcolony", *American Ethnologist*, 26(2): 279–303.

de Bruijn, M., Pelckmans, P., et al. (2015) "Communicating war in Mali, 2012: on–offline networked political agency in times of conflict", *Journal of African Media Studies*, 7(2): 109–128.

Diawara, M. (1998) *In Search of Africa*, Cambridge, MA: Harvard University Press.

Economist (2011) "The hopeful continent: Africa Rising", *The Economist*, 3 December, at http://www.economist.com/node/21541015 [accessed 01/08/2012].

Feinberg, H. M. & Solodow, J. B. (2002) "Out of Africa", *The Journal of African History*, 43(2): 255–261.

Ferguson, J. (2006) *Global Shadows: Africa in the Neoliberal World Order*, Durham, NC: Duke University Press.

Gershon, I. (2014) "Selling your self in the United States", *PoLAR: Political and Legal Anthropology Review*, 2: 281–295.

Gordon, R. J. (1997) *Picturing Bushmen: The Denver African Expedition of 1925*, Athens, OH: Ohio University Press.

Gratz, T. (2011) "Contemporary African mediascapes: new actors, genres and communication spaces", *Journal of African Media Studies*, 3(2): 151–160.

Komunte, M. (2015) "Usage of mobile technology in women entrepreneurs: a case study of Uganda", *The African Journal of Information Systems*, 7(3): 52–73.

Lutz, C. & Collins, J. L. (1993) *Reading National Geographic*, Chicago, IL: University of Chicago Press.

Mahajan, V. (2009) *Africa Rising: How 900 Million African Consumers Offer More Than You Think*, Upper Saddle River, NJ: Wharton School Publications.

Manganga, K. (2012) "The use of jokes and mobile telephony to create counterpublics in Zimbabwe", *Journal of African Media Studies*, 4(2): 243–255.

Mbembe, A. (2001) *On the Postcolony*, Los Angeles, CA: University of California Press.

Meyer, B. (1998) "'Make a complete break with the past': memory and post-colonial modernity in Ghanaian pentecostalist discourse", *Journal of Religion in Africa*, 28: 316–349.

Mitchell, T. (1991) *Colonising Egypt*, Berkeley, CA: University of California Press.

Newell, S. (2012) *The Modernity Bluff: Crime, Consumption, and Citizenship in Côte d'Ivoire*, Chicago, IL: University of Chicago Press.

Nothias, T. (2014) "'Rising', 'hopeful', 'new': visualizing Africa in the age of globalization", *Visual Communication*, 13(3): 323–339.

Nugent, P. (1995) *Big Men, Small Boys, and Politics in Ghana: Power, Ideology, and the Burden of History, 1982–1994*, London: Pinter.

Nukunya, C. K. (2003) *Tradition and Change in Ghana: An Introduction to Sociology*, Accra: University of Ghana-Legon Press.

Ochs, E. & Capps, L. (2001) *Living Narrative: Creating Lives in Everyday Storytelling*, Cambridge, MA: Harvard University Press.

Ojo, T. (2014) "Africa in the Canadian media: the *Globe and Mail*'s coverage of Africa from 2003 to 2012", *Ecquid Novi: African Journalism Studies*, 35(1): 43–57.

Perry, A. (2012) "Africa Rising", *TIME*, 3 December, at http://content.time.com/time/magazine/article/0,9171,2129831,00.html [accessed 03/12/2012]

Pierre, J. (2013) *The Predicament of Blackness: Postcolonial Ghana and the Politics of Race*, Chicago, IL: University of Chicago Press.

Poggiali, L. (2013) "We are in an ICT world: how Kenya's emergent digital discourse is shifting the flow of people, politics, and technology", ASA 2013 Annual Meeting.

Shipley, J. W. (2013) *Living the Hiplife: Celebrity and Entrepreneurship in Ghanaian Popular Music*, Durham, NC: Duke University Press.

Sumprim, A. K. (2006) *The Imported Ghanaian*, Accra: Mavrik.

Surowiec, P. (2011) "Toward norpo-nationalism: Poland as a brand", in N. Kaneva (ed.), *Branding Post-Communist Nations: Marketizing National Identities in the "New Europe"*, New York: Routledge.

Taylor, I. (2014) *Africa Rising? BRICS – Diversifying Dependency*, Woodbridge, Suffolk: Boydell & Brewer Ltd.

Tufekci, Z. & Wilson, C. (2012) "Social media and the decision to participate in political protest: observations from Tahrir Square", *Journal of Communication*, 62(2): 363–379.

UNCTAD (2012) *Economic Development in Africa Report 2012: Structural Transformation and Sustainable Development in Africa*, New York and Geneva: United Nations Conference on Trade and Development (UNCTAD).

Wadongo, E. (2014) "Africa Rising? Let's be Afro-realistic", *The Guardian*, 7 November, at http://www.theguardian.com/global-development-professionals-network/2014/nov/07/africa-rising-lets-be-afro-realistic [accessed 07/11/2014].

Wainaina, B. (2005) "How to write about Africa", *Granta*, 92: 91–95.

Warschauer, M. (2003) *Technology and Social Inclusion: Rethinking the Digital Divide*, Cambridge, MA: MIT Press.

Part III

Development and humanitarian stories

Chapter 16

Media perspectives

Is Africa's development story still stuck on aid?

Eliza Anyangwe

Before I started covering international development for *The Guardian* online, I had never heard of schistosomiasis, a chronic disease that kills 200,000 Africans per year. As parasitic illnesses go, the burden of disease from schistosomiasis – transmitted through contact with contaminated freshwater – is second only to malaria. Of the 261 million people who required preventative treatment in 2013, 90 per cent of them were in Africa. Yet this story so rarely makes the mainstream news.

Schistosomiasis seems to encapsulate so much of what is difficult with development reporting: it can be technical, so ridden with jargon as to make even the most committed journalist baulk; pilot projects are often unimpressively small; and progress is painstakingly slow.

But the coverage of development progress in Africa has its own unique set of challenges that, in my experience, stem from a dominant, often deeply rooted, neo-colonial narrative. Africa, in my view, is still perceived through the lens of a continent for the taking or one that needs saving.

It's an insidious message of African ineptitude and difference that can be traced back to the 1600s, when philosopher David Hume argued that Africans were naturally inferior to whites, a belief that was strengthened by those opposed to the abolition of slavery in the 1800s.

The narrative of the African as inferior plays out in modern-day journalism. The African development experience is almost always viewed through the lens of someone else's intervention. There are the ones we approve of – for example, British international NGOs to the rescue (more on that later) – and the ones we disapprove of, such as our Cold War enemy China spreading its tentacles across Africa.

Development reporting has become a conversation largely about aid: how much does Africa need, how badly does she need it, which developed countries are keeping their promises to give it, and where exactly does the money go? Nobody ever seems to ask: "Does Africa want aid; and if so, what kind is she looking for?"

These were sentiments shared by the Kenyan writer Binyavanga Wainaina. In an interview he gave me in 2014, Wainaina described the assumptions he felt accompanied the aid narrative: "We [the West] have already agreed that we are going to have an aid and development relationship with you [Africa]. That is non-negotiable. So the question is how do we do it more sustainably; how do we do it more empoweringly?" He laughed, then added: "I'm like no, just fuck off."

Rather than laud the inconsistent interest from much of the Western media in "development issues", I have preferred the coverage of Africa in financial publications, such as *The Economist* or *The Financial Times.* Yes, the former has been mocked in recent years for going from a "failing continent" to the "Africa Rising" narrative, but I argue that the reason it can even make that transition is because it does little of the moralising so evident in the other press.

By following the money (in other words, GDP), as fickle and as poor an indicator of sustainable development as that is, *The Economist* has been better able to recognise a changing continent than the populist press that make an exception for its own development history while expecting Africa to be green and good – but mostly grateful – from the off.

If, as the aid narrative goes, Africans have no agency, then there is little reason to recognise that they have a voice. And the lack of African voices in the mainstream media means that Africa's stories are told by someone else – more often than not, by international charities.

Here we find a rigid dichotomy between the advocacy function of an NGO, which concerns itself with challenging long-term structural and policy issues, and the fundraising arm that seeks to raise money for programmes by using the most effective tool for short-term giving: guilt and pity.

While this conflict rages on within organisations, international charities continue to grow and, as with all corporate giants, perfect their relationship with the media. They hire more journalists to work within their ranks – and as development stories fail to pique the interest of foreign news editors, writers increasingly depend on press trips organised by NGOs, an experience that can leave you with a sense of complicity that is hard to shake.

Of course, international NGOs will argue that the media are in part responsible for the rise of poverty porn, and they'd be right. The news media's obsession with death, destruction, and disease means that charities, however worthy of international media attention their work is, have to find the right language to capture an editor's imagination.

At an event I once attended on the portrayal of Africa in the media, a press officer complained that editors were only interested in the worst stories. He'd learned from experience, he said, that if you dropped the word "famine" in your call to the editorial desk, you'd increase the chances of getting a call back.

So what needs to change? I have stopped believing that simply pointing out hypocrisy or inaccuracy in the Western media's coverage of Africa, will cause a revolutionary change to take place. Ahead of Obama's historic visit to their country, Kenyans on Twitter took to the social media platform in large numbers using the hashtag #SomeonetellCNN to berate the news organisation for calling the East African country a "hotbed of terror". The rest of the press sniggered, a journalist or two were embarrassed, but nothing has fundamentally changed.

In my view, two things need to happen. The first is that African readers need to be consuming Western media in recognisably large numbers. This forces editors to rethink who their content is for. If #SomeonetellCNN was a trending hashtag every day, a deeper assessment of what the organisation gets wrong when it comes to Africa might occur.

The second thing that needs to happen is, in the long term, even more important. African media need to become internationally competitive and take up the mantle to tell Africa's development story. If Wainaina is right in saying that the conversation about development should be exclusively African, then African media need to do a much better job of telling these stories. Schistosomiasis may not matter in London, but it should matter in Lusaka.

Bibliography

Mahmood, M. & Anyangwe, E. (2014) *Binyavanga Wainaina on aid, power and the politics of development in Africa*, at http://www.theguardian.com/global-development-professionals-network/video/2014/mar/18/binyavanga-wainaina-aid-power-politics-development [accessed 01/08/2015].

Port Cities Bristol (2015) "Racist ideas", at http://discoveringbristol.org.uk/slavery/after-slavery/wider-world/black-white-in-britain/racist-ideas/ [accessed 02/08/2015].

The Global Network (2015) "Schistosomiasis", at http://www.globalnetwork.org/schistosomiasis [accessed 02/08/2015].

World Health Organization (2015) "Schistosomiasis fact sheet", at http://www.who.int/mediacentre/factsheets/fs115/en/ [accessed 01/08/2015].

Chapter 17

AIDS in Africa and the British media

Shifting images of a pandemic

Ludek Stavinoha

For more than three decades now, sub-Saharan Africa has borne much of the global HIV/AIDS burden. And, with millions of lives lost, an estimated 25.8 million people living with HIV/AIDS, and 1.4 million new infections in 2013 (UNAIDS 2015), the pandemic in SSA remains very much a crisis of the present. Yet, whereas the AIDS crisis dominated global health politics and news headlines not so long ago, a climate of "AIDS fatigue" has set in during recent years, not only in the international development arena and newsrooms, but among media scholars too (Swain 2005).

Since the 1980s, "AIDS in Africa" has played a central role in the dominant media image of the continent. Indeed, AIDS and Africa are sometimes seen as virtually synonymous; an early audience reception study of UK news coverage found that most participants associated the disease "with Africanness and blackness itself" (Kitzinger & Miller 1992: 49). However, scholarly interest in media representations of HIV/AIDS has subsided markedly since the mid-1990s, following the discovery and rollout of life-saving antiretroviral therapy (ART) across the global North. Ironically, this is precisely when the harrowing scale of the crisis in SSA was becoming evident. Since then only a few studies have investigated Western media coverage of the pandemic in Africa (e.g., Bardhan 2001; Brijnath 2007; Swain 2003), and none has examined the performance of British news media specifically. This study is an attempt to fill that gap. Drawing on a comprehensive analysis of British news coverage since the late 1980s, this chapter charts the shifts in dominant frames of "AIDS in Africa". The empirical focus is primarily on the BBC, with additional examples drawn from major UK newspapers.

Methods

The online BBC Motion Gallery archive was searched for relevant *Early* and *Late Evening News* and *Newsnight* items aired between 1 January 1987 and 31 December 2008, covering almost the entire lifespan of media coverage of the AIDS crisis in Africa. After removing items that only mentioned the pandemic in passing or were unrelated to the core research objectives (e.g., coverage of HIV-positive Africans living in Britain), the entire sample comprised 92 BBC News and 28 *Newsnight* reports. The Glasgow University Media Group's archive and the BBC website were then searched for corresponding footage. In 23 cases of missing footage, the Motion Gallery's detailed description of each news bulletin was used. All in all, 111 of the 120 items were analysed and thematically coded.

The analysis also draws on a sample of 994 articles published in *The Guardian, The Daily Mail*, and *The Financial Times* – three major newspapers that together cover a broad political spectrum of the UK media landscape – generated via the Nexis database using the search term "AIDS AND Africa" for the period from 1 January 1987 to 31 December 2008.[1]

Such a large corpus of texts inevitably opens up a range of empirical queries and analytical paths. Rather than attempting to analyse the entire 20-year period in detail, the aim was to chart the broad shifts in dominant media frames – "principles of selection, emphasis, and presentation composed of little tacit theories about what exists, what happens, and what matters" (Gitlin 1980: 6) – between three distinct phases of coverage that were identified through the analysis of news content. Particular attention was paid to competing explanations of the root causes of the AIDS crisis in SSA, or "explanatory themes" (Philo 2007). A dominant explanatory theme "gives a pattern or structure to an area of coverage" by identifying certain sources, contextual factors, and causal forces as relevant to the exclusion of others (181) and therefore carries important implications for attributions of responsibility. For example, a focus on sexual practices rather than, say, the legacy of structural adjustment programmes, generates a very different understanding of the root causes of the pandemic. In addition, the aim was to identify the "dominant spokespeople" for the pandemic (Bardhan 2001: 300) and the sponsors of rival interpretations of the AIDS crisis by analysing the sourcing patterns in news reporting.

"Death is simply a fact of life" (1987–1997)

A mysterious new "slim" disease spreading across Eastern Africa first began to appear in Western media in the mid-1980s (Treichler 1999). However, the emerging pandemic was not considered particularly newsworthy for, in the immediate post-*Live Aid* era, it merely reinforced the dominant media image of a continent plagued by endemic humanitarian disasters and where "Death is simply a fact of life" (*Guardian*, 4 February 1987). Indeed, the most striking aspect about this phase is the very paucity of coverage. "AIDS in Africa" appeared only 16 times on BBC News and on four *Newsnight* programmes between 1987 and 1997.

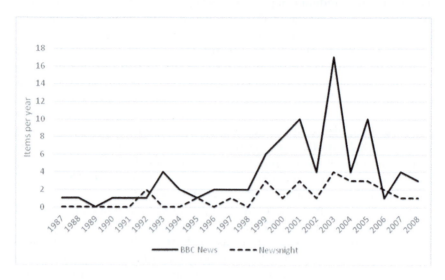

Figure 17.1 BBC coverage of "AIDS in Africa"

When AIDS *was* covered, it was framed primarily through a *biomedical* and *cultural–behavioural* lens. While the former consisted mainly of various theories about the origin of AIDS in Africa and the elusive search for an effective vaccine, central themes of the latter frame were Africans' presumed exceptional "regime of promiscuous sexual behaviour" (*FT*, 12 October 1988) and "risky" practices such as "ritual cleansing" through sexual intercourse (*Newsnight*, 10 July 1992), together with their "ignorance, and worse still, an unwillingness to listen" (BBC News, 28 January 1993). The BBC's then Harare correspondent, John Harrison, described Zimbabwe as "a country where sexual promiscuity is accepted and even celebrated" and "where for deeply rooted cultural reasons there is a refusal to accept that sexual promiscuity can kill". Alternative explanations of this terrifyingly stigmatising disease offered by a HIV patient, who related his plight to Zimbabwe's endemic poverty, were promptly dismissed: "any excuse then, from polluted water to evil spirits, anything but the truth". *The Guardian*, too, could not escape the lure of reproducing quintessential neo-colonial tropes and thinly veiled racist stereotypes typical of early Western representations of AIDS (Treichler 1999):

> The best time to observe the Nairobi hooker is at dusk when the tropical sun dips beneath the Rift Valley and silhouettes the thorn trees against the African skyline. It is then that the hooker preens itself and emerges to stalk its prey: The wazungu. (3 February 1987)

Occasionally, other dimensions of the pandemic were covered. The *FT* departed most clearly from the orthodoxy by framing AIDS as a looming development crisis, which "threatens to undermine fragile African economies" (12 October 1988). Furthermore, while biomedical experts and local health workers were the most frequently cited sources in BBC reports, space was at times given to alternative voices. For example, a campaigner from the Third World advocacy group PANOS described HIV "as a misery-seeking missile" that "homes in on social deprivation, on poverty, on disrupted families, on disadvantaged ethnic minorities, on women who have no control over their lives, on wars and civil wars, on refugees" (BBC News, 28 January 1993).

Yet, by and large, the complex aetiology of the pandemic was reduced to essentialising accounts of African culture and hypersexuality – the core explanatory themes for the unfolding crisis. Despite all the focus on "risky" sexual behaviour, the fact, for instance, that condoms were simply not available or affordable in many regions of SSA was ignored (Shelton & Johnston 2001). Furthermore, no mention was made of the effects of neoliberal reforms or Africa's debt crisis on the capacity of chronically underresourced healthcare systems to cope with an escalating pandemic (Rowden 2010), a point explored in more detail below.

By 1996, with soaring HIV prevalence rates in sub-Saharan Africa and the advent of ART, the pandemic was increasingly being framed in terms of the growing North–South divide in the fate of AIDS patients. In a report about the trial of HIV drugs in South Africa,[2] the BBC interviewed the editor of *The New England Journal of Medicine*, who raised a question that would come to define global AIDS politics several years later: "Do [the drugs] cost too much, or are they priced too high?" The report did not, however, pursue this point any further. Instead, it concluded with a statement by a UCL Medical School professor:

> The most effective way that ... they can deal with the problem in the developing world is to have good health promotion. I think it's quite unrealistic to feel that in the developing world one can buy expensive antiviral drugs. One can't do that. (BBC News, 26 November 1997)

By suggesting that limited resources to combat AIDS were most efficiently spent on prevention, the BBC thus affirmed the reigning international policy consensus that the provision of ART was technically *unfeasible* and *unaffordable* in impoverished African settings (Jones 2004), and therefore, as the *FT*'s first editorial on AIDS in the global South put it, "unthinkable" (9 July 1996). Much of that, however, would change dramatically during the next phase.

AIDS as a global crisis (2000–2003)

At the turn of the millennium, AIDS was routinely portrayed as a calamity of unparalleled proportions that is "spreading through Africa just as the Great

Plague spread through medieval Europe" (BBC News, 14 July 1999). Yet, in contrast to the earlier phase, which presented such totalising accounts of an "African" pandemic often through the sanitised language of epidemiological statistics, these were now being inflected through stories of individual suffering and family tragedies, which featured in 20 of the 48 coded BBC items between 2000 and 2003.

> Lobobo has just been rushed into Selebi-Pikwe's hospital. She can't hear or eat, she can't talk. A single victim of the silent holocaust that is enveloping the continent. In the bed next to her is Grace. She's due to get drugs that could lend her more years of life in December but may not survive the week. Grace is 25 years old and has two children who need her. ... Each death leaves an orphan. Soon there will be a quarter of a million in Botswana. (BBC News, 10 July 2003)

These deeply empathetic accounts of the human suffering to which journalists bore witness played an important role in the *rehumanisation* of the millions of people dying of HIV/AIDS across SSA. The hitherto largely nameless and voiceless Africans living with HIV/AIDS now had names, families, friends, and tangible places of origin. This combined with a growing sense of indignation at the perceived indifference of the global North to the scale and urgency of the crisis, a narrative perhaps most forcefully expressed in a three-page report in *The Mail on Sunday* (19 September 1999):

> THIS LITTLE GIRL IS ONE OF EIGHT MILLION SOUTH AFRICANS WHO WILL DIE OF AIDS WITHIN FIVE YEARS ... SO WHY DOES NO ONE CARE? IS IT BECAUSE THE VICTIMS ARE BLACK AND POOR?

A key moment that turned the AIDS crisis into one of the main news stories coming out of Africa was the July 2000 International AIDS Conference in Durban (see Figure 17.1). South Africa – the epicentre of the global pandemic – emerged as the frontline in two political battles that were particularly well predisposed to the kind of dramatic "framing contests" (Entman 2004) that tend to attract media attention. The first was the row between the international scientific community and President Thabo Mbeki over the latter's AIDS "denialism". The other was the global campaign for access to medicines, led by the South African Treatment Action Campaign in coalition with major international NGOs like Oxfam and MSF and directed against the world's largest pharmaceutical corporations, which had sued the South African government over its alleged violation of World Trade Organization (WTO) intellectual property rights rules (Smith & Siplon 2006). Consequently, over the coming months and years, AIDS would turn into the stuff of front-page headlines, op-eds, investigative reports, and high-profile celebrity campaigns.

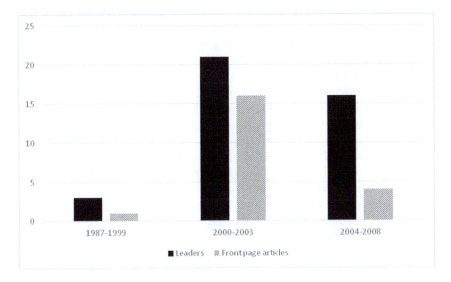

Figure 17.2 "AIDS in Africa" in the press

Note

a   All leaders and front-page articles appeared in *The Guardian* or the *FT*. AIDS in Africa never made it to the front page of Britain's second most widely read newspaper, *The Daily Mail*.

South Africa's legal battle with "Big Pharma" and the US government first featured on *Newsnight* (16 September 1999) in a special report about a "momentous, complicated and highly symbolic struggle against multinational companies. It's patented drugs that are the biggest problem. Patents create monopolies. Prices reflect patent power rather than patient interest." After giving prominent space to the Treatment Action Campaign and South Africa's Health Minister to make their case in defence of the government's 1997 Medicines Act, which allowed for the importation of cheaper generic drugs, the report then challenged Big Pharma's pricing policies in Africa. In this case, Glaxo-Wellcome's Corporate Affairs Director was in the firing line: "Don't you think it's a bit grotesque though when you go to bed at night sometimes and just think that there are countries who so need drugs and ultimately they really are not getting them?"

Such reporting broke new ground in several ways. First, alongside UNAIDS, WHO and government officials, aid workers, and biomedical experts – the dominant spokespeople for the pandemic since its outbreak – civil society campaigners had begun to play a significant role in setting the news agenda. In fact, activists and NGO campaigners were the most frequently cited source on the BBC, making up a fifth of the 113 cited sources, during this phase. Second, the *Newsnight* report was the first instance in the entire history of BBC coverage of the pandemic that featured an interview with *African* AIDS activists. Images of emaciated bodies in overcrowded hospital wards and sounds of wailing babies that had hitherto characterised televised portrayals of the pandemic gave way to Africans actively struggling against the combined devastation of the disease and the structural injustices of global capitalism, defying the crude analytical categorisation of "positive" and "negative" media representations of Africa.

Facing an unprecedented PR disaster, the South African lawsuit eventually ended with Big Pharma throwing in the towel. But with little progress in the rollout of treatment and deadlock over reform of WTO rules, the controversy over AIDS drugs continued to generate media publicity in the UK and elsewhere around the world (Owen 2013). For example, in early 2003 – the year in which the volume of BBC coverage reached its peak – *BBC Evening News* (19 February 2003) ran with the following headline news report from Swaziland, the worst-afflicted country with more than a third of its population HIV-positive:

> The 10 o'clock news has harrowing new evidence of the extent of the AIDS catastrophe in Southern Africa. According to the United Nations, several countries could be near collapse. They all face one major obstacle: access to affordable drug treatment. Today, the Chancellor Gordon Brown stepped in with a hard-hitting message to the multinational drug companies. He said they must allow poor countries to buy cheap versions of their drugs.

The access to medicines story, together with the issue of international AIDS funding, sponsored a sustained shift towards a *structural inequalities* frame during the early 2000s. Eighteen of the 48 coded BBC items contained elements that placed "AIDS in Africa" in the wider context of North–South health and economic inequalities. As a result, a radically different interpretation of the unfolding human tragedy was being relayed. No longer just "a fact of life" or one in a seemingly endless list of Africa's development crises, the pandemic was instead being framed as a profoundly *political* "global crisis" (Cottle 2012), a crisis that connects the most remote corners of the African continent to sites of global political and economic power via the living rooms of British audiences.

In the immediate aftermath of the South African court case, for example, *Newsnight* (24 April 2001) ran a report by investigative journalist Greg Palast, featuring Joseph Stiglitz, who had just publicly resigned as the World Bank's chief economist. The report framed the issue as a part of a much bigger backlash against neo-liberal globalisation, highlighting the devastation wrought by structural adjustment programmes across the global South and the imposition of healthcare user fees by the Bank in the midst of Tanzania's AIDS crisis. This was perhaps the closest that BBC coverage came to offering "a *counterframe* that puts together a completely alternative narrative, a tale of problem, cause, remedy, and moral judgement" (Entman 2004: 48).

However, it is important to emphasise its exceptionality. In fact, this was the only time in more than two decades that the AIDS crisis was explicitly linked to Africa's encounter with neo-liberalism. What is more, if we turn to the main explanatory themes, media accounts overwhelmingly continued to emphasise a combination of biomedical (e.g., unique virulence of subtype of HIV in SSA) and cultural–behavioural (polygamy, promiscuity, sexual violence, stigma, etc.) factors. Thus, for instance, when it came to explaining the root causes of Swaziland's unparalleled crisis, the BBC report cited above resorted to an emphatic *culturalisation* of the pandemic – "The Swazis' *traditions* are helping to kill them" (emphasis added). Furthermore, when socio-economic determinants such as food insecurity, lack of healthcare workers, extreme poverty, and inequality were mentioned, these were universally depicted as given and "internally generated" (Miller et al. 1998: 82).

To be sure, all of these factors contribute to the complex dynamics that have fuelled the spread of HIV in SSA and many of these cannot be attributed to external forces alone. Yet, at the same time, the unequal distribution of HIV/AIDS around the world and its concentration in Southern Africa cannot be abstracted from the systematic violation of basic socio-economic rights generated by what Stephen Lewis, the UN's former Special Envoy for HIV/AIDS in Africa, denounced as "a form of capitalist Stalinism. The credo was everything; the people were a laboratory" (2005: 16). Thus, in a highly symbolic moment of ideological closure, the BBC ended its report on South African activists' court victory in April 2001 with the words, "no more excuses, no more blaming international capitalism" (18 April 2001), as a perceptible shift towards a more *depoliticised* framing of Africa's AIDS crisis began to emerge.

Towards a depoliticalisation of AIDS (2004–2008)

Indeed, the *structural inequalities* frame had almost entirely disappeared by the mid-2000s and the impact of pharmaceutical patents on access to medicines was never mentioned again in relation to the pandemic in sub-Saharan Africa after September 2003. Instead, BBC reporting was increasingly characterised by various celebrity-endorsed charity campaigns and appeals. While advocacy NGOs and activists appeared only four times on the BBC between 2004 and 2008, HIV-positive Africans and celebrities became the two most prominent sources, accounting for 27 per cent and 17 per cent of 93 coded sources respectively. In a typical example from December 2005, BBC News carried a report about actor and UNICEF ambassador Ewan McGregor's trip to an orphanage in Malawi (14 December 2005). The report contained harrowing personal accounts of orphaned children, footage of HIV-infected babies in a dilapidated hospital, followed by

McGregor's emotional testimony. Though compassionate and empathetic, reports like these offer audiences no explanations about the structural causes of the abject poverty and suffering that form the visual and narrative backdrop. What is more, such reporting slips rather uneasily into a White Man's Burden narrative.

In 2008, all three BBC News reports about AIDS in SSA contained a celebrity focus – an arts auction by Bono and Damien Hirst (13 February), a star-studded charity gig for Nelson Mandela (27 June), and Prince Harry's trip to an AIDS orphanage in Lesotho (8 July). Against the backdrop of declining news coverage, the growing prominence of celebrities in the cultural construction of "AIDS in Africa" is further reinforced by the emergence of various "philanthrocapitalist" schemes in popular culture (Stavinoha 2014). As a result, a very different image of "AIDS of Africa" is emerging once again: a humanitarian crisis abstracted from all historical and political causalities and North–South relations of power.

Conclusion

HIV/AIDS remains the leading cause of death across much of SSA. The death toll for 2014 alone was 790,000. Another 15 million people lack access to ART (UNAIDS 2015). But body counts are no reliable predictor of media interest; the AIDS crisis has almost disappeared off the media radar in recent years.

Much of this is attributable, first, to the very real progress made in the fight against HIV/AIDS, especially the expansion of access to treatment. Second, and more worryingly, the activist groups that galvanised the attention of the media in the early 2000s "have gone or become shadows of themselves" (Heywood 2014), in part due to changing priorities of donors in the global North, the lifeline of many African AIDS NGOs (Smith 2014). But it has also something to do with the "calculus of death" (Cottle & Nolan 2007: 863) that directs cameras to instances of distant suffering according to standards of newsworthiness that remain as problematic as they were when the "slim disease" first emerged some three decades ago. The 2014 Ebola outbreak in West Africa had everything going for it in this respect. In contrast to HIV, which takes years to quietly wear away the immune system, Ebola's effects are almost immediate, graphic and gruesome, and lend themselves to the kind of hyperbolic and sensationalised reporting that swept across the world.

Given the centrality of epidemics like these to media images of Africa, what lessons can be learned from the survey of British news coverage presented here? Perhaps above all, it shows how decontextualised and depoliticised reporting of large-scale, poverty-driven epidemics like HIV/AIDS can inadvertently reproduce some of the most damaging stereotypes about the continent. Writing in the early days of the pandemic, Cindy Patton observed how,

> Linking disease and poverty in a simple way leaves the way open to the unconscious reflex of Westerners to relate *poverty* as well as disease to some transcendent racial/ethnic difference rather than situating both in larger and historically specific patterns of colonialism, capitalist statism, and a global economy increasingly controlled by supranational corporations. (1990: 82)

At the turn of the millennium, a unique set of conditions thrust "AIDS in Africa" into news headlines. This created spaces for journalists to shine the spotlight on the corridors of power of international development agencies and the executive boardrooms of pharmaceutical companies, rupturing established explanatory themes without which the mobilisation of the international effort against HIV/AIDS would have been unthinkable. While these conditions are unlikely to be repeated, the case remains that the "bodies" of those living and dying with HIV/AIDS "are the evidence of global inequality and injustice", in the words of Africa's most prominent AIDS activist, Zackie Achmat (in Oinas & Jungar 2008: 246). Consequently, as post-colonial theorists have long argued, representations of Africa that foreground "internal, indeed *intrinsic*" African characteristics to explain development crises (Andreasson 2005: 973), while masking causalities that extend beyond the spatial bounds of the continent, are projections of power, of a colonial imaginary never quite gone.

Notes

1 It should be noted that the search term – looking for articles that feature the word "Africa" – may have produced results that overstate the extent to which the news media make some of the homogenising claims about "Africa" in relation to AIDS presented below.
2 In the trial, a group of HIV-positive mothers was given a placebo, causing a furore among AIDS activists and comparisons with the infamous Tuskegee trials.

References

Andreasson, S. (2005) "Orientalism and African Development Studies: the 'reductive repetition' motif in theories of African underdevelopment," *Third World Quarterly*, 26(6): 971–986.
Bardhan, N. (2001) "Transnational AIDS–HIV news narratives: a critical exploration of overarching frames", *Mass Communication and Society*, 4(3): 283–309.
Brijnath, B. (2007) "It's about *TIME*: engendering AIDS in Africa", *Culture, Health & Sexuality*, 9(4): 371–386.
Cottle, S. (2011) "Taking global crises in the news seriously: notes from the dark side of globalization", *Global Media and Communication*, 7(2): 77–95.
Cottle, S. & Nolan, D. (2007) "Global humanitarianism and the changing aid field: 'Everyone was dying for footage'", *Journalism Studies*, 8(6): 862–878.

Entman, R. M. (2004) *Projections of Power: Framing News, Public Opinion, and U.S. Foreign Policy*, Chicago, IL: University of Chicago Press.

Gitlin, T. (1980) *The Whole World Is Watching: Mass Media in the Making and Unmaking of the New Left*, Berkeley, CA: University of California Press.

Heywood, M. (2014) "Does anybody remember AIDS?", at http://www.tac.org.za/news/letter-melbourne-international-aids-conference-does-anybody-remember-aids [accessed 01/08/2015].

Jones, P. S. (2004) "When 'development' devastates: donor discourses, access to HIV/AIDS treatment in Africa and rethinking the landscape of development", *Third World Quarterly*, 25(2): 385–404.

Kitzinger, J. & Miller, D. (1992) "African AIDS: the media and audience beliefs", in P. Aggleton, P. Davies, and G. Hart (eds), *AIDS: Rights, Risk and Reason*, London: Falmer Press.

Lewis, S. (2005) *Race Against Time*, Toronto, ON: Anansi.

Miller, D., Kitzinger, J., Williams, K., & Beharrell, P. (1998) *The Circuit of Mass Communication: Media Strategies, Representation and Audience Reception in the AIDS Crisis*, London: Sage.

Oinas, E. & Katarina, J. (2008) "A luta continua! South African HIV activism, embodiment and state politics", *Development Dialogue*, 50 (December): 239–258.

Owen, T. (2013) "From 'pirates' to 'heroes': news, discourse change, and the contested legitimacy of generic HIV/AIDS medicines", *The International Journal of Press/Politics*, 18(3): 259–280.

Patton, C. (1990) *Inventing AIDS*, New York: Routledge.

Philo, G. (2007) "Can discourse analysis successfully explain the content of media and journalistic practice?", *Journalism Studies*, 8(2): 175–196.

Rowden, R. (2010) *The Deadly Ideas of Neoliberalism*, London: Zed Books.

Shelton, J. D. & Johnston, B. (2001) "Condom gap in Africa: evidence from donor agencies and key informants", *British Medical Journal*, 323: 139–141.

Smith, D. (2014) "Funding crunch threatens TAC", *Mail & Guardian*, 7 November, at http://mg.co.za/article/2014-11-06-funding-crunch-threatens-tac [accessed 01/08/2015].

Smith, R. A. & Siplon, P. D. (2006) *Drugs into Bodies: Global AIDS Treatment Activism*, Westport: Praeger.

Stavinoha, L. (2014) "AIDS, Africa and popular culture: mediated cosmopolitanism in a neoliberal era", in A. Yilmaz, R. Trandafoiu, and A. Mousoutzanis (eds), *Media and Cosmopolitanism*, Oxford: Peter Lang.

Swain, K. A. (2003) "Proximity and power facts in western coverage of the sub-Saharan AIDS crisis", *Journalism & Mass Communication Quarterly*, 80(1): 145–165.

Swain, K. A. (2005) "Approaching the quarter-century mark: AIDS coverage and research decline as infection spreads", *Critical Studies in Media Communication*, 22(3): 258–262.

Treichler, P. A. (1999) *How to Have Theory in an Epidemic: Cultural Chronicles of AIDS*, Durham, NC: Duke University Press.

UNAIDS (2015) *World AIDS Day 2015 fact sheet*, at http://www.unaids.org/sites/default/files/media_asset/20150901_FactSheet_2015_en.pdf [accessed 01/05/2016]

Chapter 18

Media perspectives

A means to an end? Creating a market for humanitarian news from Africa

Heba Aly

The year 2007 was a tough one for Chad. The vast Sahelian central African country is often forgotten amid its headline-grabbing neighbours, but here's a taste of the challenges.

A rebellion, interethnic violence, and proxy war raged in the east; 150,000 people were displaced by the fighting; widespread food shortages led to emergency levels of malnutrition; and flooding carried away villagers and blocked relief efforts. The UN said the international community was underestimating the scale of the country's crisis and warned of a genocide in Chad on the scale of Rwanda.

But it was not until the alleged kidnapping of 103 Chadian "orphans" by French aid workers that Chad was put on the global radar that year.

It didn't surprise me that it took a Western angle to get international headlines about Chad. And I would see the same scenario unfold over and over during my time reporting from the African continent.

In the Autumn of 2008, I visited remote villages in Sudan's Darfur region, where I documented what appeared to have been government attacks on civilians. I photographed mud homes burned into ashes, bomb craters in the ground, and machine gun bullet casings strewn across the main road.

The Christian Science Monitor, the US-based but internationally minded "public service" newspaper, was then one of my regular clients. It often published my material with little editing. But when the piece about Darfur appeared online, it had a different lead – linking my report to the US vice presidential debate.

It happened again a few months later, when I told the story of a Kenyan–Somali suicide bomber who had joined Al Shabaab in Somalia. Inserted high up in the final piece was a paragraph about a Somali–American student from Minnesota reportedly killed while fighting with the militant group.

The editors needed to make these stories relevant to an American audience.

So is there an international market for humanitarian news in Africa in and of itself – in other words, without that Western connection?

Today, I run a news outlet that reports exclusively on crises, largely from countries in Africa and the rest of the developing world, and our biggest challenge is finding our place in the market. Our journey reflects the wider challenges of sustainably producing and financing this kind of news.

IRIN was the world's first humanitarian news service, founded by the United Nations after the Rwanda genocide to cover conflict, natural disasters, and the emergency aid industry. While our funding was by no means guaranteed, it required less hustle than in the outside world. For nearly twenty years, the UN (via contributions from donor governments) paid our operating costs, which grew to $11 million at IRIN's peak in 2008.

But that money came with strings: under pressure from its member states and due to operational concerns, the UN often reviewed quotations – if not entire articles – before publication and sometimes asked us to withhold certain information. Being 'part of the family' meant that our journalists often limited themselves, sometimes without even realising it. By 2013, the censorship became overt when the UN directly instructed IRIN to stop reporting on Syria (Lynch 2014).

In large part to address this, IRIN spun off from the UN in 2015 to become an independent media non-profit. But in doing so, we entered into the challenges and volatility of the news market.

Our proposition is not commercially viable. Producing original content from far-flung places of the earth is expensive. And humanitarian news simply cannot compete when held up against the market's indicators of success: eyeballs, traffic, unique visitors, audience, reach, growth.

As leading digital journalism expert Emily Bell put it recently (2015): "The inherent tension at the centre of … every news organisation … is that only the likable is reliably bankable. The relaying of trauma, devastation and cruelty is not inherently profitable".

Some for-profit outlets, like VICE News, have managed to make such news trendy. And some mainstream media do a decent job. But most are either unable or unwilling to consistently – and responsibly – cover the suffering of distant peoples.

Ultimately, with the help of outside consultants, we concluded that, while we could generate revenue to cover some operating costs, grant funding was the best bet.

We shopped around our raison d'être to many stakeholders. We explained our objective: we raise awareness about local crises among an international audience to inspire a more effective response to the world's most vulnerable people.

But as we set out on fundraising trips in Europe, the US, and the Middle East, going into donor meeting after donor meeting, writing proposal after proposal, the responses were not always encouraging.

We were too "political" for the private sector; too mainstream for the traditional aid donors; not flashy enough for the digital media donors; and not upbeat enough for the activist campaigns that inspire you but leave the world no better a place.

The non-profit media scene has seen a dramatic boom in the US in recent years, but those of us working in non-profit international news haven't seen the same level of enthusiasm, at least not yet. Many donors want to fund journalism from African countries when it has an inspiring hero or flashy solutions: the village that bucked the trend or the new mobile app that will solve refugees' problems. Headlines like "Meet this 18-year-old girl who is changing the world one headband at a time" or "This little spinning ball could help millions of people around the world" (yes, these are real) are much more popular than the failure of disarmament in the Congo or the eradication of guinea worm disease in Ethiopia.

So in this world of simple narratives and flashy visuals, how does complex humanitarian reporting survive? Where does that leave IRIN and others like us?

To be frank, it leaves us desperately trying to prove our worth. But even there, we stumble and fall.

It is now generally accepted that audience metrics are not an accurate measure of the value of non-profit news – after all, it's not numbers we're after; it's impact. Donors are increasingly attuned to this and methodologies to track impact are being developed.

We've tried to make our material more appealing and accessible to a wider audience while maintaining its substance. Striking the right balance is an hourly challenge: it colours our debates about headlines, writing style, presentation, and story selection. How far are we willing to go in pursuit of eyeballs?

War in the Central African Republic is never going to compete with the Champions League. And if bringing forgotten humanitarian stories in Africa and elsewhere to a wider public means stripping them of their nuance, complexity, and shades of grey ... if reaching a wider public comes at the cost of creating an informed public ... aren't we missing the point?

Worse, without context, our work can be deeply harmful to both the humanitarian cause and to global solidarity. When outsiders don't understand the root causes of famine in Somalia, they blame the victim. (If those stupid people can't feed themselves, why should *we* help *them?*)

We believe the world is better than that.

We believe that everyone has the right to be heard, no matter where they live; that suffering is universal; that in a financially, socially, and geographically interconnected world, one person's struggle is everyone's struggle.

We believe that countries in crisis suffer additional levels of neglect, discrimination, and stereotyping by the absence of healthy internationally tuned media.

And we believe that readers are sophisticated enough to care.

So we will continue to give an international audience those complex, nuanced narratives that don't always have happy endings or sexy taglines.

Our audience will necessarily be niche – and that's not a bad thing. In the digital age, specialised content is the only way both non-profit and for-profit outlets can maintain a value proposition.

Our funding will necessarily be a struggle – but with time, we hope that experimentation, best practice, and an increasing recognition of the opportunities created by an informed international populace will lead us to a more stable footing.

But getting these stories right undoubtedly matters – and that's something live analytics don't measure.

References

Bell, E. (2015) "Twitter's heart hits the wrong beat", *The Guardian*, 8 November.
Lynch, C. (2014) "Gag order: why is the UN censoring its own Syrian news?", *Foreign Policy*, 14 January.

Chapter 19

It was a "simple", "positive" story of African self-help (manufactured for a Kenyan NGO by advertising multinationals)

Kate Wright

Northern news organisations now face a perfect financial storm, which has been shaped by a variety of factors, including the rise of new media competitors like Google and Yahoo, regulatory change, the cost of developing new technologies, and dwindling advertising revenue (Franklin 2011). This has prompted widespread cost-cutting and the privileging of production practices geared towards producing more content, faster, and at lower cost (Phillips 2012). So it is perhaps unsurprising that news outlets' dependence upon the "information subsidies" (Gandy 1982) provided by external sources has increased, including their reliance upon the material supplied by public relations professionals (Lewis et al. 2008a, 2008b).

These changes have been compounded in the coverage of sub-Saharan Africa by reductions in the numbers of news bureaus and correspondent posts funded by international news organisations (Paterson 2011: 39–40). Those who remain, have often had to accept casualised posts that involve their being paid per item, so they struggle to leave their desks. Cuts to newsroom budgets also make it much harder for those working in the headquarters of such news organisations to justify trips to African countries themselves (Dozier 2008). Yet many journalists remain committed to representing a wide variety of people and places for a mixture of normative, legal, and commercial reasons.

In such circumstances, news outlets are increasingly turning to non-governmental organisations (NGOs) to supply them with video and photographic images representing events in more remote or dangerous locations in Africa.[1] Large, wealthy international NGOs (INGOs) tend to dominate this field of media production because they can afford to fund extensive travel and expensive communications technology, as well as hiring experienced former journalists with the cultural and social capital necessary to create and pitch such multimedia to news outlets (Fenton 2010). Thus using INGO-provided video and photos is regarded by some as improving journalism's dynamism and social engagement (Beckett & Mansell 2008), but others argue that it seriously damages the diversity and critical independence of news coverage (Cottle & Nolan 2007; Franks 2008).

Journalists' concerns about their potential complicity in enhancing the brands of powerful INGOs (Magee 2014) are often tied to other worries about some INGOs' tendency to use negative, stereotypical, and decontextualised images of Africans requiring wealthy Northerners' help (Lugo-Ocando 2015). Such arguments are underpinned by the conviction that negative media representations perpetuate chronic under-development by reinforcing notions that the entire African continent is a hopeless case. Indeed, even the former South African President, Thabo Mbeki, has asserted that international journalists have a responsibility to avoid harming African peoples' prospects and global standing through "negative typecasting" (cited in de Beer 2010: 602).

One solution, which has been explored by some British journalists, is to use photos provided by African NGOs, when these are of sufficient technical and aesthetic quality (Wright 2015). But, unless they were longstanding Africa editors, these journalists tended to assume that smaller, poorer African NGOs would be simpler and less dominated by commercial marketing practices and norms than major INGOs. So, they reasoned, disseminating such NGOs' representations of African people "helping themselves" would be more progressive, "positive", and "empowering". These assumptions were further enhanced by the ways in which these images were frequently obtained through social media, so tapping into broader hopes about the potential of digital media to foster more diverse and egalitarian modes of media production (Beckett & Mansell 2008).

The purpose of this chapter is to debunk such simplistic assumptions. It draws on Davis' theory about "promotional cultures" (2013) and Chouliaraki's work about "ironic spectatorship" (2013), as well as critiques made elsewhere in this volume about "Africa Rising" narratives, in order to analyse a particularly illuminating case study. This was constructed using internal documentation and semi-structured interviews with those who made key decisions shaping the production of a single journalistic article. It contained a still photograph produced for a campaign run by the Kenyan Paraplegic Organization (KPO), in conjunction with the telecommunications company Safaricom, and Scangroup, an Africa-wide network of advertising and marketing professionals based in Nairobi, which includes the global PR giant Ogilvy & Mather.

This article appeared in the British Sunday newspaper *The Observer* (Kiberenge 2012), although similar items about the campaign appeared outside the sampling period in one of Kenya's leading newspapers, *The Standard*, as well as in a number of prestigious international news outlets, including Al Jazeera, *The New York Times*, and *BBC News Online*. However, this case study is significant not only because the story was picked up by these major news outlets, but also because participants insisted that commercial businesses often develop media campaigns with African NGOs to enhance their reputations in the continent's highly lucrative emerging markets.

Corporate social responsibility, promotional cultures, and expats

Like many smaller NGOs, KPO lacked the financial and cultural capital needed to produce its own multimedia (Fenton 2010). So when the NGO wanted to raise money to build a new spinal injuries rehabilitation clinic in Nairobi, its leader approached an acquaintance who was a senior executive at major commercial telecommunications company Safaricom, which is also based in Nairobi. This executive was involved with Safaricom's corporate social responsibility (CSR) programme,[2] which often "adopted" local NGOs (interview 23 April 2013). This was a strategy that Safaricom's Executive Director hoped would pay handsome dividends in terms of consumer goodwill and investor interest (Baillie, cited in *Standard Digital* 2010). Indeed, Safaricom's CSR programme seems to have functioned as a specific form of public relations exercise – crisis management (Demetrious 2013). This was because it was launched in 2009, shortly after allegations of serious corruption involving the company were finally dropped in Kenya and the UK (Kenya National Assembly 2007; interview, UK Serious Fraud Office, 20 June 2014).

So KPO's campaign was shaped by highly commercialised promotional cultures (Davis 2013) long before the executive in question ever approached Scangroup, a pan-African network of advertising and communications companies that normally produces marketing campaigns for Safaricom. This executive asked Scangroup – whose members include RedSky advertising, Scanad communications, Squad Digital, and the global PR giant Ogilvy & Mather – to design a campaign with KPO on a *pro bono* basis, which would incorporate Safaricom's mobile donation platform, M-PESA (interview). As Scangroup staff explained, this was not unusual, as they were often approached by large businesses asking them to design campaigns for African NGOs as part of their CSR schemes, which were envisaged by these businesses as a key part of their brand-management strategy (interview 4 May 2013; interview 18 April 2013).

Scangroup staff also talked about the "sympathy" they had for the individual Kenyan paraplegics whom they had met, but they were far more motivated by the greater creative freedom allowed to them in *pro bono* work. In particular, working on the KPO campaign offered the European and Australian expats who dominated RedSky's creative team the opportunity to design a cutting-edge "360°" campaign, which incorporated social and mainstream media (interview). Thus they hoped to be able to compete for international industry awards in order not only to consolidate their position in the pan-African advertising market, but also to "sell" themselves in an increasingly harsh and insecure global job market. As an advertising executive at RedSky explained:

> There's a *lot* of people out there struggling with their careers and with, you know, with the global financial crisis ... [*sighs*].
> So you really need to prove that you can ... go beyond the normal. ...
> As a creative, you're always wanting to do work that gets you noticed, that *brands* you as an innovative thinker, because, on a selfish note, you know ... you're looking after your own career. (interview)

So the KPO campaign was very much designed according to the interests and norms of the commercial actors who were involved. This entailed Scangroup creating a "saleable event" (Davis 2013: 2) that its staff hoped would stimulate regular small donations from poorer Kenyan people, as well as larger donations from Kenyan elites and international audiences. First, an advertising executive at RedSky came up with the idea of asking a member of KPO to wheel himself from Nairobi to Johannesburg in South Africa – nearly three thousand kilometres away – where KPO claimed the nearest spinal injury rehabilitation centre was located. Next, this "event" was made even more "saleable" (Davis 2013: 2) by using another agency within Scangroup, Squad Digital, to track this person's progress using GPS. This information was then used in order to publish constant Facebook updates, Tweets, and embedded photo and video feeds, so stimulating a social media storm in order to attract the attention of the national and international media.

Scangroup staff then set about finding a "saleable individual" to embed in this "saleable event" (Davis 2013: 2). They interviewed a number of possible candidates before selecting Zack Kimotho, not only because of his level of fitness and determination, but also because of his marketability. As a senior figure at Scanad, who was involved in this decision-making process, explained,

> He was a vet before he got shot and he's got two kids. But, you know, he's determined to live his life, and erm ... that kind of thing was always going to go down well.
> Plus, you know, like a lot of people here, he's a very big-hearted fella and wanted to do something to help other people in his condition. ...
> And ... we thought it would be like a secondary er ... *bonus* if we got somebody, you know ... who's a good-looking guy. (interview)

So although the NGO campaign was not consciously designed in relation to mainstream news values, it was timely, involved an extensive journey, and was highly personalised, with an obvious "human interest" focus

(Harcup & O'Neill 2001). Indeed, these expat advertising and marketing executives framed the campaign in ways that were deliberately designed to persuade media audiences that the key problem was Kimotho having to continue on his arduous journey, and that the solution to this problem was for them to "Bring Zack Back Home" by giving enough money via M-PESA to enable a new rehabilitation centre to be built.

Selling representations of African "empowerment"

This emphasis on the positive but low-intensity emotions of audiences; the marketisation of suffering; the simple, immediate, and technologically delivered "solution" offered via communications technology; and on the capabilities of mediation itself, seems to mark the KPO campaign out as an example of post-humanitarian communication (Chouliaraki 2013). As such, it might be expected to be detached from the traditional grand narratives that link emancipation to solidarity (Chouliaraki 2013: 9–15). However, despite the framing of the campaign by the commercialised norms of largely European and Australian expats, it was legitimised according to normative ideas about Kenyan empowerment and collective self-help. This was because the campaign was conceptualised by the expats who developed the project as "capitalising upon" the success of the "Kenyans for Kenya" campaign, which had been run in the previous year by a coalition of charities and businesses (including Safaricom), to help those suffering from famine in the north of the country (interviews).

Indeed, the Kenyan account manager at Ogilvy & Mather said he had been appointed to deal with press enquiries because of his previous experience on that campaign, so enhancing journalists' trust via this value-laden association (interview 27 March 2013). Thus he pitched the campaign to journalists in a similar manner, arguing that "we Kenyans shouldn't all the time rely on the government or external donors ... to solve problems for us" (interview). But serious questions must be raised about the extent to which the campaign rested on principles of Kenyan empowerment, because a senior figure at RedSky, who was a British expat, said that some of KPO's lower-ranking members had objected to the plan and that he had over-ruled them. As he put it,

> What happened was some [KPO members] thought the idea [for the campaign] was too big and we were asked to do a Plan B.
>
> So I got everybody in a meeting in front of RedSky and did the "Over my *dead* body, this is not going to happen" number. "You *can't* not go with this *now*."
>
> But [some KPO members] still thought it had got out of hand and that, maybe, we were doing the wrong thing. ...
>
> Yeah ... there was a *lot* of bad feeling there. (interview)[3]

This displacement of Kenyan non-elites was not evident to Kenyan diaspora, who shared the campaign widely on Facebook and Twitter, so bringing it to the attention of a Kenyan journalist working on an internship with *The Observer* in London (interview 28 August 2012).[4] He then pitched this as a story idea to his duty editor, who pitched it to her senior editor, who agreed to allow the intern to proceed because, as he put it,

> When it comes to stories about Africa, we try and include as wide a range as possible so it's not all, well, here's another story about a disastrous situation in an African country brought about through war or poverty or what have you.
>
> Reflecting on media trends is part of our effort to have more varied coverage of the continent, which is itself extremely varied and going through some extraordinary, and often very positive, transformations. (interview 30 April 2013).

In this way, a story that was ostensibly about Kenyan empowerment and solidarity became subsumed by a broader "Africa Rising" narrative. Such narratives tend to articulate progress and self-help in privatised, technocentric, and mediacentric terms, so pose little challenge to Anglo-American cultural norms and neoliberal media markets. Thus they can be easily co-opted by Northern news organisations and used within their own commercial strategies. In this case, journalists hoped that the story would help the paper stand out from its rivals, operating as a kind of "information subsidy" (Gandy 1982) relating to market differentiation. Yet had they checked they would have found that Kenya's *The Standard* (*Standard Digital* 2012), Al Jazeera (Greste 2012), and *The New York Times* (Gettleman 2012) had already covered the KPO campaign. The BBC then covered the story two days later (BBC 2012).

In particular, *Observer* journalists hoped that the story would attract audiences because it would be uplifting and easy to read; and, as a duty news editor explained, a Sunday newspaper "cannot be all doom and gloom" (interview 23 November 2012). However, journalists' conceptualisation of this as an unchallenging, "positive" story prevented them from scrutinising the issues and values concerned: indeed, the duty news editor thought that it was not just a "light" news story but also a "simple" one, "one of the most straightforward that we do" (interview). Thus the only original research that the intern was tasked with carrying out was to call and interview Kimotho himself.

This lack of investigative research meant that neither the intern nor *Observer* journalists ever had the opportunity to discover that KPO had no plans about how to fund the equipment, staff, and running costs of a newly built rehabilitation clinic (interviews). Journalists also failed to explore the NGO's political links, even though these were detailed on KPO's website, and even though the production of this article occurred in the run-up to a Kenyan general election. In particular, the site listed the spouse of the then Prime Minister as a member of KPO's advisory panel (Kenyan Paraplegic Organization website, n.d.). However, even if *Observer* journalists had checked the website, they may not have understood what they read. This was because cost-cutting at the paper had led to the roles of the international and home news editor being merged, and the duty news editor was painfully aware of how little she understood about Kenyan politics (interview). So *The Observer* may have inadvertently boosted the cultural capital of a senior figure in KPO, who successfully ran for office for the same political party less than six months later.

"Dramatising reality"

Finally, journalists' uncritical use of the KPO photograph and the interpretative frame in which it was embedded was problematic because the KPO campaign – and all of the news stories about it – depended upon Kimotho's determination to go all the way to Johannesburg if necessary. Yet no logistical plans, financial budgets, fundraising licences, or travel permits had ever been put in place to allow him to continue over the Kenyan border. This was because none of those involved had anticipated that Kimotho would need to go that far before enough money had been raised (interviews). So the KPO campaign was based on a kind of "pseudo-event" (Boorstin 1961).

Indeed, Kimotho had already stopped his journey by the time that the Kenyan intern made his call on behalf of *The Observer*. The intern said the PR person at Ogilvy & Mather told him that this was a temporary break because Kimotho was exhausted and because Safaricom needed to apply for a new fundraising licence (interview). But more senior figures in the campaign said that Kimotho's journey was also curtailed because donations had already tailed off (interviews).[5] When challenged about why those in charge of the campaign had not been more transparent with *The Observer* about the extent of Zack's journey, those involved in commercial marketing and advertising insisted that they had not intended to mislead journalists. Instead, they had acted according to the commercialised, "promotional" logic (Davis 2013) normal in their lines of work. As one put it,

> We [were] just *dramatising* it ... like in advertising. It is just [using] creative licence ... to move towards an objective. It is [about creating] a mood, a goal, a feeling – in our case, that was to fundraise, yeah? (interview)

Indeed, all of those involved repeatedly described news coverage as a form of "advertising" or "publicity" donated by media owners (interviews).

Observer journalists, like others in the broader study from which this piece is drawn, were not aware of the problems caused by their uncritical acceptance of the image produced for the KPO campaign and the narratives in which it was embedded. Much of this was due to the dominance of multiskilling, which led to widespread redundancies among photojournalists and picture editors. This meant that overworked subeditors were routinely expected to source, select, and attribute photos, even though they had little or no image-related training. The ways in which specialised understandings about visual meaning had been marginalised in news outlets also meant that journalists tended to regard pictures as simply "illustrating" the written story. So when subeditors omitted or made mistakes with pictorial attribution in their haste to carry out all of their tasks before deadlines, these errors weren't seen as being particularly significant.

In this case, when the senior editor at *The Observer* was made aware that the photo had been taken by commercial actors working for an NGO campaign, and that it had not been attributed at all because of a subeditor's error, he claimed that no serious harm had been done (interview). Instead, he reasoned that, because the article was about the KPO campaign and because the photo showed Kimotho in his wheelchair in front of a long road, it was "obvious what it's about" (interview). But even the photo itself was not what it seemed to be – it was a still taken from a staged TV advertisement.

Conclusion

This case study shows that Northern journalists are in danger of losing the critical judgement they need to analyse images of Africa circulated by others through social media at the same time as they have become more dependent upon them. Widespread redundancies among photojournalists and picture editors have made contributed photos seem like attractive "information subsidies" (Gandy 1982), while news outlets have become far less able to evaluate their visual meanings. Role-merging, multiskilling, and the sheer speed of news production have also combined to erode journalists' ability to interrogate and contextualise contributed material using traditional forms of investigative research grounded in geographic specialisation.

However, journalists' inability to exercise critical judgement has also been shaped by their desire to counteract what they believe to be common, negative stereotypes about Africa. This is simultaneously a normative and a commercial intention: encompassing considerations about attracting larger media audiences and differentiating news output in a fiercely competitive market, as well as moral/political commitments to "diversity" and African "empowerment". But appealing and positive "human interest" stories about the continent were rarely seen by journalists as meriting detailed investigation of specific political and economic alliances, vested interests, or areas of contention.

This problem was then compounded by journalists' assumptions about the uncommercial and "simple" nature of NGOs in Africa, when compared with the slick, professionalised marketing operations of well-known INGOs (Cottle & Nolan 2007; Magee 2014). Yet this misses a very basic, logical point: that it is precisely because such organisations are comparatively small and resource poor, that they may need to rely on more powerful actors in order to achieve media impact. These actors include expat executives working for major advertising and public relations multinationals, who are not only keen to break into the continent's emerging markets, but also adept at generating the upbeat, technically sophisticated, and highly visual campaigns likely to go viral on Twitter and Facebook.

What's particularly interesting is that these expats deliberately crafted a value-laden and emotive story about Kenyan self-help and empowerment, while simultaneously maintaining interpretative control over the campaign in ways that served their own economic interests. Thus republishing the material they produced within the context of an uncritical, "positive" news story about "Africa" was potentially just as harmful as endlessly reproducing "negative" stories about the continent. This was because it played into simplistic grand narratives about "Africa Rising" that normalised and legitimised privatised and media-centric conceptualisations of empowerment, while effacing profound socio-economic disparities. It also gave Scangroup and Safaricom commercial advantages in the continent's emerging markets and political advantages to a particular party during a sensitive pre-election period, without addressing either of these issues explicitly. But most of all, it both entrenched and obscured the ascendance of commercial norms and practices over rigorous analysis and truth-telling in news coverage of the continent.

Notes

1   The findings of a broader research project (Wright 2015) are referred to throughout this chapter in order to contextualise the case study in question.
2   This participant has since left the company.
3   This account of events was supported by other participants who were present, although it should be noted that in later correspondence a more senior executive at RedSky, who was not part of the study, denied that any argument had occurred.
4   This was part of a scheme funded by a news-related INGO, the David Astor Trust.
5   In total, 73 million Kenyan Shillings had been raised (nearly £500,000), although this was not enough to finish building the clinic.

References

BBC (2012) "The man pushing himself across Africa", *BBC News Online*, 21 August, at http://www.bbc.co.uk/news/world-africa-19316955 [accessed 01/07/2014].

Beckett, C. & Mansell, R. (2008) "Crossing boundaries: new media and networked journalism", *Communication, Culture and Critique*, 1(1): 92–104.

Boorstin, D. J. (1961) *The Image: A Guide to Pseudo-Events in America*, New York: Vintage.

Chouliaraki, L. (2013) *The Ironic Spectator: Solidarity in the Age of Post-Humanitarianism*, Cambridge: Polity Press.

Cottle, S. & Nolan, D. (2007) "Global humanitarianism and the changing aid-media field: everyone was dying for footage", *Journalism Studies*, 8(6): 862–878.

Davis, A. (2013) *Promotional Cultures: The Rise and Spread of Advertising, Public Relations, Marketing and Branding*, Cambridge: Polity Press.

De Beer, A. S. (2010) "News from and in the 'Dark Continent': Afro-pessimism, news flows, global journalism and media regimes", *Journalism Studies*, 11(4): 596–609.

Demetrious, K. (2013) *Public Relations, Activism and Social Change: Speaking Up*, New York: Routledge.

Dozier, K., speaking at the Frontline Club (2008) "The news carers: are aid groups doing too much real newsgathering?", at http://www.frontlineclub.com/the_news_carers_are_aid_groups_doing_too_much_real_newsgathering_-_new_york_-_fully_booked/ [accessed 04/02/2009].

Fenton, N. (2010) "NGOs, new media and the mainstream news: news from everywhere", in N. Fenton (ed.), *New Media, Old News: Journalism and Democracy in the Digital Age*, London: Sage.

Franklin, B. (2011) "Sources, credibility and the continuing crisis in UK journalism", in B. Franklin and M. Carlson (eds), *Journalists, Sources and Credibility: New Perspectives*, London: Routledge.

Franks, S. (2008) "Aid agencies: are we trusting too much?", *The Political Quarterly*, 79(3): 316–318.

Gandy, O. H. (1982) *Beyond Agenda Setting: Information Subsidies and Public Policy*, Norwood, NJ: Ablex.

Gettleman, J. (2012) "Kenyan paraplegic is on a 2,500-mile journey by wheelchair", *The New York Times*, 29 June, at http://www.nytimes.com/2012/06/30/world/africa/kenyan-paraplegic-is-on-a-2500-mile-journey-by-wheelchair.html [accessed 01/07/2014].

Greste, P. (2012) "Wheeling across Africa for the disabled", at http://www.aljazeera.com/video/africa/2012/06/201262785348857806.html [accessed 01/07/2014].

Harcup, T. & O'Neill, D. (2001) "What is news? Galtung and Ruge revisited", *Journalism Studies*, 2(2): 261–280.

Kenya National Assembly Official Record of Proceedings (2007), Government of Kenya: Nairobi.

Kenyan Paraplegic Organization (n.d.) "Organization structure", at http://www.kenyanparaplegic.or.ke/organizationstructure.html [accessed 02/10/2013].

Kiberenge, K. (2012) "Wheelchair hero's 2,485 mile journey to raise funds for Kenya's first spinal injury rehab unit", *The Observer*, 19 August.

Lewis, J., Williams, A., & Franklin, B (2008a) "A compromised fourth estate?", *Journalism Studies*, 9(1): 1–20.

Lewis, J., Williams, A., & Franklin, B (2008b) "Four rumours and an explanation", *Journalism Practice*, 2(1): 27–45.

Lugo-Ocando, J. (2015) *Blaming the Victim: How Global Journalism Fails Those in Poverty*, London: Pluto Press.

Magee, H. (2014) "The aid industry: what journalists really think", International Broadcast Trust, London, at http://www.ibt.org.uk/documents/reports/TheAidIndustry.pdf [accessed 15/01/2015].

Paterson C. (2011) *The International Television News Agencies: The World from London*, New York: Peter Lang.

Phillips, A. (2012) "Faster and shallower: homogenisation, cannibalisation and the death of reporting", in P. Lee-Wright, A. Phillips, & T. Witschge (eds), *Changing Journalism*, London: Routledge.

Standard Digital News (2012) "Bring Zack Back Home", at http://www.standard media.co.ke/ktn/video/watch/2000058360/-bring-zack-back-home [accessed 01/07/2014].

Standard Digital News (2010) "Corporate social responsibility now a priority", at http://www.standardmedia.co.ke/article/2000025099/corporate-social-responsibility-now-a-priority?articleID=2000025099&story_title=corporate-social-responsibility-now-a-priority&pageNo=3 [accessed 1 July 2014].

Wright, K. (2015) "A quiet revolution: the moral economies shaping journalists' use of NGO-provided multimedia in mainstream news about Africa", PhD thesis, Goldsmiths, University of London, London.

Chapter 20

Media perspectives
Africa for Norway: challenging stereotypes using humour

Nicklas Poulsen Viki

You will have seen it a hundred times: charities trying to raise money using stereotypical images of poverty. Charity campaign adverts frequently depict their beneficiaries as apathetic victims: they have swollen stomachs, terrible living conditions, flies in their eyes. Often these adverts include little – if any – information about who these "victims" actually are, the structural issues that contribute to their situation, or the active and creative attempts they have made to improve their wellbeing. In these representations, there is an artificial distinction between us and them: *we* are the resourceful agents of change, and *they* are the passive others in need of benevolence. This gap between "us" and "them" creates little room for understanding or empathy. Instead, it fosters a well-meaning and infantilising sense of pity.

Using parody as a tool for change

Numerous writers, politicians, activists, and organisations from the global South have made similar critiques of the way African countries are portrayed in Western media and in fundraising campaigns. To us, Band Aid's "Do They Know It's Christmas?" stood out as the epitome of this genre. But rather than presenting a lofty critique of this campaign, we decided to take a more lighthearted approach; we created a parody video called "Radi-Aid: Africa for Norway". Instead of singing about "a world of dread and fear/Where the only water flowing is the bitter sting of tears", we turned it around. In our video, African pop stars offer their sympathy to the poor, freezing people of Norway facing yet another hard winter. Without preaching, the video comments on the simplicity and the patronising notion of "saving" anyone.

The following year we made another spoof called "Let's Save Africa!", in which a director is exasperated by his cynical African stars who won't conform to the victim archetypes he wants to include in his charity advert: they can't carry jugs on their heads, and they just don't seem to be "sad enough". In 2015, a still photo with a very similar message became a viral internet meme: a Ugandan child wearing dirty clothes and a wry expression is giving what the BBC (2015) describes as "the mother of all side-eyes" to a white woman squatting next to him in the dirt. The meme, sometimes called "Sceptical Third World Child", has been used as a shorthand to parody charity campaigns. Its popularity suggests a large appetite – especially within Africa – to question the motives of those who want to "help" and "save" (also see Nyabola's chapter in this volume).

In 2014 we made the video, "Who Wants to Be a Volunteer?", which parodied the clueless volunteers who travel to Africa wanting to "save" the continent, but who know very little about the context; in the video, volunteers throw food at people who are already eating, and take selfies with black children for their Facebook accounts. In the final scene, the volunteer is unable to answer the simple question, "How many countries are there in Africa?"

The videos have now been seen more than 5 million times on YouTube, and they have sparked a debate on the power of language. Their simple message is: stereotypes harm dignity. We have been trying to communicate this same message for years, but it was not until we started to use humour in our work that we have been able to reach such a wide audience, and go beyond the choir that we usually preach to in the aid sector. Humour is more "shareable" in social media, and it is, we hope, more constructive. It is sometimes hard for audiences to know what to do with negative or critical pieces about Africa's media image. Humour and parody, however, invite viewers to interact, play with, and share the content; they can take the messages on board without experiencing forms of compassion fatigue.

Awarding the Goldies and shaming the Rusties

In addition to our parody videos, SAIH (solidarity organisation of students and academics in Norway) also arranges the Radiator Awards, where a prize is awarded to the best and the worst fundraising and awareness-raising campaigns. In our critical awards, we are particularly focused on adverts that employ reductive and damaging stereotypes, and which deny the dignity or agency of the people they purport to be helping. In 2014 the "prize" for worst advert went to a video called "Feed a child" from South Africa. The advert showed a wealthy white South African woman hand-feeding a black child scraps of food, as if the child were a dog. The video concluded with the line: "The average domestic dog eats better than millions of children. Help feed a child." And it received scathing reviews from our Jury:

[One of the judges] had to turn it off after 10 seconds. ... This was produced by one of the biggest advertising companies in the world, and how they got it so very wrong. ... The poor are already depicted as incapable of their own rescue, now they are being compared to dogs. What next? Is there a score worse than 0? (SAIH 2015)

In 2015, we awarded the prize to – who else? – Band Aid 30, for "Do They Know It's Christmas?" The jury noted that this video contributed to the spread of misinformation and stereotypes presenting Africa as a single country filled with misery and diseases – despite the fact that the Ebola outbreak occurred in only three countries in West Africa. Summarising their reasons for the award, the jury commented:

> We resent the idea of a bunch of celebrities joining forces together, giving the impression that they are saving Africa from Ebola. Furthermore, they just make it so much more about themselves! Highly offensive and awful in every way possible. Celebrities cannot stop Ebola. (SAIH 2015)

While the worst of these videos are depressing and frustrating, there are also, increasingly, examples of good fundraising videos and campaigns from aid organisations that are finding new ways to tell these stories. Creative professionals are engaging with Africa on different, more equal terms, and we see many reasons to be positive as we go forward. The nominations for our "Golden Radiators" showcase campaigns where citizens speak on their own terms about their own issues and solutions. These adverts include compelling storytelling and innovative production techniques, and have often gone viral on social media. Their success suggests that audiences around the world welcome new approaches to these old challenges.

References

BBC (2015) "What a viral picture tells us about child poverty in Africa", BBC Trending, 2 November, at http://www.bbc.co.uk/news/blogs-trending-34678592 [accessed 17/03/2016].

SAIH (2015) "The Rusty Radiator Award", at www.RustyRadiator.com [accessed 17/03/2016].

Chapter 21

Bloggers, celebrities, and economists

News coverage of the Millennium Villages Project

Audrey Ariss, Anya Schiffrin, and Michelle Chahine

Understanding how the media cover the large question of economic development in Africa brings into relief ongoing ideological debates over the roles of government, foreign aid, free markets, and technology. In the case of the Millennium Villages Project, reporting carried out by journalists also shows how a range of constraints affects coverage of complex, ongoing subjects and initiatives that are located in distant locations. This chapter[1] describes how the Millennium Villages Project (MVP) was covered in the African, US, and UK media and blogosphere between 2004 and 2015. Delving deep into the press coverage of the MVP provides a case study that allows us to examine how some of the standard theories about the media have played out in reality, over time, and across countries.

Launched in 2004, the MVP was an ambitious development project that aimed to promote an integrated and holistic approach to economic development in Africa. The Project began with the selection of a dozen pilot villages, or clusters of villages, in ten sub-Saharan African countries. Through a range of interventions in areas such as health, education, and agriculture, it was hoped that these villages would develop rapidly, standards of living would rise dramatically, and the interventions and benefits would be replicated throughout rural Africa. Despite the large scale of the project (and the central role the planners hoped the media would play in spreading news of their success), there has been limited research into how the MVP has been reported in the world's media. One of the main avenues for dissemination about the successes and failures of the MVP is, of course, the media. However, if the MVP were to actively disseminate all research results this would provide credibility to the project but might risk undermining enthusiasm.

We analysed more than ten years of press coverage of the villages, including the differences between legacy media reporting and the emerging blogosphere focused on development.

We found marked differences between the coverage in sub-Saharan African outlets and the UK/US press coverage, as well as between traditional media and blogs focused on development. Reporters in the UK and US wrote longer stories and did more investigative journalism than the African reporters. African media coverage was overwhelmingly more deferential, enthusiastic, and press release driven than the US/UK coverage. The most critical media were bloggers and online publishers, who devoted more space to development theories and the details of the Millennium Villages than did many of the journalists in the legacy media.

The US economists on the blogosphere who pushed for quantitative evaluations of the village project certainly effected broader press coverage in the US/UK, but this debate was not picked up in Africa, as far as we could see. However, we concluded that the analysis available in the development blogosphere offset the scant press coverage.

Background on the Millennium Villages Project

In 2000, country representatives at the United Nations' Millennium Summit promised to end poverty by 2015 and drafted eight goals, the Millennium Development Goals (MDGs), to be met by 2015. Several development projects, with the aim of achieving the MDGs, sprang up across the world's poorest countries and areas, spearheaded by various United Nations (UN) agencies. One of the largest projects focused on achieving all of the MDGs was the Millennium Villages Project (MVP) in sub-Saharan Africa, which brought together the UN, academics from the Earth Institute (EI) at Columbia University in New York, donors, foundations, governments, and business. Its emphasis on integrated solutions in the villages meant that instead of focusing on one or two aspects of development (like education or infrastructure) the MVP aimed to overhaul many aspects of village life simultaneously.

The first village projects began in Sauri, Kenya (2004) and Koraro, Ethiopia (2005), with further projects implemented in Malawi, Mali, Nigeria, Rwanda, Senegal, Tanzania, Ghana, and Uganda. Each community received financial support to improve five main areas: food production, education, health, essential infrastructure (such as roads and access to clean water), and business development. The plan was that these communities would strengthen healthcare and the education of their children, boost agricultural productivity, and start exporting products in order to raise revenue and join the global trading system. The Earth Institute does not provide a total figure for how much the MVP costs, but more than $190 million was pledged during phases 1 and 2 of the project (Munk 2013: 226–227). The project was guided and promoted by the influential economist Jeffrey Sachs. Over time, the MVP polarised leading voices in international development, primarily as a reaction to the lack of evidence around the MVP's efficacy versus costs and the contentious sustainability of the measures implemented.

Our study

We conducted a content analysis of digital and print newspaper in the US, UK, and sub-Saharan African countries. We conducted an initial digital search of the newspapers with the highest recorded circulations, using "Millennium Village", "Millennium Villages Project", and the names of the MVP clusters as search terms for the period from August 2004 to April 2015. The sample was then checked for relevance of articles and duplicates, and then supplemented by an online search, using the same terms, in magazines and development blogs. Our total sample included 369 print and digital articles from 69 different publications – newspapers, magazines, and blogs from Ethiopia, Ghana, Kenya, Malawi, Mali, Nigeria, Rwanda, Senegal, Tanzania, and Uganda – the countries in which the MVPs have taken place – as well as the US and the UK. Articles were quantitatively coded for their length, genre, sources, and tone; and they were qualitatively read for the variety and depth of information they contained.

We supplemented our content analysis with 15 interviews with journalists, economists based in New York, Washington, and Uganda as well as Earth Institute and UNDP communications staffers based in New York and Uganda. Interviews were carried out over Skype, by email, over the phone, and in person in New York and Kampala in July 2012. The interviews were designed to explore the journalistic cultures, resources, and approaches to covering the MVPs.

One limitation of our research was that it does not include radio coverage, a significant source of information in the African countries in our study. Even in the case of Uganda, one of the countries in which we found the largest number of articles about its MVP, radio dominates the media and journalism profession (Khamalwa 2006). Another limitation was that the analysis excluded articles that are not accessible online.

The above methods identified 369 articles in total, which were spread across the 10-year period, with the most concentrated coverage falling between 2009 and 2011.

Findings

In the sub-Saharan publications studied, news coverage of the MVP was scant. Articles were mostly short and driven by press releases and/or coverage of officials. As noted in Figure 21.1, there were very few feature pieces exploring the MVP in depth. Rather, the vast majority of coverage consisted of news stories focusing on official announcements, events, new projects, donations, partnerships, or official progress reports. Feature stories were in a distant second place and opinion pieces in third. There were no articles that could be classified as investigative reporting. The most quoted sources in the MVP country coverage were high-level government officials, and representatives from companies contributing to the MVP. Less than 15 per cent included interviews with local villagers. Only two pieces cited academics as independent critics, and none refers to African academics or other critical thinkers or external evaluators.

A notable feature of the local MVP country reporting was the dominance of press releases, and the use of official language, statistics, and interpretations within news stories. This use of press release language, quotes, and reported statistics was evident in the detailed information given about how the MVPs are progressing. The use of official press releases and reports from the MVPs is most evident in Uganda, Kenya, and Ghana. After the villages of Ruhiira, Sauri, and Bonsaaso were featured in an MVP three-year progress report, "Harvest of development in rural Africa: The Millennium Villages after three years", the numbers quoted in the report were repeated in newspaper articles that appeared around the same time.[2] Several articles used the publication of the report as the news peg. Others simply lifted or paraphrased material from the report and presented it as fact without any attribution. For instance, "A report on the achievement of the project, in efforts to meet the eight Millennium Development Goals, shows the yield of the crop tripled from eight bags an acre to 24" (Mosota 2009).

In addition to press releases from the UNDP and MVP, a number of corporate press releases became part of the coverage. For example, when the telecom companies Zain/Celtel and Ericsson announced they would expand cellular networks to the villages, they placed a press release on their website. Nine days later, Kenya's *The EastAfrican* published a news article that reprinted almost half of the press release verbatim (Ngunjiri 2008).[3] The most frequently cited examples were Ericsson and MTN's "Connect to Learn" initiative (10 per cent of articles in African press). Others include Unilever's contributions for "Global Handwashing Day". Articles with titles such as "Rural empowerment – Governor lauds MTN, Ericsson" exemplify the extent to which corporate press releases informed the local news coverage.

By contrast, the press coverage in the United Kingdom and the United States gave significantly more space to feature reporting, interviewing, editorials, and opinion pieces. In addition, using the villages as a news peg, US and UK journalists and commentators wrote about more general development issues. The journalists explored themes such as: whether

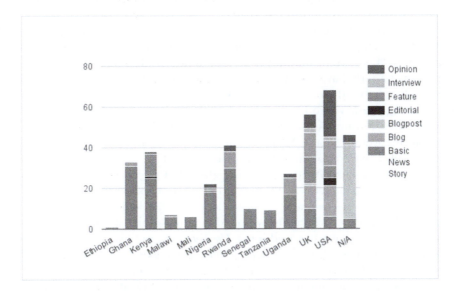

Figure 21.1 Number of articles by type and country

aid was necessary and how the money was being spent; the people and personalities involved in the debates; and whether the MVP achieved its stated aims. These three themes dominated much of the press coverage as well as the back-and-forth on social media and in the blogosphere.

While in the sub-Saharan African press the coverage was mostly based on press releases and used statistics published by representatives of the MVP, Western media focused on evaluations and commentary from other international development professionals as well as academics and economists. Notable in this reporting was the publication in 2007 of long-form magazine articles by Nina Munk, Sam Rich, and Vicky Schlesinger about their visits to the Villages.

Within the US and UK coverage, there was a heavy emphasis on the clash of ideologies between different economists working on and writing about African economic development. The media coverage covered the disagreements, sometimes characterising them as conflicts between Zambian economist Dambisa Moyo and William Easterly on one side and Jeffrey Sachs on the other. Moyo as well as US economists Glenn Hubbard and William Easterly all criticised "big aid", with Moyo and Hubbard arguing that foreign investment and private sector growth would be better for Africa. Easterly called Sachs a "planner" who was raising vast amounts of money for development projects that would be ineffective. The disagreements between Moyo/Easterly and Jeff Sachs were played out in *The Washington Post* (Sachs 2001, 2005) and in op-ed pages of various newspapers such as the *Los Angeles Times* (Sachs 2006, Easterly 2006) as well as at conferences and discussions throughout the world.

One article that encapsulated how the UK and US media treated the debate is Memphis Barker's 2013 contribution in *The Independent*, in which he writes: "Like two economically literate sumo wrestlers, Jeffrey Sachs and William Easterly have spent much of the past decade belly to belly, each struggling to put the other on his back."

Among the MVP countries, the tone of articles on the MVP was over-whelmingly favourable (see Figure 21.2). Remarkably there was almost no negative coverage of the MVP. Of the articles whose main focus was the MVP, only five were found to be decidedly critical.

As with the local African coverage, the US/UK coverage was initially positive. Articles such as "In Ethiopian Hills, five years to create something out of nothing" in *The New York Times* (Cooper 2005) depicted the potential of the MVPs: "If poverty can be whipped here in Koraro, it can be whipped anywhere. The place has nothing." *The Guardian* published articles with headlines such as, "In the village where aid makes a vital difference" (Bloomfield 2006). However, as the MVP entered its second phase, US/UK journalists and bloggers increasingly focused on indications of potential failure. In the total sample, the US and UK coverage had far more reports that were coded as either balanced or critical, such as Rosen's 2013 piece for *The Atlantic*, "It's the politics, stupid: what Jeffrey Sachs' development

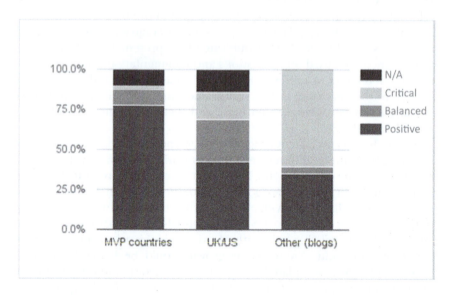

Figure 21.2 Tone of articles

work is missing", in which he criticises Sachs' approach for ignoring crucial institution-building.

The most critical space for debating the MVPs was in the blogosphere. On this online media platform, 61 per cent of articles were critical. Unsurprisingly, the majority of the positive articles (90 per cent) were those published on the MVP blog or by people directly involved in the MVP. By contrast, only 16.5 per cent of US/UK articles were critical, and only a very small proportion - 2 per cent - of the articles in sub-Saharan publications were unfavourable. Websites such as A View from the Cave; the Global Development pages on *The Guardian* online, and Nick Kristof's *On the Ground* site hosted by *The New York Times* provided space for journalists and others writing about development. Notably, the digital media sphere (in contrast to traditional media) included blog posts, reports, and websites written by development economists and accessible to public audiences. Many of these were critical of the MVP and urged an evidenced-based approach to their evaluation. Critical pieces included: "The Millennium Villages, evaluated? A skeptical view" (Blattman 2011), "From Kenya to Harlem: the search for impact" (Green 2010); and "Millennium Villages: don't work, don't know, or don't care?" (Freschi 2010). Prolific, critical writers, and fora included Chris Blattman and Michael Clemens, writing on the Center for Global Development blog, and William Easterly and Laura Freschi on *Aid Watch*. The call for more evidence and evaluation was in keeping with larger trends in the development community. As Madeline Bunting wrote in her 2010 *Guardian* article: "Why the drama? Well, a lot of money has been poured into the Millennium Villages project."

When the first official evaluation of the MVP appeared in Spring 2012, it was again online fora that provided the most significant space for critical debate, and watchdog journalism. In May 2012, the UK medical journal *The Lancet* published an article by Jeffrey Sachs and several colleagues claiming that infant mortality had fallen dramatically as a result of the MVP intervention (Pronyk et al. 2012). Clemens, a high-profile critic of the MVP, publicly disputed the findings of the evaluation. Clemens noted that there were problems with the evaluation methodology, and that the MVPs had been depicted "in an excessively positive light" (Clemens & Demombynes 2013). This was a significant article that led to the *Lancet* article's partial retraction and Pronyk's leaving the employ of Columbia University. The controversy was discussed in the UK/US with comment and news pieces appearing in *Nature* (Gilbert 2012), the Letters column of *The Lancet*, in *Foreign Policy* (Starobin 2013), and on multiple blogs that cover development including A View from the Cave, *The Economist*, and Retraction Watch. However, the discussion was largely ignored by the African press, with only one article appearing on allAfrica.com (Taylor 2012), the site that aggregates news from African magazines and newspapers that are archived online.

Discussion: constraints on reporting

The Ugandan journalists we interviewed suggested several logistical reasons for the dearth, brevity of their reporting, and reliance on press releases. The MVP villages were often far away, and difficult or expensive to access. Most of the journalists we spoke to lacked resources to pay to visit and stay in the villages. In some cases journalists who did visit were directly funded by UN and MVP officials. One magazine reporter we interviewed was paid by the MVP, and one informant told us of an African newspaper editor who was working part time for the UNDP. Being hosted by these organisations may well have come with direct or indirect pressure to publish positive articles and/or to disseminate the official perspective on the MVPs.

In addition to these resource constraints, the interviews confirmed other soft pressures that likely contributed to the positive news coverage in the articles examined. In many countries in sub-Saharan Africa, there is a tradition of development journalism, and a history of governments calling on journalists to help build national unity and advance economic development (Ansah 1993; Bourgault 1995, 228; Hachten 1971). "This self-censorship is not driven by anything so simple as fear, repression, or any such violation of the right to free speech; rather, it is the product of an implicit contract between journalists and state officials," explains Jennifer Hasty, after experiencing this phenomenon firsthand at the *Daily Graphic* in Ghana (Hasty 2005: 78).

Interestingly, the most critical piece in an African publication was an article in *The Star* (Kenya) that responded to a favourable piece about the MVP in Bonsaaso, Ghana written by journalist John Mulholland and published in the British newspaper *The Guardian* in 2012. Andrea Bohnstedt, who runs a country risk consultancy in Kenya, took Mulholland to task, saying,

> I'm left scratching my head because I don't quite recognise Ghana and certainly don't find an assessment of Ghana's progress, nor do I find an assessment of how aid worked or maybe didn't work in Ghana. I do, however, find a neat PR exercise for Bono's and Sachs's organisations. ... To my mind this reads like a campaign advert. A straight report would surely have mentioned that there is some debate about the long-term effectiveness of Sachs's Millennium Villages concept or given one example at least of the critics. (Bohnstedt 2012)

Implicit in the coverage was an uncritical view of the projects and the assumption that it is in each country's interest to promote the success of the project and thereby help it expand. While Ugandan journalists told us of the constraints they faced *before* publication, US journalists tended to emphasise pressures they faced *after* publication. Nina Munk (see above), for example, who wrote a long research article on the villages for *Vanity Fair*, did not experience the resource constraints the Ugandan journalists had to grapple with. In addition, as an outsider, Munk was not constrained by any local pressure to report favourably. However, after she had written her article – and especially after she had developed it into a longer book – the response from the Sachs camp was severe, including a Twitter storm of response.

Journalists told us that the Sachs team responded in a robust manner to coverage they felt was critical. On several occasions, Sachs had legal counsel send letters when he felt he had been unfairly criticised (Sachs 2005; Haddad 2011; Sachs 2011). Additional emails and letters were regularly sent by Sachs and his communication team. One journalist described the experience: "The pushback is off the charts." Another stated: "Sachs' currency is intimidation" (author interviews and correspondence, New York, 2015).

Conclusion

Sachs, Munk, and others do agree on one matter: the need for more in-depth coverage of development issues. Sachs has said that press coverage of poverty is "pretty sporadic" and has lamented the absence of coverage of the UN's Millennium Development Goals (Hanrahan 2009). That the Millennium Villages Project is a long-term response to a historical phenomenon, and not a short-term crisis or emergency, has also dictated the amount of attention it has received. As noted by sociologist Craig Calhoun, "Events supposed to be extraordinary have become so recurrent that aid agencies speak of 'emergency fatigue'" (Calhoun 2008: 87). As a result, extreme poverty, lack of infrastructure, poor healthcare, limited education, and insufficient agricultural production are not on the same radar of "emergency" as they are constant, the status quo, in many regions of Africa.

The MVP was a complicated subject to cover. There were relatively few articles in the earlier period and these mostly described the excitement of the initial stages of the project. By 2012 the media, sometimes influenced by the expert blogging community, had begun to question whether the project actually worked. The presence of development economists in the blogosphere influenced mainstream press coverage as UK/US journalists spoke to a range of sources about their views of the MVP. The involvement of celebrities also helped boost the amount of coverage. However, our interviews with journalists and bloggers found a chilling effect from the soft pressure put on journalists reporting on MVP, including angry letters, emails, and phone calls. The effect this has had, and continues to have on coverage, is a question for future research

While journalists in the UK/US and Africa grappled with a number of constraints that limited their reporting, the persistence of economists who

Table 21.1 Breakdown of publications

Country	Total	Publication	Count
Ethiopia	1	The Reporter	1
Ghana	33	All Ghana News	2
		Daily Heritage	1
		Ghana Nation	5
		Ghana Web	4
		Ghanadistricts.com	3
		Ghanaian Chronicle	6
		Ghana Business News	9
		Graphic Online	3
Kenya	39	Daily Nation	5
		Nairobi Star	1
		The East African	18
		The Nation	3
		The Standard	12
Malawi	7	Malawi Voice	1
		The Nation	6
Mali	6	L'Essor	1
		L'Independent	1
		Lafia Revelateur	2
		Le Segovien	2
Nigeria	23	Business Daily	1
		Daily Champion	1
		Daily Independent	2
		Leadership	1
		The Daily Trust	2
		This Day	14
		Vanguard	2
Rwanda	42	Focus Media	1
		The New Times	41
Senegal	10	Le Soleil	1
		Senenews.com	1
		Rewmi	8
Tanzania	9	The Citizen	7
		The Guardian	2
Uganda	27	Daily monitor	12
		New Vision	11
		The Independent	2
		The Observer	2
United Kingdom	56	Financial Times	13
		The Guardian/The Observer	25
		The Independent	6
		The Economist	10
		The Times/Sunday Times	2

U.S.A.	70	Forbes	3
		Foreign Policy	1
		Harper's Magazine	2
		The L.A. Times	2
		Newsweek	2
		Pacific Standard	1
		Seattle Post	1
		The Atlantic	3
		The Daily Beast	3
		The Huffington Post	25
		The New York Times/ International Herald Tribune	19
		The New Yorker	1
		The Philadelphia Inquirer	3
		The Wall Street Journal	1
		The Washington Post	1
		The Wilson Quarterly	1
		Vanity Fair	1
Other	46	Irin	6
		Project Syndicate	4
		A View From The Cave	1
		Aid Watch	12
		Center for Global Development Blog	7
		Chris Blattman Blog	6
		Humanosphere	2
		Millennium Villages Blog	5
		The World Bank Blogs	3
Total			369

blogged about the MVP and the commitment of a number of writers ensured that (for a reader who sought out the information) there was detailed coverage that included a range of voices, and provided fuel for more mainstream media to discuss these development issues. These findings suggest that, despite the financial and technical challenges the legacy media faces, as well as the soft pressures put on journalists before and after publication, the reporting in the blogosphere and the availability of open data transformed the framing of the narrative of the MVP. Having expert opinion online as well as accessible information helped journalists in the legacy media who wanted to find multiple viewpoints and sources of information.

It is to be hoped that other development stories - in Africa or other parts of the world - will benefit from this expanded ability to transmit and share ideas across borders, thus adding to the knowledge available and helping policy-makers and citizens act in the public interest.

Notes

1 Some of the materials in this chapter appeared in the unpublished paper, 'When a tree falls in the forest', written by Michelle Chahine and Anya Schiffrin, available on academia.edu.
2 Several newspaper articles published at the same time as the report use similar language, although they vary slightly in their wording (bags of maize instead of tons, for example). This may be because a different, perhaps earlier version of the report was distributed locally to key journalists in each country. Or it may be that the journalists made mistakes when reprinting the information from the report.
3 For example, the article read, "According to Chris Gabriel, Celtel's chief executive officer, people in this remote part of Africa will have access to basic but effective mobile Internet access over an EDGE network", and the press release read, "Chris Gabriel, CEO of Celtel, says: 'It is wonderful that the people in this remote part of Africa will have access to basic, but effective mobile internet access over an EDGE network.'" This paraphrasing of the press release was repeated throughout the entire article.

Bibliography

African Media Development Initiative (2006) "Research summary report", *AMDI Reports*, BBC World Service Trust.

Ansah, P. (1993) "Kwame Nkrumah and the Mass Media", in A. Kwame (ed.), *The Life and Work of Kwame Nkrumah*, Trenton, NJ: Africa World Press.

Barker, M. (2013) "Ending poverty is a huge ambition: it's too much to ask of foreign aid", *The Independent*, 14 October, at http://www.independent.co.uk/voices/comment/ending-poverty-is-a-huge-ambition-its-too-much-to-ask-of-foreign-aid-8879704.html [accessed 03/03/2015].

Blattman, C. (2011) "The Millennium Villages, evaluated? A skeptical view", 29 November, at http://chrisblattman.com/2011/11/29/the-millennium-villages-evaluated-a-skeptical-view/ [accessed 04/04/2016].

Bloomfield, S. (2006) "In the village where aid makes a vital difference", *The Independent*, 20 September, at http://www.independent.co.uk/news/world/africa/in-the-village-where-aid-makes-a-vital-difference-416878.html [accessed 11/08/2015].

Bohnstedt, A. (2012) "Africa: continent must wean itself off aid trap", *The Star*, 21 January, at http://allafrica.com/stories/201201230813.html [accessed 11/08/2015].

Bourgault, L. (1995) *Mass Media in Sub-Saharan Africa*, Bloomington, IN: Indiana University Press.

Bunting, M. (2010) "The Millennium Villages project: Could the development 'wonk war' go nuclear?", *The Guardian*, 4 November, at http://www.theguardian.com/global-development/poverty-matters/2010/nov/04/millennium-villages-sachs-clemens-demombynes [accessed 04/04/2016].

Calhoun, C. (2008) "The imperative to reduce suffering: charity, progress and emergencies in the field of humanitarian action", in M. Barnett and T. G. Weiss (eds), *Humanitarianism in Question: Politics, Power, Ethics*, Ithaca, NY: Cornell University Press.

Clemens, M. (2010) "Why a careful evaluation of the Millenium Villages is not optional", Center for Global Development, 18 March, at http://www.cgdev.org/blog/why-careful-evaluation-millennium-villages-not-optional [accessed 21/04/2015].

Clemens, M. & Demombynes, G. (2013) "The new transparency in development economics: lessons from the Millennium Villages controversy", *World Economics*, 14(4): 71–97.

Cooper, H. (2005) "In Ethiopian hills, five years to create something out of nothing", *New York Times*, 27 April, at http://www.nytimes.com/2005/04/27/opinion/in-ethiopian-hills-five-years-to-create-something-out-of-nothing.html [accessed 11/08/2015].

Easterly, W. (2006) *The White Man's Burden: Why the West's Efforts to Aid the Rest Have Done So Much Ill and So Little Good*, New York: Penguin.

Eviatar, D. (2004). "Spend $150 billion a year to cure world poverty", *The New York Times Magazine*, 7 November.

Freschi, L. (2010) "Millennium Villages: don't work, don't know or don't care?', at http://www.nyudri.org/aidwatcharchive/2010/10/millennium-villages-dont-work-dont-know-or-dont-care [accessed 04/04/2016].

Gilbert, N (2012) "Development project touts health victory but critics question data and cost estimates from the Millennium Villages Project", *Nature*, 485: 158–159.

Green, E. (2010) "From Kenya to Harlem: the search for impact", at http://chrisblattman.com/2010/10/13/from-kenya-to-harlem/ [accessed 04/04/2016].

Hachten, A. (1971) *Muffled Drums: The News Media in Africa*, Ames, IA: The Iowa State University Press.

Haddad, L. (2011) "Jeff Sachs: LVP of the MVP?", at http://www.developmenthorizons.com/2011/10/jeff-sachs-lvp-of-mvp.html?spref=tw [accessed 18/03/2016].

Hanrahan, J. (2009) "World poverty: so important but so little coverage", *Nieman Watchdog*, 14 October.

Hasty, J. (2005) *The Press and Political Culture in Ghana, Bloomington and Indianapolis*, Bloomington, IN: Indiana University Press.

Henwood, D. (2011) "Introduction to Jeffrey Sachs", *Left Business Observer*, 26 November.

Hubbard, G. & Duggan, W. (2010) *The Aid Trap: Hard Truths About Ending Poverty*, New York: Columbia Business School Publishing.

Khamalwa, J. W. (2006) "Uganda: research findings and conclusions", *AMDI Reports*, BBC World Service Trust.

McKenzie, D. (2011) "Jeff Sachs, the Millennium Villages Project and misconceptions about impact evaluation", at http://blogs.worldbank.org/impactevaluations/jeff-sachs-the-millennium-villages-project-and-misconceptions-about-impact-evaluation [accessed 13/03/2016].

Milburn, R. (2013) "Idealism's reality check", 12 September, at http://blogs.barrons.com/penta/2013/09/12/idealisms-reality-check/ [accessed 09/04/2015].

Mosota, M. (2009) Village records increased crop yield, attains MDGS, *The Standard*, at http://www.standardmedia.co.ke/archives/InsidePage.php?id=1144025933&cid=4 [accessed 03/04/2011].

Moyo, D. (2009) *Dead Aid*, New York: Farrar, Straus and Giroux.

Munk, N. (2007) "Jeffrey Sachs's $200 billion dream", *Vanity Fair*, at http://www.vanityfair.com/news/2007/07/sachs200707 [accessed 07/09/2009].

Munk, N. (2013) *The Idealist: Jeffrey Sachs and the Quest to End Poverty*, New York: Doubleday.

Ngunjiri, P. (2008) "Celtel to give internet services to Millennium Villages", *The East African*, at http://allafrica.com/stories/200805190468.html [accessed 03/04/2011].

Nielsen (2012) "The diverse people of Africa", at http://www.nielsen.com/content/dam/nielsenglobal/ssa/docs/reports/2012/the-diverse-people-of-africa-march-2012.pdf [accessed 09/04/2015].

Polman, L. (2010) *The Crisis Caravan: What's Wrong with Humanitarian Aid*, New York: Metropolitan Books.

Pronyk, P. (2012) "Errors in a paper on the Millennium Villages Project", *The Lancet*, 379 (9830): 1946–1947.

Pronyk, P. M., Muntz, M., Nemser, B., et al. (2012) "The effect of an integrated multisector model for achieving the Millennium Development Goals and improving child survival in rural sub-Saharan Africa: a non-randomised controlled assessment", *The Lancet*, 379 (9832): 2179–2188.

Rich, S. (2007) "Africa's village of dreams", *The Wilson Quarterly*, Spring.

Rosen, A. (2013) "It's the politics, stupid: what Jeffrey Sachs' development work is missing", *The Atlantic*, at http://www.theatlantic.com/international/archive/2013/01/its-the-politics-stupid-what-jeffrey-sachs-development-work-is-missing/267054/ [accessed 04/04/2016].

Sachs, J. (2005) *The End of Poverty: Economic Possibilities for Our Time*, New York: Penguin.

Sachs, J. (2005) "Up from poverty", letter to the editor, *The Washington Post*, 27 March, at http://www.washingtonpost.com/wp-dyn/articles/A64541-2005Mar24.html [accessed 11/03/2015].

Sachs, J. (2011) "Letter to the editor", *The Economist*, 17 December.

Sachs, J. (2011) "The Millennium Villages Project is working well", *The Guardian*, 31 October.

Sachs, J. (2014) Interview with Russ Roberts, Econtalk Episode, 17 March, at http://www.econtalk.org/archives/2014/03/jeffrey_sachs_o.html [accessed 07/04/2015].

Sachs, J. (2015) Informal conversation with author, Beijing, China, with reference to MVP, "Millennium Village programs now in more than 20 countries", 29 August 2013, at http://millenniumvillages.org/field-notes/millennium-village-programs-now-in-more-than-20-countries/ (details of funding are not included) [accessed 02/04/2015].

Sachs, J. & Singh, P. (2011) "Learning in and from the Millennium Villages: a response to Lawrence Haddad", *Millennium Villages Blog*, 16 October. (As of February 2013, this post was no longer accessible on the *Millennium Villages Blog*.)

Schlesinger, V. (2007) "Rebranding African poverty", *Harper's Magazine*.

Starkman, D. (2014) *The Watchdog That Didn't Bark: The Financial Crisis and the Disappearance of Investigative Journalism*, New York: Columbia University Press.

Starobin, P. (2013) "Does it take a Village?", *Foreign Policy*, 24 June, at http://foreignpolicy.com/2013/06/24/does-it-take-a-village/ [accessed 05/04/2015].

Taylor, M. (2012) "Africa: Michael Clemens vs. Jeffrey Sachs – the Millennium Villages and evaluating impact assessments", at http://africanarguments.org/2012/07/06/michael-clemens-vs-jeffrey-sachs-the-millenium-villages-and-evaluating-impact-assessments-%E2%80%93-by-magnus-taylor/UN.org [accessed 21/04/2015].

UN News Centre (2011) "UN-backed Millennium Villages Project in Africa launches second phase, at http://www.un.org/apps/news/story.asp?NewsID=39914#.VRMUzPnF98E [accessed 09/09/2012].

Wanjala, M. & Muradian, R. (2013) "Can big push interventions take small-scale farmers out of poverty? Insights from the Sauri Millennium Village in Kenya", *World Development*, 45: 147–160.

Politics in the representation of Africa

Part IV

Politics in the representation of Africa

Africa through Chinese eyes: new frames or the same old lens?

African news in English from China Central Television, compared with the BBC

Vivien Marsh

The screen fills with close-ups of smiling African faces against a black-and-orange background: the carefree child, the gap-toothed man with smoke curling from his pipe. The faces retreat into an outline of a map of Africa as the saccharine background music dissolves into birdsong. The silhouette of an acacia tree appears. This is not the much-derided Western romantic stereotype of the continent: it is an extract from a promotional trailer on CCTV Africa,[1] the embodiment of China's "soft power" drive and a spearhead of Chinese state television's overseas expansion. Yet this image is at variance with the English-language channel's professed ambitions. The Chinese premier, Li Keqiang, himself declared that "CCTV embraces the vision of seeing Africa from an African perspective and reporting Africa from the viewpoint of Africa" (CCTV News 2014).

These contradictory messages prompt fundamental questions about CCTV's expansion into Africa. Are the channel's English-language news bulletins aimed at African or Chinese viewers? What kind of Africa – and indeed China – do they represent, and could the framing of African events by CCTV News provide an alternative to the perspective of international rivals? Is CCTV's main mission in Africa to provide news or to act as mouthpiece of the Chinese Communist Party and state? This chapter addresses these questions by applying a cross-cultural variant of framing theory to the news content of CCTV's *Africa Live* and that of its closest direct competitor, *Focus on Africa* from BBC World News TV.

News for Africa made "more African" – *Africa Live* and *Focus On Africa TV*

CCTV Africa, Chinese television's first overseas network news centre, was launched in Nairobi in January 2012 as part of state media's 6bn USD expansion or "going out" policy in English and several other languages. It was aimed at giving China a global voice commensurate with its economic might, in the pursuit of international influence through co-optive "soft power" (Nye 2011). This mission suggested that "Voice of China" would be a better summary of CCTV's English ambitions than the long-debated notion of a "Chinese CNN" (Jirik 2010; Dong & Shi 2007). At CCTV Africa, nonetheless, about two-thirds of the staff were African (Gagliardone 2013), exemplifying the trend among international broadcasters to "globalise" their workforces to bring them culturally closer to their audiences. By mid-2015, CCTV Africa provided twice-daily African news (*Africa Live*), a daily business programme (*Global Business by CCTV Africa*), and weekly current affairs, features, and specialist sports programming (*Talk Africa, Faces of Africa*, and *Match Point*). As CCTV expanded into Africa, China Radio International and the Xinhua news agency also enhanced their African presence, the English-language *China Daily* launched a weekly African edition, and China built telecommunications facilities in Africa and began training African journalists.

China's African agenda can be evaluated most usefully through a direct comparison with a programme launched just five months after *Africa Live* and with very similar declared objectives. The BBC's *Focus on Africa* went to air on weekdays on the World News channel with the aim of broadening the reporting of Africa beyond what its editor described as an "agenda of death, disease and destruction" (in Marsh 2016). Like *Africa Live, Focus on Africa* used predominantly African journalists on screen. Initial quantitative content analysis of the new programmes indicated that the BBC, in particular, made space for reporting on African entrepreneurship and culture (Marsh 2016). However, the main diet of both programmes remained conflict, security, and politics, setting them the challenge of improving on the "episodic, simplistic and relentlessly negative content" (Bunce 2015: 42) for which international news coverage of Africa is often criticised.

CCTV: a new type of news for Africa?

Chinese media, with its official role as promoter of government policies and shaper of public opinion, may seem an unlikely source of an alternative discourse on Africa, yet there have been signs that CCTV News is using Africa as a testing ground for ways of challenging the dominant Anglo-American news narrative (Zhang X. 2013). However, this does not necessarily allow for greater editorial licence: CCTV News (English) is broadcast in China as well as worldwide despite the original announcement (CCTV 2009) that it would be an overseas-only service. For more than thirty years, the Central Propaganda Department has championed what it calls "positive news" as a way of ensuring unity and stability. Gagliardone (2013) says that by tapping into the "Rising Africa" narrative through positive reporting, CCTV Africa has positioned China alongside Africans trying to overturn their continent's negative image. Wekesa and Zhang (2014), however, define such reporting as constructive journalism, involving the leavening of negative events through a solution-focused spin. Using constructive journalism, according to Zhang (Y. 2014), CCTV reports on Africa's problems while presenting its people as actively engaged in solving them.

Africa might indeed represent fertile ground in which China could plant an alternative model of reporting. China comes to Africa without the colonial baggage of Western powers and with a history of developmental engagement. Friction over China's exploitation of African raw materials can be set against growing African interest in China's new political model of an authoritarian market economy. China's anti-imperialist record in Africa may give its news media greater traction there (Hu et al. 2013). However, Western champions of constructive journalism have distanced it from "government-influenced 'development journalism'" (Constructive Journalism Project n.d.). The academic jury is still out in any case on whether governments – East or West – can hope to gain influence by force-feeding soft power to other countries through their media.

Framing theory with a Chinese twist

The choice of framing was prompted by contrasting perspectives on CCTV News and BBC World News of the conflict in South Sudan (Marsh 2016). Framing, as defined by Entman (1993: 52), selects "some aspects of a perceived reality and make(s) them more salient ... in such a way as to promote a particular problem definition, causal interpretation, moral evaluation, and/or treatment recommendation". The BBC witnessed the South Sudanese conflict from the battlefield and relayed images of human suffering from refugee camps, while CCTV focused on peace negotiations, prioritising the hoped-for outcome.

The framing categories (Table 22.1) for this cross-cultural comparison were based on a streamlined and extended version of Semetko and Valkenburg's study of European political coverage in Dutch national news (2000: 100). Their five news frames were conflict, economic consequences, human interest, attribution of responsibility, and morality. Added to those were two new categories – stability and harmony – which, it will be argued, might take greater account of Chinese perspectives. As a consequence of the Chinese academic interest in constructive journalism, the frame governing the attribution of responsibility was split into two. This distinguishes the blame for a problem from the drive for a solution.

Harmony and stability

It was under the leadership of Hu Jintao that the Chinese objective of a harmonious society (*hexie shehui*) and its foreign policy offshoot, harmonious world (*hexie shijie*), came to the fore (Delury 2008; Zheng & Tok 2007). The leadership was responding in part to discord caused by widening social divisions in

China, but the external application of "harmony" also signalled the emergence of a more assertive and focused China abroad. "Harmonious society" has faded from official pronouncements since Xi Jinping took power in 2012 (Qian 2014). However, the concept of harmony has a long tradition in China, with roots in ancient Eastern philosophies including Confucianism. The presence (actual or potential) of harmony is a much stronger frame evocation than a simple absence of conflict. Gagliardone et al. (2010) see a link between China's harmony and the South African concept of *ubuntu*, along with other traditions across Africa that place the community ahead of the individual.

Stability has long featured in official Chinese discourse. Currently, stability preservation (*weiwen*) alludes to social disorder, which the authorities have made it their priority to avoid (Qian 2012). References to (in)stability have permeated China's English-language media, including reports on events abroad.

The data were derived from content analysis of the two daily African news programmes over two constructed weeks in May/June 2014, assembled through recording every third day of output for six weeks. Only the

Table 22.1 Categories for comparison of British and Chinese news about Africa

Framing categories	
Conflict*[a]	Does the story involve disagreement or accusations between parties (including countries) or refer to two or more sides to a problem or issue?
Economic consequences*	Does the story mention financial losses, gains or costs, or the economic consequences of following or ignoring a course of action?
Human interest*	Is there a human angle to the coverage, does it show how individuals or groups are affected, or does it depict scenarios that might prompt outrage, sympathy, compassion, or empathy?
Responsibility* (cause)	Does the report contain a suggestion that an individual, group, or level of government is responsible for the issue or problem?
Responsibility* (solution oriented)	Does the report indicate solutions or suggest that officials or government are capable of solving or easing the problem?
Morality*	Does the story bear a moral message or appear to tell viewers how to behave?
Stability	Is reference made to the stability (or lack of it) of a country, government or society, or fears or hopes about future stability?
Harmony	Is reference made to harmonious relations (actual or possible) between or among nations, ethnic groups or different sectors of society, or peaceful coexistence?

Note

a   Categories asterisked summarise those employed by Semetko and Valkenburg (2000:100).

"hard news" elements of the programmes were sampled: headlines, pro-motional material, and discrete business and sports slots were disregarded. The African news on the sampled dates was dominated by three issues: insurgency (Boko Haram in West Africa and Al-Shabab in the East), the elections in Malawi, and the problems of African migration and refugees. Coverage of these subjects on BBC *Focus on Africa* and CCTV *Africa Live* (N = (19 + 32 =)51) was examined for presence of the eight frames, and tran-scribed for textual and visual analysis. This produced specific rather than generalisable results, but the focus of the research was sharpened through same-day comparison, representing what Esser (2013) categorises as inten-sive rather than extensive comparative study.

Analysing the frames

Table 22.2 shows the data gathered through framing analysis. The num-bers represent the percentages of stories sampled per channel that were observed to contain a given frame.

Insurgency: Boko Haram and Al-Shabab

In West Africa, bomb attacks in the central Nigerian city of Jos and several north-eastern villages from mid-May to early June 2014 were blamed on the Islamist militants of Boko Haram, as the authorities deliberated on how to rescue 200 schoolgirls kidnapped by the group. In East Africa, the focus was on multiple killings on Kenya's coast in mid-June 2014: the Somali Islamist group Al-Shabab said it had carried out the attacks, while the government insisted local political networks were to blame.

BBC *Focus on Africa* framed the insurgencies as conflict – in the sense of a straightforward fight between the authorities and the militants – twice as fre-quently as CCTV's *Africa Live*. The BBC repeatedly asked, "Is the (Nigerian) government losing the battle against Boko Haram?" (Okwoche 2014) and ran reports and interviews questioning the authorities' competence to handle the insurgency (*Focus on Africa* 2014a, 2014b, 2014c). In Kenya, the BBC asked a government spokesman why Kenyans should believe President Kenyatta's safety assurances, "considering he's made previous statements on enhanced security and the attacks have continued" (Igunza 2014). CCTV ran President Kenyatta's statement denying Al-Shabab's involvement without challenge: in the same report, it reflected more controversial issues from a distance, saying, "critics have again questioned Kenya's ability to keep its people safe" (Kiyo 2014c).

While the BBC highlighted governments' inaction just as often as it credited them with offering solutions, CCTV made the intervention of the authorities a focal point of its coverage. In Nigeria, CCTV asserted that "everyone wanted to know the official reaction" (Badmus 2014a), that

Table 22.2 Framing analysis

Frame (Items)>	BBC Focus on Africa				CCTV Africa Live			
	Insurgency (11)	Election (4)	Migration (4)	Total (19)	Insurgency (18)	Election (4)	Migration (10)	Total (32)
Conflict	72.73	100.00	25.00	68.42	38.89	75.00	30.00	40.63
Economic	0.00	25.00	25.00	10.53	5.56	25.00	60.00	25.00
Human Interest	36.36	50.00	50.00	42.11	44.44	0.00	100.00	56.25
Responsibility – cause	54.55	50.00	50.00	52.63	22.22	75.00	10.00	25.00
Responsibility – solution	54.55	50.00	25.00	47.37	77.78	100.00	20.00	62.50
Morality	0.00	25.00	25.00	10.53	0.00	0.00	0.00	0.00
Stability	45.45	0.00	25.00	31.58	38.89	25.00	50.00	40.63
Harmony	9.09	25.00	30.00	10.53	33.33	25.00	30.00	31.25

"everyone is waiting to ... get the side of the government" (Mrenje 2014). A local man, shown on CCTV, asked the government to "work hard" and rescue Nigerians from the insurgency (*Africa Live* 2014b). The stability frame was invoked more often by the BBC than CCTV in covering the insurgencies because of BBC reporters' repeated questioning of people's safety. However, CCTV availed itself of the harmony narrative by featuring the international help (led by China) offered to Nigeria to free the kidnapped girls (*Africa Live* 2014a). According to CCTV, the then president Goodluck Jonathan was also "turning to his neighbours to help combat Boko Haram" (Kiyo 2014a), and Ghanaian people were seen supporting pleas for the Nigerian government to act (*Africa Live* 2014b).

The two broadcasters' catchlines for the insurgency in west Africa were strikingly different. On 21 May, CCTV's headline on a suspected Boko Haram massacre carried a strapline reading, "Nigeria's War On Terror" (*Africa Live* 2014b). The BBC's backdrop bore the phrase, "The Enemy Within" (*Focus on Africa* 2014b). Both terms arise from othering processes, but enemies or an enemy (from) within are reminiscent of McCarthyite and Thatcherite accusations of Cold War subversion and indicate a much more intractable ideological conflict than that denoted by the binary, impersonal "war on terror". Moreover, the language and cultural background of "war on terror" are those of the West – specifically, of George Bush and Tony Blair – and not of either China or Africa.

Deployment of reporters affected the strength of the frame. The BBC's use of the conflict and human interest narratives in Nigeria was strengthened by the footage of its correspondent picking his way across the devastated site of a bombing in Jos (Gatehouse 2014). By contrast, CCTV's reporter was interviewed hundreds of kilometres away standing outside his office (Badmus 2014b). However, on 17 June both broadcasters reported from the scene of massacres near Lamu in Kenya initially blamed on Al-Shabab: here, the strength of the frame was determined by the running orders. For the BBC, the human interest frame was paramount and the programme opened with the strongest images – those of frightened villagers in Mpeketoni (Soy 2014) – followed by a dissection of President Kenyatta's reaction to the killings. CCTV, conversely, gave priority to the much less televisual statement by the president before showing its correspondent in Mpeketoni speaking to worried survivors amid smouldering rubble (Nagila 2014a). Three days later the two broadcasters gave opposing interpretations of security in coastal Kenya. The BBC grilled a government spokesman on the adequacy of security precautions and featured a Kenyan citizen saying he did not feel safe (*Focus on Africa* 2014d); CCTV reported from Mpeketoni on the increased, if belated, security presence and said the town was "slowly coming back to life" (Nagila 2014b).

Elections: the vote in Malawi

CCTV and the BBC both portrayed the 2014 elections in Malawi as conflict – in terms of the contested outcome of the presidential poll and the ensuing legal battles over a recount. The BBC's *Focus on Africa* interviewed people waiting for hours to vote ("Does that make you angry?" "Yes, we are very angry." (Maseko 2014a)) and referred to "court case after court case" (Maseko 2014b). CCTV's *Africa Live* spoke of an electoral process in "disarray" (Oyola 2014a) and featured complaints of voting irregularities (*ibid.*; *Africa Live* 2014b; Sumbuleta 2014). However, CCTV also gave space to the Malawi Electoral Commission and reported its justification of its actions (*Africa Live* 2014b, 2014c). After the new president, Peter Mutharika, was finally installed, the accusations and conflict frame on CCTV fell away. The new president was "tasked with reviving the economy and uniting Malawians" (*Africa Live* 2014d), and a supporter interviewed at the inauguration said people were prepared to "wait patiently" for progress (in Kiyo 2014b). The BBC's reporter at the ceremony, by contrast, spoke of a "messy and disputed outcome" to the elections, "riddled with accusations of foul play and rigging", although she also mentioned President Mutharika's promises to revive Malawi's fortunes (Maseko 2014c).

Migration and refugees

It was on migration and refugees that the two broadcasters diverged most widely. They covered the same news only once, on 20 June, World Refugee Day. The BBC's *Focus on Africa* briefly summarised overall refugee figures before dealing at length with how displaced people could be integrated into other African societies, focusing on individuals through the frames of human interest and economic consequences. CCTV's *Africa Live* interpreted the human interest frame mostly through a macro lens. It highlighted the scale of the refugee crisis and dwelt on basic survival needs, illustrating this with wide-shots of families standing in desolate camps and close-ups of malnourished children having their limbs measured. CCTV returned to the angle of human suffering on other days, featuring the threat of starvation and disease in South Sudan (Harper 2014; Mwongeli 2014; Khamsin 2014) and the refugee exodus from the Central African Republic (Galang 2014a; Oyola 2014b). Its reporting style was distant, involving footage narrated from headquarters in Nairobi or the United Nations. On migration, the BBC was close to the action, its correspondent accompanying a Mediterranean coastguard patrol to track Africans' dangerous boat journeys to Europe (Sommerville 2014). A similar story on CCTV was covered from European Union headquarters in Brussels using agency footage of a Mediterranean rescue (Barton 2014). Its strapline was non-African: "Europe struggles with migrants influx".

The divergence in the two broadcasters' framing of migration and displacement coincided with CCTV's disproportionate use of non-original footage. Reliance on material from Western television news agencies or non-governmental organisations inevitably means a loss of control of the news agenda (Paterson 2011) and constraints on alternative news flows. While China's *Africa Live* made use of stock images of refugee camps and United Nations appeals, however, the BBC's *Focus on Africa* – admittedly with less airtime to fill – appeared to eschew routine news agency coverage. This is in line with a recently reiterated emphasis on "distinctive, original journalism" at the BBC (Harding 2014) in the light of steep budget cuts.

The Chinese elephant in the room

News about China or Chinese people in Africa was omitted from this frame analysis because previous research indicated that CCTV Africa gave it a positive gloss (Zhang X. 2013, Marsh 2016). This separation of data prevented major distortions of the general sample, although China is too involved in Africa for its state broadcaster to be considered a disinterested observer. China was mentioned once in the BBC *Focus on Africa* output studied, when Hong Kong authorities burned a stockpile of illegal ivory (Liu 2014). This event was not covered on CCTV *Africa Live*, although CCTV did report on the seizure of elephant tusks packed for export from Kenya to an undisclosed destination (Liao 2014). Otherwise, CCTV mentioned China only positively – in connection with joint counter-piracy exercises with the Nigerian navy (Galang 2014b), attempts to help restore stability in South Sudan (*Africa Live* 2014e), a photo exhibition of China–South Africa relations (*Africa Live* 2014a), and the rise of martial arts in Ethiopia (Girum 2014).

CCTV Africa: a different but occluded perspective

The results of the frame analysis (Table 22.3) indicate that, on these three key topics at least, CCTV Africa's coverage of the continent does differ from that of the BBC, but its emerging alternative voice is not yet clearly defined.

CCTV's overall preference for the solution-oriented responsibility frame indicates that – consciously or not – it is adopting some elements of "constructive journalism". This framing of African events does indeed diverge from the norms of Western coverage, but it is also marked by a lack of critical focus on China and a reluctance to hold African leaders and officials to account. The absence in CCTV Africa's coverage of the frame indicating that an individual, group, or government is held responsible for a problem may suggest a general distaste for a critical perspective. Just as CCTV halted criticism of Peter Mutharika once he was installed as president of Malawi,

Table 22.3 Top five frames in the analysis of three key issues on the BBC's and
CCTV's African news programmes

	CCTV Africa Live	BBC Focus on Africa TV	Semetko & Valkenburg
1	Responsibility (solution)	Conflict	Responsibility
2	Human interest	Responsibility (cause)	Conflict
3	*Stability*[a] }	Responsibility (solution)	Economic consequences
4	Conflict	Human interest	Human interest
5	*Harmony*	*Stability*	Morality

Note

a   Items in italics: new frames, not present in Semetko and Valkenburg's analysis.

it showed itself on numerous other occasions to be much more deferential towards officials than the BBC. Viewers and rivals may increasingly look to CCTV Africa to tackle questions about the conduct and security of Chinese citizens abroad as China expands its involvement in Africa, and to examine China's policies and economic ties with the continent. Beijing's avowed non-interference in other countries' affairs has enabled its official media to take a non-confrontational approach on many issues outside its immediate neighbourhood: however, this policy is becoming strained as China's global power grows. The Chinese navy's unprecedented evacuation of foreigners along with Chinese nationals from Yemen to Djibouti (Xinhua 2015) was confirmation of an increasingly assertive and interventionist foreign policy that may yet prompt changes of approach in China's official foreign news reporting.

The presence of the stability and harmony frames suggests that official domestic Chinese policy priorities have permeated CCTV's English news discourse. The conflict frame ranks much lower with CCTV Africa than with the BBC's African programme, possibly because CCTV's reporters often keep more of a distance from news events – physically and mentally – than their counterparts at the BBC. CCTV's tendency to prioritise officials and government pronouncements militates against the picture-led imperative for which Western television news has been criticised, while still favouring a dialogue of the elite rather than providing a truly alternative perspective. Further work is needed to broaden the issues compared through frame analysis, and to test whether constructive journalism is equipped to deal with a wider range of news.

The silhouette of the acacia tree in the CCTV Africa video hints at the view of an outsider: the content analysis indicates that its news editors, too, have international as well as African viewers in mind. In this study, CCTV's *Africa Live* sometimes fell back on stereotypes of Western coverage in its depiction of refugees in camps, reliance on broad-brush statistics, or references to "war on terror". The use of news agency pictures to cover displacement and migration, along with infrequent deployment of reporters to the scene of breaking news, had the effect of allowing rivals to dictate the visual agenda. As international broadcasters scramble to Africanise their coverage, CCTV Africa certainly appeared to be testing an alternative voice, but it had yet to reveal a consistent strategy or a fully distinctive way of reporting the news.

Note

1 *Africa Live* promotional video, CCTV News channel, 17:15 GMT, 18 February 2015.

References

Africa Live (2014a) Nairobi: CCTV News, 15 May. GMT: 17.00.
Africa Live (2014b) Nairobi: CCTV News, 21 May. GMT: 17.00.
Africa Live (2014c) Nairobi: CCTV News, 27 May. GMT: 17.00.
Africa Live (2014d) Nairobi: CCTV News, 2 June. GMT: 17.00.
Africa Live (2014e) Nairobi: CCTV News, 23 June. GMT: 17.00.
Badmus, D. (2014a) In: *Africa Live*. Nairobi: CCTV News, 15 May. GMT: 17.00.
Badmus, D. (2014b) In: *Africa Live*. Nairobi: CCTV News, 21 May. GMT: 17.00.
Barton, J. (2014) In: *Africa Live*. Nairobi: CCTV News, 20 June. GMT: 17.00.
Bunce, M. (2015) "International news and the image of Africa: new storytellers, new narratives?", in J. Gallagher (ed.), *Images of Africa: Creation, Negotiation and Subversion*, Manchester: Manchester University Press.
CCTV (2009) "Increase the overseas influence of CCTV and build world-class media", 26 June, at http://english.cctv.com/20090626/111181.shtml [accessed 09/07/2015].
CCTV News (2014) "Li speaks to CCTV News about China–African ties", at http://www.china.org.cn/video/2014-05/12/content_32361564.htm [accessed 17/04/2015].
Constructive Journalism Project (n.d.) "What is constructive journalism? What is it not?", at http://constructivejournalism.org/about/ [accessed 17/04/2015].
Delury, J. (2008) "'Harmonious' in China", *Policy Review*, April–May, Hoover Institution.
Dong, S. & Shi, A. (2007) "Chinese news in transition", in D. Thussu (ed.), *Media on the Move: Global Flow and Contra-Flow*, Abingdon: Routledge.
Entman, R. (1993) "Framing: towards clarification of a fractured paradigm", *Journal of Communication*, 43(4): 51–58.
Esser, F. (2013) "The emerging paradigm of comparative communication enquiry: advancing cross-national research in times of globalization", *International Journal of Communication*, 7: 113–128.
Focus on Africa (2014a) London: BBC World News, 15 May. GMT: 17.30.
Focus on Africa (2014b) London: BBC World News, 21 May. GMT: 17.30.
Focus on Africa (2014c) London: BBC World News, 5 June. GMT: 17.30.
Focus on Africa (2014d) London: BBC World News, 20 June. GMT: 17.30.
Gagliardone, I. (2013) "China as a persuader: CCTV Africa's first steps in the African mediasphere", *Ecquid Novi: African Journalism Studies*, 34(3): 25–40.

Gagliardone, I., Repnikova, M., & Stremlau, N. (2010) *China in Africa: A New Approach to Media Development?*, report, Programme in Comparative Media Law and Policy (PCMLP), University of Oxford.

Galang, M. (2014a) In: *Africa Live.* Nairobi: CCTV News, 27 May. GMT: 17.00.

Galang, M. (2014b) In: *Africa Live.* Nairobi: CCTV News, 30 May. GMT: 17:00.

Gatehouse, G. (2014) In: *Focus on Africa.* London: BBC World News, 21 May. GMT: 17.30.

Girum, C. (2014) In: *Africa Live.* Nairobi: CCTV News, 2 June. GMT: 17:00.

Harding, J. (2014) "James Harding and BBC News Group Board – presentation to BBC News staff", 17 July, BBC Media Centre, at http://bbc.co.uk/corporate2/mediacentre/speeches/2014/james-harding-news-plans [accessed 17/07/2014].

Harper, N. (2014) In: *Africa Live.* Nairobi: CCTV News, 21 May. GMT: 17.00.

Hu, Z., Zhang, L., & Ji, D. (2013) "Globalization, social reform and the shifting paradigms of communication studies in China", *Media, Culture and Society,* 35: 147–155.

Igunza, E. (2014) In: *Focus on Africa.* London: BBC World News, 17 June. GMT: 17.30.

Jirik, J. (2010) "24-hour television news in the People's Republic of China", in S. Cushion and J. Lewis (eds), *The Rise of 24-Hour News Television: Global Perspectives,* New York: Peter Lang.

Khamsin, W. (2014) In: *Africa Live.* Nairobi: CCTV News, 5 June. GMT: 17.00.

Kiyo, J. (2014a) In: *Africa Live.* Nairobi: CCTV News, 21 May. GMT: 17:00.

Kiyo, J. (2014b). In: *Africa Live.* Nairobi: CCTV News, 2 June. GMT: 17:00.

Kiyo, J. (2014c) In: *Africa Live.* Nairobi: CCTV News, 17 June. GMT: 17:00.

Liao, L. (2014) In: *Africa Live.* Nairobi: CCTV News, 5 June. GMT: 17:00.

Liu, J. (2014) In: *Focus on Africa.* London: BBC World News, 15 May. GMT: 17.30

Marsh, V. (2016) "Mixed messages, partial pictures? Discourses under construction in CCTV's Africa Live compared with the BBC", *Chinese Journal of Communication,* 9(1): 56–70.

Maseko, N. (2014a) In: *Focus on Africa.* London: BBC World News, 21 May. GMT: 17.30.

Maseko, N. (2014b). In: *Focus on Africa.* London: BBC World News, 27 May. GMT: 17.30.

Maseko, N. (2014c) In: *Focus on Africa.* London: BBC World News, 2 June. GMT: 17.30.

Mrenje, K. (2014) In: *Africa Live.* Nairobi: CCTV News, 2 June. GMT: 17.00.

Mwongeli, S. (2014) In: *Africa Live.* Nairobi: CCTV News, 27 May. GMT: 17.00.

Nagila, R. (2014a) In: *Africa Live.* Nairobi: CCTV News, 17 June. GMT: 17.00.

Nagila, R. (2014b) In: *Africa Live.* Nairobi: CCTV News, 20 June. GMT: 17.00.

Nye, J. (2011) *The Future of Power.* New York: Public Affairs.

Okwoche, P. (2014) In: *Focus on Africa.* London: BBC World News, 21 May. GMT: 17.30.

Oyola, C. (2014a) In: *Africa Live.* Nairobi: CCTV News, 27 May. GMT: 17.00.

Oyola, C. (2014b) In: *Africa Live.* Nairobi: CCTV News, 2 June. GMT: 17.00.

Paterson, C. (2011) *The International Television News Agencies: The World From London,* New York: Peter Lang.

Qian, G. (2012) *Watchwords: Reading China through its Political Vocabulary,* JMSC Working Papers, University of Hong Kong, at http://jmsc.hku.hk/2012/11/jmsc-series-unlocks-political-jargon-china/ [accessed 04/04/2015].

Qian, G. (2014) *Reading Chinese Politics in 2014,* China Media Project, 30 December, China Media Project, at http://cmp.hku.hk/2014/12/30/37469/ [accessed 28/03/2015].

Semetko, H. & Valkenburg, P. (2000) "Framing European politics: a content analysis of press and television news", *Journal of Communication,* Spring: 93–109.

Sommerville, Q. (2014) In: *Focus on Africa*. London: BBC World News, 30 May. GMT: 17.30.

Soy, A. (2014) In: *Focus on Africa*. London: BBC World News, 17 June. GMT: 17.30.

Sumbuleta, A. (2014) In: *Africa Live*. Nairobi: CCTV News, 30 May. GMT: 17.00.

Wekesa, B. & Zhang, Y. (2014) "Live, talk, faces: an analysis of CCTV's adaption to the African media market", discussion paper, Stellenbosch University, May.

Xinhua (2015) "China helps 10 countries evacuate nationals from Yemen", 3 April, at http://news.xinhuanet.com/english/2015-04/03/c_134120671.htm [accessed 06/07/2015].

Zhang, X. (2013) "How ready is China for a China-style world order? China's state media discourse under construction", *Ecquid Novi: African Journalism Studies*, 34(3): 79–101.

Zhang, Y. (2014) "Understand China's media in Africa from the perspective of constructive journalism", paper for the China and Africa Media, Communications and Public Diplomacy conference (CMI), Beijing.

Zheng, Y. & Tok, S. (2007) "'Harmonious society' and 'harmonious world': China's policy discourse under Hu Jintao", *Briefing Series* (26), China Policy Institute, University of Nottingham, Nottingham.

Chapter 23

Media perspectives

New media and African engagement with the global public sphere[1]

Sean Jacobs

Is new media helping Africa "reclaim its voice" in the global public sphere? Certainly some African citizens have engaged via new technologies and social media to extend a voice well beyond the nation state and indeed the continent. But it is not the high-profile social media campaigns such as the #Kony2012 or #BringBackOurGirls campaign, that best illustrate the transformative potential of new media. Rather, it is the way these media are being utilised by less celebrated actors within civil society: diaspora journalists, youth culture, and church groups (to name a few) that best encapsulate Africa's new forms of engagement with the global public sphere.

#Kony2012 was arguably the most significant event in the short history of Africa's place in the global public sphere. Despite criticisms about the "film" and Invisible Children, Inc. (including after the public meltdown of its founder), at least for a while this will remain the template for how "the global public sphere" will engage with African issues and Africans. Similar dynamics – Western storytellers framing issues of African suffering in the global sphere – could be seen in the #BringBackOurGirls campaign.

Initial criticism of #Kony2012 centred on demands for more "African voices". Obviously, the lack of African voices from the regions in which the Lord's Resistance Army operates (or once operated) was part of the problem in this "activist" film, with its easy "to do" list of solutions aimed at those who are often mockingly described as "Facebook slacktivists".

But it is not clear how being "authentically African" makes someone a necessarily useful purveyor of opinion on the issue. Even Invisible Children has "African voices" on its staff. In fact, this was part of the filmmakers' defence when they responded to criticisms. Africans can also draw uninformed (or purely self-interest-driven) conclusions about what's going on in the continent. So it is unclear if the "authenticity" of the Africans engaged in (or critiquing) any given "African" situation is the solution, per se. It is important to think about what these voices have to say.

More promising, perhaps, are the implications of #OccupyNigeria, a series of protests that brought that country to a standstill for the first two weeks of January 2012 following an announcement by President Jonathan that he would scrap a fuel subsidy that most Nigerians considered their birthright. Hundreds of thousands of Nigerians streamed onto the streets to join marches and rallies. The national strike was only suspended after the government, following a deal brokered with trade unions, partially restored the subsidy.

Media coverage of Nigeria during #OccupyNigeria mostly focused on alleged violence associated with protesters – it rarely attempted to hold the politicians themselves to account. However, a great deal of pressure did come from activists on social media – and crucially the Nigerian diaspora. Online activists targeted celebrities (Nollywood actors and popular singers like D'Banj), who were forced to declare their allegiance with the strike. And anger was directed towards Nigeria's political class, who were frequently lampooned online. Two websites stood out: the Nigeria-based Chop Cassava (which produces video reports) and Sahara Reporters, based in New York City.

Of these, Sahara Reporters has had a larger impact. Sahara Reporters has become a media force inside Nigeria largely because it is not in Nigeria. The website's base in New York City places Sahara Reporters beyond the reach of the politicians and corporations that the site often reports on. What appeals to its audience is the nature of the stories it reports, which includes eyewitness accounts, and information about sensitive issues that the press in Nigeria is often too afraid to report. This has included extensive coverage of a huge oil spill in the Niger Delta; revealing the corruption of a state governor who was eventually tried in a British court; and events surrounding the illness, absence from Nigeria, and eventual death of President Umaru Yar'Adua in May 2010.

Ordinary Nigerians have warmed to Sahara Reporters' reporting and support it publicly. It has also attracted the attention of those in power. In some instances, Jonathan's office has released media statements directly addressed to the site. In one celebrated case, Sahara Reporters' story of 32 aides accompanying Nigeria's first lady on an official trip to an African Union summit in Ethiopia resulted in the presidential spokesperson releasing a press statement aimed specifically at Sahara Reporters. What makes Sahara Reporters' reporting "global" is not just the fact that it is transnational but also the flow and counterflow of information between New York City, Lagos, and elsewhere in Nigeria. There's also the reciprocity between Sahara Reporters' editors, audience, contributors, and sources, as well as its targets.

Civil society voices

There are other important civil society actors within Africa, who are utilising new media to engage with the global public sphere. One important – and under-studied – group are youth. Irreverent youth culture – both by ordinary Africans on the continent and in the diaspora – contributes to online political culture with real effects and, in doing so, creates new forms of African modernity. In Nigeria, satirical memes of an unsympathetic and awkward Goodluck Jonathan created critical pressure in the important run-up to the Nigerian national elections. Another high-profile example was the satirical memes that circulated widely after longtime Zimbabwean President Robert Mugabe fell over. These responses to political events are creating new discourse, which, in turn, shapes politics itself, creating space for new political voices.

Indeed, hashtag politics are now ubiquitous in a number of countries on the continent, with actual movements named for hashtags, whether #RhodesMustFall and #FeesMustMall (movements on South African for free education and to deracialise university campuses in 2015), #WalktoWork (opposition party protests in Uganda), or #Mpigs (against increases in MPs salaries in Kenya). This is largely due to youth culture within and beyond the continent. International solidarity and support are often key features of these movements.

Beyond youth culture and social movements, researchers also need to pay more attention to forms of evangelical Christianity that are exported from parts of West Africa (and increasingly smaller countries like Zimbabwe or Zambia), creating powerful celebrities out of their leaders like the Nigerian "super pastor" TB Joshua. Joshua's followers spread their brand of African evangelical Christianity by building churches in shop fronts around major Western, East Asian, and South American cities and, more importantly, through posting his sermons on YouTube. These YouTube videos have receive view counts in the millions, and the "Comments" spaces below them are lively forums where the pastor's followers vigorously defend TB Joshua and his Synagogue Church of All Nations. It is these forms of media – seldom mentioned or discussed by researchers – that create powerful images of Africa and ways of being to millions of diaspora and church groups. These less-celebrated actors – youth culture, religious groups, and diaspora media – increasingly come to determine the outlines of how Africans enter and operate in the global public sphere.

Note

1 Some of these comments are based on an earlier essay that appeared on the analysis website *African Futures*, 21 February 2013.

Chapter 24

Shifting power relations, shifting images

Herman Wasserman

Representations are central to power relations. When considering media images of Africa, we have to take cognisance of how these power relations are shifting, as such shifts will be linked to changing media images. The primary set of power relations that has defined discourses on Africa over the years, has been that of imperialism and colonialism. The impact of the discourse of Empire on images on Africa is well established in critical post-colonial studies. The discursive Othering of Africa, in the process that Spivak (1988: 280) called "epistemic violence", has also been included in post-colonial critiques of the position that the global South occupies in global media (and media studies) (see Shome and Hegde 2002).

Even in the post-colonial era, after the continent has seen vast changes as part of the "third wave" of democratisation (Blankson 2007: 19) that included economic liberalisation, political renewal, and media reforms, the legacy of colonialism remains visible. This legacy can be seen in the continent's geography, global economic position, and the symbolic frameworks within which it is embedded. The discourses of colonialism can still be heard in the media as well. As McMillin (2007: 55, 66) points out, the media have historically played a role in the reproduction of imperial power, and their position in contemporary global power relations often show similarities to that earlier era. Journalistic narratives often still repeat discourses of "civility and barbarity", and even positive reports on Africa are frequently marked by a "patronisingly subtle tone that works as a constantly reminder that this is a hopeless region that needs salvation and can only achieve 'success' – in itself a loaded term – if it manages to reproduce Western institutions and values" (Conboy et al. 2014: 5). The extent to which existing evidence bears out the assumption that the global media are Afro-pessimistic has been called into question (Scott 2015), but it is agreed that at least the widespread assumption of this negativity can inform politics and policymaking.

However, not only do the echoes of colonial discourse reverberate through journalism about Africa, but the vocabulary of imperialism has also provided an interpretative framework for contemporary geo-politics. In the post-colonial era, the impact of globalisation on communication has itself been equated with "cultural imperialism", "media imperialism", or similar terms (Hamelink 2015: 193), not only in terms of representation but also with regard to the political economy of media ownership and control. Strong critiques of global media saw it complicit with the spread of corporate capitalism that has wreaked disaster on Africa and the global South as a whole (Herman & McChesney 1997: 11).

This scholarly concern with the representation of Africa in global media, in particular the legacy of imperialism on media discourses and political economy, has up until now focused on the continent's image in Western media. A recent article (Scott 2015), for instance, surveying the literature on global representations of Africa, limits itself to "US and UK media", which is an understandable approach given the historic baggage of Western involvement in Africa as well as Western dominance of global media ownership (Conboy et al. 2014: 6). In recent years, however, important shifts in geo-political developments have taken place, which have brought new dimensions to the way Africa is located within global media discourses. These shifts have again produced questions regarding the nature of foreign engagement with the continent, the role of the media in these engagements, and whether the emerging power relations repeat older imperialist forms of domination and exploitation.

Perhaps the development most clearly seen as indicating a geo-political shift has been the formation of the bloc of rising economic powers Brazil, Russia, India, China, and South Africa, the so-called BRICS countries. The emergence of this new power bloc, signifying the "Rise of the Rest" (Zakaria 2011: 2), has widely been seen as heralding a shift away from the declining metropolitan powers (although critics such as Bond and Garcia (2015) see this group as collaborators rather than competitors of these old centres of financial power). Despite the fact (pointed out by Sparks 2015: 42) that the members of the BRICS group vary greatly in terms of the size of their economies and their media systems, these countries have all seen "exponential growth" in their media industries, raising questions about "the impact this might have on global communication" (Thussu & Nordenstreng 2015: 1). Already an increase in intra-BRICS coverage and movement of capital and personnel can be observed (Wasserman et al. 2015).

Within these shifting patterns, the emerging relations between China and Africa have become a particular point of focus for scholars of African media. This is partly because this relationship has frequently again been cast in terms of imperialism by its critics, and partly because the media has been central to China's "soft power" strategy on the continent.

A central question that relates to the issue of geo-political power struggles as they pertain to African media is therefore how China's increased involvement on the African continent has been *mediated*. This question regarding mediation includes the movement of media capital between the two regions, as well as the representation of China–Africa relationships in the media.

China–Africa media relations[1]

The emerging media relations between China and Africa come on the back of a wider engagement, largely economic in nature but also including political contacts. Chinese involvement in Africa has a long history, but it gained momentum in recent years as a result of the need for China to find new sources of energy and natural resources to support its rapid economic development.

This intensified political–economic relationship, viewed against the background of the geo-political shifts indicated by, among others, the rise of the BRICS grouping as mentioned above, has raised questions as to what the impact would be on African politics, its economy, and its media. These concerns included the perceived support for African leaders in undemocratic regimes, Chinese companies' labour practices, and commitment to environmental sustainability (Sautman & Hairong 2007).

These questions about the impact of China's increased engagement with Africa have also been applied to the media. This is because the media have been central to the extension of China's influence on the continent. The establishment of Chinese media houses in Africa, as well as the investment in local media infrastructure and training or exchange programmes for journalists, have been interpreted mostly as a "charm offensive" (Kurlantzick 2007) aimed at extending China's "soft power" (Nye 2004) on the continent.

Besides signalling the extent to which the shifting geo-political relations between Africa and China are being mediated, these heightened exchanges between media capital, content, and personnel will also have implications for the way Africa is represented in the media.

The implications for Africa's media image

The coverage of Chinese involvement in Africa in the Western media has frequently been negative. It could be argued that the way that the Sino-African relationship has been portrayed, also displays a certain paternalistic attitude towards Africa. In media accounts of Chinese involvement in Africa, the continent is often depicted as falling prey to a new imperialism, while African agency to resist exploitation or negotiate the terms of engagement is frequently underplayed. Such reporting usually emphasises the threat China poses to African countries, often drawing on Orientalist tropes (Daly 2009; Sautman & Hairong 2007). Attempts to counterbalance these discourses of imperialism often make use of an equally simplistic frame of solidarity (Zeleza 2008).

The introduction of Chinese media in the continent has, however, the potential to construct alternative frames through which the continent can be viewed. As Gagliardone (2013: 26) points out, it has been the aim of CCTV Africa not only to improve the perception of Chinese involvement in Africa, but to do so by promoting ways of looking at Africa differently, through an approach of "positive reporting" of the continent.

While the positive representation of Africa by Chinese media like CCTV seems to be an instrumentalist approach aimed at amplifying China's soft power, it also fits into a broader philosophy of "constructive journalism" that offers a different normative model to the critical, "watchdog" approach mostly espoused by the Western media. On the one hand, this alternative approach can provide new ways of doing journalism in and about Africa, but on the other it has also raised concerns. Incidentally, the concept of "constructive journalism" has also recently surfaced in Western journalism literature (Haagerup 2014). As in the case of the Chinese media, this notion has met with some criticism for its resonances with the older approach of covering Africa in terms of "development journalism" that also eschewed harsh criticism of governments (WEF 2014).

Although the resistance against "constructive journalism" can be linked to the journalistic mantra of objectivity that abhors media bias (Yanqiu & Matingwina 2016), the criticism of the Chinese version of "constructive journalism" is predominantly based on political–economic grounds. Chinese media are state owned, and therefore they have a vested interest in portraying China–Africa relations as cordial and beneficial, and African states as worthy of investment – in other words, Chinese media can be seen as protecting the interests of the Chinese state (Yanqiu & Matingwina 2016). This is also the reason why many observers have expressed concerns that Chinese media in Africa might have a detrimental influence on robust, critical journalism and press freedom on the continent. The notion of positive or constructive journalism has been linked to a subservient, government-controlled Chinese media at best, and at worst as leading to censorship, as has been the case in Chinese domestic media. Chinese media involvement in Africa has therefore often been feared as having a potentially negative influence on media freedom on the continent (e.g., Keita 2012). As Gagliardone (2013: 28) has pointed out, these fears are ironic to the extent that they are based on the assumption that Chinese media will export and promote their normative models for the media just as Western countries have done since colonial times.

The debates that have followed these investments centred on a wider concern for press freedom on the continent and China's potential influence on editorial independence and professional values (Keita 2012). These concerns are summed up in Harber's (2013: 151) statement that the "authoritarian, top-down Beijing media model will not sit easily in a country such as South Africa, with its strong tradition of independent and outspoken media, which are highly critical of authority." Harber's comments have been echoed by critics such as Thamm (2015), who has observed that the

South African government might take lessons in media repression from its Chinese counterparts, and Allison (2014), who took the media company Naspers to task for profiting from the Chinese platform Tencent while it cooperates with the Chinese government's repression of free speech. What is important to note from these criticisms are that they are mostly linked directly to concerns about media freedom at home, such as the imprisonment of Ethiopian journalists (Keita 2012) or the ANC government's renewed attempts to stifle media criticism (Harber 2013; Thamm 2015). In other words, global geo-politics are evaluated through the prism of local, domestic politics and media–state relations.

Conclusion

The rise of the BRICS alignment of emerging states has had a significant impact on Africa's position in geo-political networks of power and, concomitantly, on the representation of the continent in global media discourses. One of the major points of focus in these discourses has been the growing relations between China and Africa. This relationship has led to shifts in media representations of Africa in that the continent has become located in discourses of changing geo-politics. Furthermore this relationship has also led to the increasing exchange of media capital and personnel. These shifts have raised questions as to what the impact on media images, practices, and value systems might be in the longer term. Although these shifts have arguably located Africa within a new power bloc, they have also borne echoes of earlier discourses about the continent's vulnerability to exploitation, its lack of agency, and its proneness to undemocratic politics. Again the "patronisingly subtle tone" (Conboy et al. 2014) that constructs Africa as a region that needs salvation from either the West, or the East, or that has to be rescued from the East by the West, is unmistakably heard in media discourses. Africa still serves as a space where contests for geo-political domination plays out – also in the form of discursive struggles over meaning, images, and representations.

Note

1   This section draws on Wasserman 2013 and 2015.

References

Allison, S. (2014) "TenCent, WeChat and Chinese censorship: does Naspers have a free speech problem?", *Daily Maverick*, at http://www.dailymaverick.co.za/article/2014-11-20-tencent-wechat-and-chinese-censorship-does-naspers-have-a-free-speech-problem/ [accessed 27/08/2014].

Blankson, I. A. (2007) "Media independence and pluralism in Africa: opportunities and challenges of democratization and liberalization", in I. A. Blankson and

D. Murphy Patrick (eds), *Negotiating Democracy: Media Transformation in Emerging Democracies*, Albany: SUNY Press.

Bond, P. & Garcia, A. (2015) "Introduction", in P. Bond and A. Garcia (eds), *BRICS: An Anti-Capitalist Critique*, Johannesburg: Jacana.

Conboy, M., Lugo-Ocando, J., & Eldridge, S. (2014) "Livingstone and the legacy of Empire in the journalistic imagination", *Ecquid Novi: African Journalism Studies*, 35(1): 3–8.

Daly, J. C. K. (2009) "Feeding the dragon: China's quest for African minerals", in A. Waldron (ed.), *China in Africa*, Washington DC: The Jamestown Foundation.

Gagliardone, I. (2013) "China as a persuader: CCTV Africa's first steps in the African mediasphere", *Ecquid Novi: African Journalism Studies*, 34(3): 25–40.

Haagerup, U. (2014), *Constructive News*, Hanoi, New York, Pretoria, and Rapperswil: Inno Vatio Publishing.

Harber, A. (2013) "China's soft diplomacy in Africa", *Ecquid Novi: African Journalism Studies*, 34(3): 149–151.

Hamelink, C. J. (2015) *Global Communication*, London: Sage.

Herman, E. S. & McChesney, R. W. (1997) *The Global Media: The New Missionaries of Corporate Capitalism*, London and New York: Continuum.

Keita, M. (2012) "Africa's free press problem", *The New York Times*, 15 April, at http://www.nytimes.com/2012/04/16/opinion/africas-free-press-problem.html?_r=0 [accessed 01/09/2015].

Kurlantzick, J. (2007) *Charm Offensive: How China's Soft Power Is Transforming the World*, New Haven, CT: Yale University Press.

McMillin, D. C. (2007) *International Media Studies*, Malden, MA: Blackwell

Nye, J. (2004) *Soft Power: The Means to Success in World Politics*, New York: Public Affairs.

Sautman, B. & Hairong, Y. (2007) "Fu Manchu in Africa: the distorted portrayal of China's presence in the continent", *South African Labor Bulletin* 31(5): 34–38.

Scott, M. (2015) "The myth of representations of Africa: a comprehensive scoping of the literature", *Journalism Studies*, August, DOI: 10.1080/1461670X.2015.1044557.

Shome, R. & Hegde, R. S. (2002) "Postcolonial approaches to communications: charting the terrain, engaging the intersections", *Communication Theory*, 12(3): 249–270.

Sparks, C. (2015) "How coherent is the BRICS grouping?", in K. Nordenstreng and D. K. Thussu (eds), *Mapping BRICS Media*, London: Routledge.

Spivak, G. C. (1988) "Can the subaltern speak?", in C. Nelson & L. Grossberg (eds), *Marxism and the Interpretation of Culture*, Urbana, IL: University of Illinois Press.

Thamm, M. (2015) "Media freedom: South African government sees how it's done in China", *Daily Maverick*, 27 July, at http://www.dailymaverick.co.za/article/2015-07-27-media-freedom-south-african-government-sees-how-its-done-in-china/ [accessed 26/08/2015].

Thussu, D. K. & Nordenstreng, K. (2015) "Introduction: contextualizing the BRICS media", in *Mapping BRICS Media*, London: Routledge.

Wasserman, H. (2013) "China in Africa: the implications for journalism", *Ecquid Novi: African Journalism Studies*, 34(3): 1–5.

Wasserman, H. (2015) "South Africa and China as BRICS partners: media perspectives on geopolitical shifts", *Journal of Asian and African Studies*, 50(1): 109–123.

Wasserman, H., Molina, F., Paulino, F., Pietiläinen, J., & Strovsky, D. (2015) "Intra-BRICS Media Exchange", in K. Nordenstreng & D. K. Thussu (eds), *Mapping the BRICS Media*, London: Routledge.

WEF (World Editors' Forum) (2014) "Constructive journalism: emerging mega-trend or a recipe for complacency?", *The Media Online*, at http://themediaonline.co.za/2014/11/constructive-journalism-emerging-mega-trend-or-a-recipe-for-complacency/ [accessed 01/09/2015].

Yanqiu, Z. & Matingwina, S. (2016) "Constructive journalism: a new journalistic paradigm of Chinese media in Africa", in X. Zhang, H. Wasserman, and W. Mano (eds), *China's Soft Power in Africa: Promotion and Perceptions*, New York: Palgrave Macmillan.

Zakaria, F. (2011) *The Post-American World: Release 2.0*, New York: WW Norton & Co.

Zeleza, P. T. (2008) "Dancing with the dragon: Africa's courtship with China", *The Global South*, 2(2): 171–187.

Chapter 25

Communicating violence

The media strategies of Boko Haram

Abdullahi Tasiu Abubakar

A grainy video showing about 136 girls, dressed in full-length grey and black hijabs, reciting Qur'anic verses, appeared on global television screens on 12 May 2014 (BBC 2014). The following morning the image was splashed across the front pages of many tabloids and broadsheets around the world. It was the first picture of roughly half of the school-girls abducted four weeks earlier by Boko Haram insurgents in north-eastern Nigeria (BBC 2014). It came from a 27-minute video delivered by an emissary of the group to journalists in northern Nigeria, including a correspondent of the *Agence France-Presse* (Smith 2015). The French news agency, from which the global media bought the footage, is one of the media organisations that have been receiving such materials from the group because they have been covering the insurgency for many years. This particular video was produced by the group to prove that they were indeed holding the schoolgirls. A week earlier they had released a 57-minute film showing their leader, Abubakar Shekau, claiming the abduction of the girls and threatening to sell them as "slaves" (Sahara TV 2014; Smith 2015). It provoked a global outrage – as indeed did the abduction itself – but it didn't erase doubts about the group's culpability. The second video did.

The release of these videos – and many more before them – was just one of Boko Haram's methods of drawing public attention to their activities, of showing off their prowess, and of intimidating their enemies. From hawk-ing audio cassettes in street corners to staging headline-grabbing attacks, the Nigerian jihadists have adopted a range of media strategies that both utilise and defy modern public relations logic. But they are not the first jihadi group to employ media to advance their cause. Al Qaeda, the group they sometimes eulogise and often ape, is well known for its deft deploy-ment of media to spread its ideology (Lynch 2006). And Al Qaeda's off-spring-turned-rival, the so-called Islamic State, has demonstrated an even greater mastery of this, "using social media and cyber technology to recruit fighters and intimidate enemies" (Farwell 2014: 49). In Africa itself, mem-bers of Al Shabaab – Somalia's extremist group whose militancy extends to

Kenya – have used social media so viciously in their insurgency that they were dubbed "Twitter terrorists" (Greenwood 2013).

Employing media strategies to advance organisational goals is nothing new, and entities ranging from business conglomerates to advocacy groups regard it as an integral part of their work. There are also numerous studies showing how different media strategies were – or could be – deployed by organisations as diverse as political parties (Arterton 1984), the intelligence services (Shpiro 2001), the military (Jensen 2011), and environmental groups (Merry 2012) to achieve their objectives. But many scholars argue that the media's ideological leanings do also play a role in determining the scope and colour of their coverage of events both elsewhere and in Africa (Maloba 1992; Ibelema 1992). This may perhaps explain why, for instance, the Western media in the 1950s generally demonised the Mau Mau (Maloba 1992) – the Kenyan nationalist movement that fought against British colonialism – but largely gave positive portrayal of Biafra (Jorre 1972; Bamisaiye 1974; Ibelema 1992; Waters 2004), the entity that sought to secede from Nigeria in the 1960s. It would, of course, be argued that Biafra did employ smart media strategies in its campaign (Jorre 1972), but, as Bamisaiye (1974) argues, the media's entrenched interest too could not be discounted. Western media's current Islamist fixation in their coverage of events is largely responsible for the massive attention they have been giving to jihadi groups. And because the jihadists too seek such attention, for their own purposes, a convergence of a sort has emerged.

Methodology

This chapter unveils Boko Haram's media strategies and examines their efficacies and deficiencies. The data were drawn from interviews with journalists and people who had had direct contacts with the insurgents, analysis of the group's audio and video contents, the author's personal reflections, and library and online research. Twenty-two journalists who have covered the Boko Haram crisis for local and/or international media were interviewed – 13 of them face to face in the Nigerian cities of Yola, Maiduguri, and Abuja, and the rest on the telephone from London. Nineteen of the interviews were conducted between 11 August 2014 and 15 July 2015 specifically for this research. The rest had earlier been conducted (between June 2009 and January 2012) for another research project concerning Boko Haram, part of the primary data of which was relevant for this study. Three people who had had close contact with Boko Haram founder Muhammad Yusuf – two were his former students, while the third person had studied Islamic education with him – were also interviewed between 11 August 2014 and 6 April 2015. Two former friends of a suspected Boko Haram bomb-maker, Abdulrasheed Abubakar – who was arrested in 2009 (BBC 2009) – were separately interviewed in Yola in October 2009. Boko Haram's audio and video messages (seven of which they uploaded directly to YouTube and their Twitter account @*Al-Urwah al-Wuthqa*, while five were sent by them to journalists via emissaries) were also gathered and analysed. This chapter also draws from my own personal reflections on reporting about the group between July 2009 and January 2015, since I have covered the insurgency myself as a journalist working for both the BBC World Service and Nigeria's Media Trust, two of the media organisations that have given the crisis comprehensive coverage.

Boko Haram background

To understand Boko Haram's media strategies, it is essential to know the group itself. First, the name Boko Haram – meaning "Western education is prohibited" – is not the group's real name; its members actually detest it. They call themselves *Jama'atu Ahlus Sunna lid Da'awatu wal-Jihad* (approximately, "Movement for the Propagation and Enthronement of Righteous Deeds"). Boko Haram is an extremist Islamic sect that claims to be rooted in Salafism (Meijer 2009). Founded by Muhammad Yusuf in north-eastern Nigeria around 2002 (Herskovits 2012), it began as a peaceful movement before liaisons with politicians and encounters with security operatives turned it into a violent outfit blamed for the most dreadful attacks in the country (Abubakar 2012; Amnesty International 2015). It became a full-fledged insurgent group after the killing of its founder by the police in July 2009 following an uprising in which more than 800 people, mostly its members, were killed (Smith 2015). The remaining members went underground and resurfaced a year later under a new leader, Abubakar Shekau, with deadly attacks including bombing of schools, churches, mosques, and markets as well as kidnapping for ransoms – and for sexual enslavement. They also engaged in bank robberies, cattle rustling, and plundering of towns and villages to raise funds for their campaigns in Nigeria and in neighbouring Niger, Chad, and Cameroon. Although it was their abduction of 276 schoolgirls from Chibok in Borno State in April 2014 that gave them global notoriety, they have committed far worse crimes, such as individual beheadings and mass executions (Amnesty International 2015). They also seized swathes of territory in north-eastern Nigeria, which they declared as their caliphate. By January 2015 they were controlling a territory the size of Belgium, on which they imposed their own version of Islamic law, beheading suspected spies and stoning to death those they convicted of adultery (Amnesty International 2015). But a multinational force comprising Chadian, Nigerien, and Cameroonian troops along with the Nigerian military fought back and retook the territory. By September 2015 the insurgency has claimed an estimated 20,000 lives and displaced over two million people. Researchers have linked the emergence of Boko Haram – variously – to Nigeria's endemic corruption, youth unemployment, chronic poverty, poor governance, incompetent security services, the rise of jihadi ideology in response to the West's war on terror, British colonial legacy, and a lack of proper education (Abubakar 2012; Herskovits 2012; Smith 2015). With an estimated force of 15,000 fighters (Amnesty International 2015), Boko Haram derived its power through the use of brutal force, but it also craved soft power. So, although it did not spare journalists and media houses in its brutal attacks (Abubakar 2012; Smith 2015), it relentlessly sought their attention using diverse means.

Media strategies

Seeking publicity has always been on Boko Haram's priority list. So significant is propaganda to the group that it is, in fact, an integral part of its original name. *Da'awatu* – Arabic for propagation – is a key component of *Jama'atu Ahlus Sunna lid **Da'awatu** wal-Jihad*; and as such enormous resources were devoted to it. Long before gaining strength, Boko Haram had established its "Public Awareness Department", which handled matters ranging from propaganda to recruitment of members. Interviews with those close to its founder and journalists revealed that the group had established this department before the commencement of its insurgency. It also had an official spokesman variously known as Abul Qaqa or Abu Darda or Abu Zaid – all are pseudonyms and at times they all called themselves Abul Qaqa (Idris 2012) – who ran the media arm. The spokesman was a senior member of the group's *Shura* (Supreme Council) and was very close to its leader (Idris 2012).

Cassette radicalisation

Boko Haram's mediated engagement with the public began with the use of what Mohammadi and Sreberny-Mohammadi (1994) call "small media": audio cassettes and leaflets. Specifically, they started with the recording and selling of their leaders' sermons in audio cassettes – reminiscent of the way Ayatollah Khomeini's cassettes were used to mobilise Iranians for the 1979 revolution against the Shah (Mohammadi & Sreberny-Mohammadi 1994). In Boko Haram's case the sermons and speeches of its founder Muhammad Yusuf – and sometimes those of his deputies, Shekau and Muhammad Nur, the suspected mastermind of the August 2011 UN building bombing in Nigeria's capital Abuja (Smith 2015) – would be recorded in audio cassettes and sold in street corners mainly to their followers but also to the general public, as their sermons were popular due to their condemnation of alleged corrupt practices and injustice in Nigeria. As Smith (2015) notes, Yusuf was a charismatic leader and talented orator whose sermons many people, including non-Muslims, could easily relate to. The role of the small media in the daily lives of Nigerians has been well documented by Larkin (2008), who argues that they were deeply entrenched into the country's cultural, political, and economic landscapes. Boko Haram utilised them effectively. "They started with audio cassettes in the early 2000s before moving to CDs when CDs became more popular," recalled Ahmed Mari, a reporter of the Lagos-based *Champion* newspaper, who has covered the group for over seven years. Some of the sermons have since been digitalised and uploaded on YouTube (Yusuf 2011).

Mainstream media relations

As his sermons brought him into the public arena, the Boko Haram founder began to attract the attention of the mainstream media. Soon, his speeches, often made at Muslim youth conferences, were being aired at the local broadcast stations in Borno State. They were, however, stopped when his criticisms of the government became unbearable to the authorities, according to journalists and people close to him. And when his group attracted strong scrutiny from security agencies, especially in the middle of 2009, a dispute between them ensued, drawing journalists' attention. It was then that the group began to hold news briefings at its headquarters in Maiduguri. Journalists who attended those briefings said the group's founder would first complain about alleged harassment of his followers by security operatives and then denounce Western culture and express his desire to turn Nigeria into a Salafist state. Yusuf also granted many interviews to journalists around that period. In one of them, he told a BBC stringer that Western education "spoils the belief in one God" (Boyle 2009). Bilkisu Babangida, a BBC Hausa Service reporter who had done interviews with him and some of his lieutenants, said Yusuf would talk calmly but firmly emphasising his points.

Boko Haram's most open interactions with journalists happened from mid-June 2009 to the end of July 2009, when its members were in violent confrontations with the police and the army. At that time Yusuf spoke frequently with journalists threatening retaliations over the killings of his followers (Smith 2015). When the clashes culminated in the July 2009 uprising leading to the death of over 800 people including Yusuf himself and his father-in-law Baba Fugu Mohammed – both of whom were killed in police custody (Abubakar 2012; Smith 2015) – the group went underground, ending its open relationship with the mainstream media.

Guerrilla media strategy

Going underground did not quench Boko Haram's thirst for publicity, but its members knew that it would be fatal to approach journalists openly, and so they devised a guerrilla media relations strategy. This consisted of using anonymous mobile phone lines to deliver messages to journalists, emailing materials to media houses using fake addresses, and organising teleconferences from secret locations. The first sign that they had resorted to using this strategy emerged shortly after Yusuf's death. A video recording of his interrogation by the army after his arrest was emailed to some journalists and media houses. This was followed by a video of his corpse after his killing by the police. It was unclear who exactly sent the videos because while some journalists said it originated from a policeman and was shared by a journalist, others said it was shared by Boko Haram members. "It is hard to know who the original senders were, but they had all the trappings of Boko Haram," one of the journalists who received them but preferred to remain anonymous said. A few weeks later a video of the execution of many Boko Haram members by the police in Maiduguri was also being circulated. It later found its way to Al Jazeera, which aired it in February 2010 (Al Jazeera 2010). For several months after that nothing was heard from Boko Haram, until some audio and video clips of Yusuf's successor Shekau, who was thought to have been killed in the July 2009 uprising, began to circulate. And by the end of December 2010 another video, this time showing Shekau claiming responsibility for a bomb attack in the north-central city of Jos on that year's Christmas Eve, was also circulating (Smith 2015), removing any doubt about Boko Haram's return and their guerrilla media strategy.

The group then added a teleconferencing technique using mobile phones. In this, its spokesman – Abul Qaqa or Abu Zaid or Abu Darda (all pseudonyms) – would call journalists from an undisclosed location with a concealed phone number, urge them to gather in one place, and hold a mobile phone news conference. Journalists who attended these conferences in Maiduguri revealed that they would gather and listen to his briefing, ask him questions, and write their reports based on the veracity of his claims. Hamza Idris, the Maiduguri Bureau Chief of the Abuja-based *Daily Trust* newspaper who had attended many of them, said: "In most cases, there would be few of us, correspondents of national newspapers and stringers for international media organisations, but our colleagues who weren't there would also pick the stories from us." These teleconferences often took place when the group wanted to claim responsibility for certain attacks or issue warnings against the government. The technique worked well for several months until the Nigerian secret police tracked down and killed one of the spokesmen in Kano and arrested another in Kaduna in February 2012 (Idris 2012).

Direct dropping strategy

When the teleconferencing technique died with the disappearance of the spokesmen, Boko Haram leaders devised other means of reaching the media. They focused on producing audio and video messages, which they would then distribute discreetly to journalists. They would also produce leaflets and drop them in places where journalists and other people would see. The leaflets would often contain warnings to the public against supporting the government's anti-insurgency campaign. Alternatively, they would seek public support for the group, or claim responsibility for carrying out attacks, or justify them. Many journalists interviewed said the insurgents also dropped their leaflets in the areas they raided. One of such incidents happened when the group raided Gombe city on 14 February 2015, the day Nigeria's presidential election was originally scheduled to be held before it was delayed by six weeks due to the insurgency. They dropped their leaflets, warning people against participating in the election (Vanguard 2015).

However, it was their distribution of videos to journalists that became their most potent propaganda tool. They would produce videos – containing speeches of their leader, showcasing their "successes" (often seizing of towns and weapons), and displaying their brand of punishments including beheadings and mass executions – and give them to journalists via emissaries. Journalists who had received those videos disclosed that the insurgents were initially sending them on CDs but later advanced to memory sticks. It was through this method that the video of the abducted schoolgirls reached the global media (Sahara Reporters 2014; Smith 2015). Of course, it was the act of the abduction itself that primarily provided the story and the accompanying publicity – partly enhanced by the Bring Back Our Girls campaign (Smith 2015) – but it was the release of the video that took them to new levels. Indeed, even the kidnapping itself and the group's other acts of savagery were all part of its overall publicity-seeking strategy. As Lynch (2006: 50) aptly observes in the case of "Al-Qaeda the organization" becoming "indistinguishable from Al-Qaeda the media phenomenon", Boko Haram the organisation could hardly be distinguished from Boko Haram the media phenomenon.

Despite the efficacy of the videos-dropping technique, however, it too was disrupted by security agents who also reportedly arrested "a team of cameramen believed to be handling media matters for Boko Haram" (Soriwei 2014). But they have not destroyed the group's media relations skills.

The online drive

Blocked from delivering their videos to the mainstream media, the insurgents, like Al Shabaab in East Africa (Greenwood 2013), turned to the online media for their propaganda. They would now upload their messages directly on YouTube (AFP 2015). They also launched an Arabic-language Twitter account, *@Al-Urwah al-Wuthqa*, on 18 January 2015 and began to upload their messages on it (BBC Monitoring 2015). The account was promptly promoted by "media operatives" linked to the so-called Islamic State, fuelling speculation of collaboration between the two groups (BBC Monitoring 2015). This was reinforced in March 2015 when Boko Haram pledged allegiance to the Islamic State group (Callimachi 2015) and later renamed itself *Wilaayat Gharb Ifriqiyyah* – (Islamic State's) West Africa Province (ISWAP). A significant change in both the content and form of the Boko Haram propaganda was also conspicuous. The grainy "amateurish footage" the group used to produce gave way to slick and expertly produced content featuring "music, graphics and slow motion shots" (AFP 2015).

Significantly, Boko Haram's newfound ability to bypass the mainstream media did not steer them away from journalists. They kept contacting journalists and directing them to their contents whenever they uploaded them. "They still alert us to where their new releases are," said AFP Northern Nigerian correspondent Aminu Abubakar, who regularly received their tapes. "It is much safer for us now. The original system of direct delivery was very dangerous. You never know who will harm you first: Boko Haram or security personnel." But the group's online drive too was not without trouble. Its Twitter account was suspended many times and YouTube regularly removed its videos (AFP 2015; BBC Monitoring 2015). In most cases, however, before the account would be suspended or the videos removed, the uploaded content would be picked up by journalists and the message would reach the public – if deemed newsworthy.

Conclusion

From being an obscure Salafi sect stuck in north-eastern Nigeria to becoming a media phenomenon hitting international headlines, Boko Haram has undergone quite a rapid transformation within a few years. Its media relations skills – rudimentary though some of them were – may have played a part here, but in reality most of this was as much the result of the group's unfettered barbarity as it was the consequence of the changes taking place in our complex media environment. The advancement of communication technology, the Western media's obsession with jihadi-related stories, and the fluid nature of the Nigerian media landscape did unwittingly aid Boko Haram's publicity drive. On many occasions it was the militants – not the media or the Nigerian authorities – who seemed to be dictating the news agenda of many media outlets. They were achieving this not necessarily by skilful manipulation of the media, but mainly by the depths of their depravity.

The global media's passion for covering dramatic events partly facilitated this. As Maloba (1992: 60) has argued, the "media in the West looks at Africa as an area of peripheral interest and only reports those stories that are dramatic and graphic." And so a combination of Boko Haram's media strategies and international media's approach to African news coverage has helped produce an image of Nigeria as a nation ravaged by jihadists' barbarism. Stories such as those of the schoolgirls' abductions and of teenage girls being used as suicide bombers, seemed to dominate the coverage – with Boko Haram's jihadi tag giving the stories a stronger appeal to sell to global audiences. The focus was on the series of atrocities being committed by the militants but not on the context in which they were able to do so. Nigeria's complex historical and socio-economic milieus that bred and sustained the insurgency were often ignored. The local media didn't fare better, as colonial legacy, lack of capacity (both human and material), and imitation mentality led them sometimes to regurgitate the content of the international media.

However, to be fair to both the local and international media, although historically jihadi insurgency is not a new phenomenon in West Africa, this one seemed to have caught them unawares. Worse still, it was being carried out by a group that combined dynamism with unscrupulousness. Boko Haram insurgents demonstrated exceptional abilities to adapt to changing scenarios and to adopt techniques suitable to them – albeit for a warped ideological intent. The speed with which they graduated from producing crude audio cassettes to manning Twitter accounts loaded with slick videos (even if with outside help), the extent to which they maintained relationships with the media, and the manner with which they surmounted various obstacles to reach the wider public have indicated the level of their capabilities. Studying them has not only provided some insights into the inner workings of the group itself and offered opportunities for designing preventative measures, but it has also enhanced our understanding of the media's relationship with an African jihadi insurgency.

References

Abubakar, A. (2012) "The media, politics and *Boko* blitz", *Journal of African Media Studies*, 4(1): 97–110.

AFP (2015) "Boko Haram: changing media strategy for a wider conflict?", *Daily Mail*, 20 February, at http://www.dailymail.co.uk/wires/afp/article-2961665/Boko-Haram-changing-media-strategy-wider-conflict.html [accessed 21/02/2015].

Al Jazeera (2010) *Nigeria killings caught on video*, at http://english.aljazeera.net/news/africa/2010/02/20102102505798741.html [accessed 12/02/2010].

Amnesty International (2015) *"Our job is to shoot, slaughter and kill": Boko Haram's reign of terror in north-east Nigeria*, AFR44/1360/2015, London: Amnesty International.

Arterton, F. (1984) *Media Politics: The News Strategies of Presidential Campaigns*, Lexington, MA: Lexington Books.

Bamisaiye, A. (1974) "The Nigerian civil war in the international press", *Transition*, 44: 30–35, at http://www.jstor.org/pss/2935103 [accessed 18/06/2010].

BBC (2009) "Nigerian 'trained in Afghanistan'", at http://news.bbc.co.uk/1/hi/world/africa/8233980.stm [accessed 03/09/2009].

BBC (2014) "Nigeria kidnapped girls 'shown in Boko Haram video'", at http://www.bbc.co.uk/news/world-africa-27373287 [accessed 12/05/2014].

BBC Monitoring (2015) "Is Islamic State shaping Boko Haram media?", at http://www.bbc.co.uk/news/world-africa-31522469 [accessed 07/03/2015].

Boyle, J. (2009) "Nigeria's 'Taliban' enigma", at http://news.bbc.co.uk/1/hi/world/africa/8172270.stm [accessed 12/08/2009].

Callimachi, R. (2015) "Boko Haram generates uncertainty with pledge of allegiance to Islamic State", *The New York Times*, 7 March, at http://www.nytimes.com/2015/03/08/world/africa/boko-haram-is-said-to-pledge-allegiance-to-islamic-state.html?smid=nytcore-iphone-share&smprod=nytcore-iphone&_r=0 [accessed 08/03/2015].

Farwell, J. (2014) "The media strategy of ISIS", *Survival: Global Politics and Strategy*, 56(6): 49–55.

Greenwood, C. (2013) "The Twitter terrorists: how killers boasted of Kenyan mall carnage with live commentary as they murdered dozens of people", *Daily Mail*, 23 September, at http://www.dailymail.co.uk/news/article-2429660/Kenya-attack-How-killers-boasted-Nairobi-Westgate-shopping-mall-carnage-Twitter.html [accessed 24/09/2013].

Herskovits, J. (2012) "In Nigeria, Boko Haram is not the problem", *The New York Times*, 2 January, at http://www.nytimes.com/2012/01/02/opinion/in-nigeria-boko-haram-is-not-the-problem.html?_r=1&ref=global [accessed 03/01/2012].

Ibelema, M. (1992) "The tribes and prejudice: coverage of the Nigerian civil war", in B. Hawk (ed.), *Africa's Media Image*, New York: Praeger.

Idris, H. (2012) "Boko Haram spox Abul Qaqa captured", *Daily Trust*, 2 February, at http://www.dailytrust.com.ng/index.php?option=com_content&view=article&id=153791:boko-haram-spox-abul-qaqa-captured&catid=2:lead-stories&Itemid=8 [accessed 02/02/2012].

Jensen, R. (2011) "British military media strategies in modern wars", *Global Media and Communication*, 7(3): 193–197.

Jorre, J. (1972) *The Brothers' War: Biafra and Nigeria*, Boston, MA: Houghton Mifflin.

Larkin, B. (2008) *Signal and Noise: Media, Infrastructure, and Urban Culture in Nigeria*, Durham, NC: Duke University Press.

Lynch, M. (2006) "Al-Qaeda's media strategies", *National Interest*, 83: 50–56.

Maloba, W. (1992) "The media and Mau Mau: Kenyan nationalism and colonial propaganda", in B. Hawk (ed.), *Africa's Media Image*, New York: Praeger.

Meijer, R. (ed.) (2009) *Global Salafism: Islam's New Religious Movement*, New York: Columbia University Press.

Merry, M. (2012) "Environmental groups' communication strategies in multiple media", *Environmental Politics*, 21(1): 49–69.

Mohammadi, A. & Sreberny-Mohammadi, A. (1994) *Small Media, Big Revolution: Communication, Culture and the Iranian Revolution*, Minneapolis, MN: University of Minnesota Press.

Sahara Reporters (2014) *Boko Haram video showing kidnapped school girls*, at http://saharareporters.com/videos/full-video-boko-haram-video-showing-kidnapped-school-girls [accessed 25/05/2014].

Sahara TV (2014) *Boko Haram leader Shekau releases video on abduction of Chibok girls*, at https://www.youtube.com/watch?v=wrfWS_vL0D4 [accessed 06/05/2014].

Shpiro, S. (2001) "The media strategies of intelligence services", *International Journal of Intelligence and Counterintelligence*, 14(4): 485–502.

Smith, M. (2015) *Boko Haram: Inside Nigeria's Unholy War*, London: I.B. Tauris.

Soriwei, F. (2014) "Military arrests Boko Haram media aides in Adamawa", *Punch*, 8 December, at http://www.punchng.com/news/military-arrests-boko-haram-media-aide-in-adamawa/ [accessed 09/12/2014].

Vanguard (2015) "Hundreds of Boko Haram Islamists invade Gombe", *Vanguard*, 14 February, at http://www.vanguardngr.com/2015/02/hundreds-boko-haram-islamists-invade-restive-city-gombe/ [accessed 15/02/2015].

Waters, K. (2004) "Influencing the message: the role of Catholic missionaries in media coverage of the Nigerian civil war", *The Catholic Historical Review*, 90(4): 697–718.

Yusuf, M. (2011) *Tafsirin Tuba* [The interpretation of Qur'anic verses on confession], at https://www.youtube.com/watch?v=R3NcgQv-LVM [accessed 20/07/2011].

Chapter 26

Perceptions of Chinese media's Africa coverage[1]

James Wan

From huge infrastructure projects to ubiquitous cheap goods, evidence of China's presence across Africa today is unavoidable. But over the past few years, there is one area in which China's deepening footprint on the continent has been particularly notable – turn on the radio, switch on the TV, or check out the newsstands, and China's expansion into Africa's media is clear to see.

Chinese journalists have been present in Africa for a long time, but as the China–Africa relationship has flourished, there has been a concerted effort from Beijing to build its media agencies in Africa and around the world so they can compete with the likes of the BBC, CNN, and Al Jazeera. As certain international media houses have been cutting back on foreign reporting budgets, Beijing in 2009 allocated a whopping $7 billion to increasing China's state-owned media presence around the world.

In Africa, audience numbers are reportedly struggling, but the scale of China's media expansion in terms of its presence has been remarkable. On television today, CCTV Africa's host of programmes provides up-to-date coverage on a wide range of issues; stories from Xinhua feature frequently in national newspapers across the continent; *China Daily Africa* rolls off the press once per week; and China Radio International confidently rides the African airwaves.

As many of these strides were first being made, some on the continent and beyond raised concerns about what they saw as the rise of Chinese "propaganda". Beijing was explicit about its desire to create a more positive view of China in Africa, and the fear was that Chinese media would only churn out uncritical stories about China with its reporters prohibited from covering controversial issues.

However, Chinese media journalists on the continent – the vast majority of whom are African – tend to deny this has been the case the past few years.

"I can guarantee you that we have been 100 per cent in control of our own editorial content," says Beatrice Marshall, the anchor of Talk Africa, CCTV Africa's flagship news analysis show. "Are there any red lines? Up until this point, absolutely not."

Media experts who have conducted content analyses of Chinese media since their expansion on the continent concur that these news organisations have covered several contentious issues and offered critical views – up to a point.

"If you look at Chinese news agencies in the early 1990s, there was no room at all for criticism of certain African leaders," says Bob Wekesa, a research associate at the University of the Witwatersrand, South Africa, and specialist on Chinese media. "Nowadays, they increasingly don't shy away from this, though they might not go the whole hog. China still operates under a communist system in which criticism is not really appreciated and there are still no-go zones."

Wekesa's study of Talk Africa, for instance, found that the show has not avoided controversial stories such as mining strikes in South Africa, political turmoil in Egypt, and conflict in South Sudan. However, his analysis also suggested that the activities of Chinese and African governments in attempting to address problems are almost always framed in a positive light.

Part of this may be down to the Chinese media's stated goal of improving perceptions of China and the continent, an objective perhaps facilitated by African journalists who, if not directly influenced by Beijing, are required to self-censor their stories to an extent.

However, according to some theorists, while there may be instances of direct control from China in some instances, this explanation as a whole could be overly reductive – the usual criticism of Chinese state-owned media being little more than propaganda may be missing an important point. Rather than simply being constrained, they suggest, Chinese media may also have a different philosophy of journalism to begin with.

"There are a lot of superficial opinions of Chinese media in the West in the same way that there are many superficial opinions of Western media in China, but the reality is more complex," says Zhang Yanqiu, director of the Africa Communication Research Centre at the Communication University of China. According to her, the Western media typically adopt a kind of "watchdog" role, while Chinese media come closer to what she calls "constructive journalism".

"Constructive journalism can be both positive and negative, but the purpose is to find solutions," explains Zhang. "The idea is to give a new kind of balance and shine a new kind of light on the continent. Instead of just reporting on the situation, it asks, 'How can we help them?' The Western media may be telling the truth, but if you are telling the truth and things are just getting worse and people are afraid of travelling to Africa, for whose good is this?"

Constructive journalism therefore purports to be more "solutions based", something that Marshall claims is at the heart of CCTV Africa's ethos.

"When you look at Western media, a lot of the time their strategy is to be combative," she says. "But what we want to do is say, 'This is the issue, this is the challenge, and this is how it's being solved' rather than getting people to argue."

It is for this reason, she says, that CCTV Africa focuses on a wide range of developmental issues and why in its coverage of the run-up to the 2015 Nigerian elections, for instance, it focused on security measures put in place to help people vote rather than the security *threats* that might prevent them from voting. "It may be the same story, but the difference in framing is important," she says.

Observers disagree over the extent to which this approach is a genuine reflection of a different media philosophy and to what extent it is merely the result of interference from Beijing. But in terms of audiences in Africa, researchers have typically found that most viewers tend to shy away from, and remain sceptical of, Chinese state-owned media.

Additionally, while broadly sympathetic to the Chinese approach, Wekesa points out that, "The people who seem to appreciate the positive or constructive journalism of Chinese media most are those who are in power and certain elites with close business interests with the Chinese."

However, while Chinese media struggles to present itself as credible, its presence may already be changing Africa's media landscape for the better, albeit not necessarily in ways Beijing intended.

"Both Western and Chinese media are problematic for different reasons, but there is also a lot that each can, and is, learning from the other," says Wekesa. "For me, the ideal would be a mix of the more adversarial Western approach with the more constructive Chinese approach, and I think there is evidence of them being influenced by one another already.

"Ultimately, this can only be good for Africa and for Africa's media."

Note

1   The quotes that appear in this article are the result of interviews conducted by the author in 2015.

Chapter 27

New imperialisms, old stereotypes

Chris Paterson

A theme of this book is the extent to which Africa's external representation corresponds to the realities of a fast-changing continent. It has often proven the case that media portrayals seem unable to keep pace with real changes that signal a break from old colonial ties and mindsets, but in this chapter I'll suggest that an imperial grip on Africa has altered shape, but not disappeared, and that it is supported rather than challenged in media reporting. By focusing here on competing US military and Chinese commercial imperialisms that have come to exert unprecedented power across Africa, this chapter assesses the shift from a Cold War-driven news agenda concerning Africa's relations with global superpowers to a post-Cold War agenda that camouflages a no less imperialistic and exploitative modernity. The second half of this chapter assesses how these dual imperial processes, together potentially as exploitative and asymmetrical as the relations between centre and periphery that shaped modern Africa, are represented by three global media organisations: CNN, the BBC, and Al Jazeera English.

In the two decades since this author wrote in the original *Africa's Media Image*, proxy wars in Mozambique and Angola (where 7 per cent of the Angolan population was killed in the US-backed post-colonial civil war, Easterly 2006: 288) were exchanged for a fragile stability marked by tremendous wealth for the privileged few and little material improvement for the rest (Burgis 2015). These Lusophone countries epitomise the consequences of new imperialisms that transpire continent wide with rare critique from global media, cynically fuelling an "Africa Rising" narrative suggesting increasing African autonomy while obscuring processes of neo-imperialism that have mostly seen concessions of African political and financial sovereignty. As economic "reform" made Mozambique a favourite of Western governments through the structural violence of neo-liberal policies (Jones 2005), oil endeared Angola to Chinese and Western oil companies (French 2014).

This chapter explores the extent to which these contemporary imperialisms driven by the US and China are made visible by global media.

The reporting on these forms of neo-imperial expansion contributes to both Afro-pessimist and Afro-optimist discourses, but in each case positions Africa as an exploitable object lacking an ability to develop and thrive independently of external powers – thereby reinforcing enduring stereotypes.

Western commercial expansion and the neo-liberal structural adjustment regimes that enable it have been widely celebrated and condemned (e.g. Easterly 2006), just as fast-paced Chinese state-backed expansion across Africa has been hailed and condemned in equal measure for its differences from those approaches. This research was inspired by an awareness of the lack of investigation into the global media image of Chinese and US expansion in Africa (despite increasing attention to Chinese *media expansion* in Africa, e.g. Banda 2009; Wasserman, Chapter 24 in this volume), in conjunction with the military turn in the West's approach to Africa, whereby a single imperial power has established a military presence across most of the continent for the first time in modern history and US-originating religious fundamentalism has been implicated in human rights concerns and in acting as a driver for that military expansion. The last decade of secretive US military expansion across Africa, with US forces active in nearly every African country, has been exposed by investigative journalists like Turse (2014, 2015a, 2015b) and Scahill (2013), but the present research finds that core international news organisations more commonly follow the familiar pattern of telling a story orchestrated by the US government.

Trends in reporting Africa

Limited investment by larger Western news organisations in Africa has long resulted in a dependence on international news agencies by most media, and for most coverage (Bunce, Chapter 1 in this volume; Paterson 2011). A news agency focus on both conflict and on the movement of capital has contributed to replicating what Hawk (1992) called "the primitive archetype", the image of an Africa both available for exploitation and dependent on the benevolence of Northern countries. In the post-9/11 period, which is the focus of this chapter, the largest television news agency (Associated Press Television News) halved the amount it spent on Africa to shift resources to parts of the world it considered more interesting to the largest global broadcasters (Paterson 2011: 37–41).

Television news agency managers have been consistent in stating, over the decades, that their top-paying clients don't demand broad and consistent coverage of Africa (Paterson 2011). Studies of US television coverage of Africa during the 1980s found that information sources were mostly non-African and tended to reinforce both images of Africa as a powerless victim dependent upon aid, and images of US power and goodwill (Paterson 1992). In her study of how US media construct the topic of hunger in Africa, Kogen found the issue framed "as irrelevant to the public sphere, [with] the victim as removed from political action, and the reader as politically impotent" (2015: 3). But Kogen also observed (in an echo of Bennett 1990) that when the US Congress expresses interest in a story, overall news coverage increases and news stories that propose solutions are more likely.

However, Africa is now covered for the world both by an international press corps more attuned to critiques of Afro-pessimist reporting (see Parts I and II of this book), and by powerful global news organisations that claim to challenge what is widely perceived as stereotype-laden Western coverage and limited news frames. Xin explains how the world's largest news agency, and voice of the Chinese government, Xinhua, is deeply embedded in Africa, with over twenty bureaus in place by 2009. But Xin notes that, while Xinhua has an influence on the news coverage of local media outlets in Africa (largely through the provision of free or cheap content), its editorial agenda, like that of most global media, is still significantly shaped by the leading Western news agencies (Xin 2009; also see Marsh, Wan, and Wasserman, in this volume). The other significant new global player in international coverage of Africa is Al Jazeera, to which we turn shortly, after examining the characteristics of the new imperialisms this chapter addresses.

New imperialisms

Chinese neo-imperialism in Africa is well described, if not by media reporting, at least by recent books like those of French (2014) and Burgis (2015), so in this section I focus on the less well documented characteristics of US neo-imperial expansion in Africa. Since the onset of the US "war on terror", analysts have been warning of a militarisation of Africa stemming from a struggle for resources and influence. Klare and Volman peg the start of that programme of militarisation to April 2002, when the former US ambassador to Chad told the US Congress, "It's been reliably reported that, for the first time, the two concepts – 'Africa' and 'US national security' – have been used in the same sentence in Pentagon documents" (2006: 298). US military interest in Africa is rooted in the Cold War, but was then conducted by proxy and supported by friendly media coverage in the US (Windrich 1992).

Through the period of its build-up in Africa since the mid-2000s, the US military has taken precautions to avoid the appearance of a permanent presence in all but a few countries, while developing operational capabilities in most of them (Turse 2014); this comes in the context of research suggesting the US operates 700 to 800 military bases in over sixty countries (Dufour 2013; Vine 2015), and, by their own admission, conducted military operations in 135 countries in 2015 (Turse 2015a). Bilmes and Intriligator (2013) argued that the United States is – unsustainably – fighting five simultaneous wars, including one in Somalia (in addition to Iraq,

Afghanistan, Pakistan, and Yemen). Turse found that one US Army division "carried out 128 separate 'activities' in 28 African countries" in 2013, and in that same year reported that his analysis of official documents and open source information revealed "that the U.S. military was involved with at least 49 of the 54 nations on the African continent during 2012 and 2013 in activities that ranged from special ops raids to the training of proxy forces" (Turse 2014); the collaboration extends to militaries in Africa that have been accused by international human rights organisations and the US government of human rights violations, and, in the case of Mali, the overthrow of the elected president (Turse 2015b; Whitlock 2012). This has been accompanied by a massive expansion of US arms sales to African countries; some of these are sold by the US government directly, or through providing credit, while other arms are bought directly from US manufacturers with State Department oversight. Countries that spent vast sums on US arms through these programmes in the mid-2000s were Djibouti, Kenya, Botswana, Eritrea, Ethiopia, Nigeria, Uganda, Angola, Nigeria, Senegal, and South Africa (Klare & Volman 2006: 299).

In *The New Scramble for Africa*, Carmody concluded that "US interests in Africa will continue to be dictated by the twin and interlinked concerns of oil and security and the continent will also play an increasingly important role in the global struggle for political influence between the United States and China" (2011: 65). Klare and Volman similarly warned that, though small in relation to military activity in other parts of the world, US and Chinese rivalry over resources in Africa "encourage[s] African regimes to continue to rely on oil-based development, rather than pursuing broader economic development strategies that promote local manufacturing and agriculture", adding, "the possession of oil by countries in Africa and other parts of the developing world nearly always leads to political repression, corruption, and violence" (Klare & Volman 2006: 306–307).

Another form of US expansionism that has swept across Africa over the past decade is evangelical Christianity. Like US military expansionism, it is well funded and has been implicated as a threat to human rights, but it also, similarly, has met with little external media critique, despite the presence, as noted by van Klinken, of "an emerging narrative of American conservative evangelicals and other right-wing Christian groups exporting the 'culture wars' on homosexuality, which they are losing at home, to Africa, using their money to promote homophobia and anti-homosexual legislation" (van Klinken 2016: 494). Analyses link US evangelicals with lobbying for anti-gay laws, such as the draconian anti-gay law passed in Uganda in 2014 (Kaoma 2014; Walker 2014), and one US social justice think tank wrote that these groups "frame their agendas as authentically African, in an effort to brand human rights advocacy as a new colonialism bent on destroying cultural traditions and values" (Smith 2012). De Witte (2011: 190) observed that in Ghana, following the sweeping deregulation of the media in the 1990s, "churches, and Charismatic–Pentecostal ones in particular, have now jumped into the new media spaces, opened up by the liberalization, to exploit their religious, commercial and political possibilities to the fullest and capture new religious audiences," adding that, around Africa, "media liberalization has enabled new, public manifestations of religion as religious groups assert a powerful and transformative presence in new public spheres" (de Witte 2011: 191).

De Witte (2011) wrote that the US-based evangelical television networks Christian Broadcasting Network (CBN), Trinity Broadcasting Network (TBN), and the Catholic Eternal World Television Network (EWTN) have established programme supply agreements with new commercial broadcasters in Ghana and around Africa. As *Review of African Political Economy* editor Roy Love commented (2006: 619), "The Cold War has been replaced by a new global confrontation whose proponents couch their ideological stances in religious and indeed 'fundamentalist' terms." US involvement in Sudan was largely driven by US religious groups pressuring policymakers (Huliaras 2008), and similarly, the viral Kony2012 video, while rife with stereotypes and misinformation, was a tremendously effective lobbying campaign and cover for further US military expansion in central Africa (Paterson & Nothias 2016). But van Klinken also cautions that, "exportation of American culture wars to Africa has been criticized as a too American-centered perspective on African socio-political dynamics" and that other international and local forces at play, as well as the agency of Africans, can be negated by such a focus (2016; also see Jacobs, Chapter 23 in this volume).

The view from global online news

Research by this author with Nothias[1] set out to systematically identify and critically analyse instances when three leading global news organisations made reference to these "new imperialisms" in their online output, while determining the extent and nature of those references. The three news organisations were Al Jazeera English (AJE), the BBC, and CNN. These were chosen due to the longstanding hegemonic position in global news provision of the BBC and CNN, along with their important agenda-setting role (Xie & Boyd-Barrett 2015). AJE is the dominant example of a news organisation promoting alternative narratives to those of these established providers, and it is the only such global news organisation with a popular online international news provision, extensive global newsgathering apparatus of its own, and global reach. As with the Venezuela-based TeleSur, AJE has demonstrated audience demand for challenges to traditional US/Europe-dominated news frames. The timeframe for this study was the start of 2011, when the creation of South Sudan and the Libyan civil war marked milestones in the US and Chinese expansions we focused on, to September 2014, providing the most recent data available at the time of the analysis.

We do not assert that the news coverage of these outlets is representative of all media coverage or, indeed, of the limits of global debate on these issues, but we hoped to demonstrate trends in this coverage that could suggest avenues for exploration of a broader range of media.

We found that China's economic expansion across Africa was given less prominence overall than the US military expansion, and that US religious expansion across Africa was all but invisible. These media outlets gave ample coverage to AFRICOM, but also were generally eager partners in constructing a public image of AFRICOM to be "one of humanitarian missions and benign-sounding support for local partners" (Turse 2014).

As research over many years has found, external news coverage of Africa is mostly coverage of a small portion of African countries (Paterson 1992), while most are all but ignored (a problem replicated in *research about news coverage,* as Scott observes in this volume). In the case of US military expansionism, coverage was limited to a small number of countries, and there was almost no coverage indicating the continental nature of the US military project. However, coverage by the three media organisations we examined that addressed China mostly referred to Africa in its totality, emphasising a continent-wide role for China (while still drawing from examples in fairly few countries, and nearly ignoring countries with the most significant Chinese financial presence, like Angola, or human presence, like Zambia). Through a negative tone, conflation of activities, and implicit distrust of Chinese intentions, the coverage we examined is at risk of contributing to a denigration of China and feeding, as Mawdsley (2008) identified in an examination of UK newspaper representations of the Chinese presence in Africa, a "yellow peril" discourse.

The United States was, by contrast, almost entirely portrayed as a benevolent provider of humanitarian interventions and small-scale military support to capture war criminals and fight terrorists. Few stories reviewed for this study presented US military involvement in Africa as anything other than legitimate and benign, reinforcing Easterly's lament of an efficient postmodern imperialism that uses the cover of militarised humanitarianism to pretend that armies exist for purposes other than enforcing the will of one state on another (Easterly 2006). Across the three media outlets, we found the US generally portrayed as a positive force for change in Africa, while China received less coverage overall (despite now being Africa's largest trade partner: *Economist* 2013) and was most often portrayed as predatory and caring only for its economic interests.

The two forms of powerful and transformative transnational religious expansions taking place in Africa – the fundamentalist variants of the Abrahamic religions Christianity and Islam (as opposed to the religions in a general sense) – share characteristics in that both have been implicated in the persecution of minority groups, both are substantially dependent on foreign money and the localisation of a foreign ideological brand, and both depend heavily on media campaigns for their expansion (e.g., Love 2006; De Witte 2011; Abubakar, Chapter 25 in this volume), but this research found a near absence of coverage of Christian fundamentalism by the media examined (Smith 2014, is a recent exception, but falls outside our sample).

Conclusion

This chapter has argued that imperialism in Africa remains pertinent in the form of the largely under-the-radar expansionist exercises of China and the United States – the one mostly commercial though largely state financed (French 2014), the other supplementing the commercial with a poorly understood project of military and religious expansion. This research suggests that global media don't ignore US military activity in Africa, but they do fail to portray it as continental in nature, and as anything more than humanitarian and consisting of a wholly legitimate "anti-terrorism" and humanitarian role, confirming Cook's (2013) view of reporting of US African policy "filtering out the logic of plunder."

Chinese expansion is conversely portrayed in mostly negative terms: one superpower portrayed as morally legitimate, the other not. Critique of US imperialism was rare in the media analysed for this research, although Al Jazeera English did provide exhaustive critiques of US military expansion (for example, *The New Scramble for Africa* 2014), while always separating these generally well-evidenced commentaries from news content, which was broadly similar to that of the BBC and CNN; a large number of AJE mentions of AFRICOM were in commentaries.

This international news coverage of the most dramatic "new imperialisms" in Africa, as summarised here, offers little agency to Africans. The coverage by three leading international news services that was examined for this research suggested an ongoing external image of Africa as undifferentiated, threatening, eminently exploitable, and reliant on outsiders. Such coverage perpetuates colonial and Cold War discourses that have for so long shaped Africa's external image, while critiquing "imperialism" in entirely European and American terms.

Note

1 The study performed a critical framing analysis of 492 news articles. This full study is published as Paterson & Nothias 2016, where further detail of the methodology and findings are available.

References

Banda, F. (2009) "China in the African mediascape: a critical injection", *Journal of African Media Studies*, 1(3): 343–361.

Bennett, W. L. (1990) "Toward a theory of press–state relations in the United States", *Journal of Communication*, 40: 103–127.

Bilmes, L. & Intriligator, M. D. (2013) "How many wars is the US fighting today?", *Peace Economics, Peace Science and Public Policy*, 19(1): 8–16.

Burgis, T. (2015) *The Looting Machine: Warlords, Oligarchs, Corporations, Smugglers, and the Theft of Africa's Wealth*, New York: PublicAffairs.

Carmody, P. (2011) *The New Scramble for Africa*, Cambridge: Polity.

Cook, C. R. (2013) "Coverage of African conflicts in the American media: filtering out the logic of plunder", *African and Asian Studies*, 12(4): 373–390.

de Witte, M. (2011) "Business of the spirit: Ghanaian broadcast media and the commercial exploitation of Pentecostalism", *Journal of African Media Studies*, 3(2): 189–204.

Dufour, J. (2013) "The worldwide network of U.S. military bases", *Global Research*, 17 February.

Easterly, W. (2006) *The White Man's Burden: Why the West's Efforts to Aid the Rest Have Done So Much Ill and So Little Good*, New York: The Penguin Press.

Economist (2013) "Africa and China: more than minerals", 23 March.

French, H. (2014) *China's Second Continent: How a Million Migrants are Building a New Empire in Africa*, New York: Knopf.

Hawk, B. (1992) "Metaphors of African coverage", in B. Hawk (ed.), *Africa's Media Image*, New York: Praeger.

Huliaras, A. (2008) "The evangelical roots of US Africa policy", *Survival: Global Politics and Strategy*, 50(6): 161–182.

Jones, B. G. (2005) "Globalisations, violences, and resistances in Mozambique", in C. Eschle and B. Maiquashca (eds.), *Critical Theories, International Relations, and "the Anti-globalisation Movement": The Politics of Global Resistance*, London: Routledge.

Kaoma, K. (2014) *American Culture Warriors in Africa: A Guide to the Exporters of Homophobia and Sexism*, Somerville, MA: Political Research.

Klare, M. & Volman, D. (2006) "America, China & the scramble for Africa's oil", *Review of African Political Economy*, 33(108): 297–309.

Kogen, L. (2015) "Not up for debate: US news coverage of hunger in Africa", *International Communication Gazette*, 77(1): 3–23.

Love, R. (2006) "Religion, ideology & conflict in Africa", *Review of African Political Economy*, 33(110): 619–634.

Mawdsley, E. (2008) "Fu Manchu versus Dr Livingstone in the Dark Continent? Representing China, Africa and the West in British broadsheet newspapers", *Political Geography*, 27(5): 509–529.

Paterson, C. (2011) *The International Television News Agencies*, New York: Peter Lang.

Paterson, C. (1992) "Television news from the frontline states", in B. Hawk (ed.), *Africa's Media Image*, New York: Praeger.

Paterson, C. & Nothias, T. (2016) "China and the US in Africa in online global news", *Communication, Culture & Critique*, 9(1): 107–125.

Scahill, J. (2013) *Dirty Wars: The World is a Battlefield*, New York: Nation Books.

Smith, D. (2012) "US evangelical Christians accused of promoting homophobia in Africa", *The Guardian*, 24 July, at http://www.theguardian.com/world/2012/jul/24/evangelical-christians-homophobia-africa [accessed 08/11/2015].

Smith, D. (2014) "Why Africa is the most homophobic continent", *The Guardian*, 23 February, at http://www.theguardian.com/world/2014/feb/23/africa-homophobia-uganda-anti-gay-law [accessed 08/11/2015].

The New Scramble for Africa (2014) Al Jazeera, 7 July, at http://www.aljazeera. com/programmes/empire/newscrambleforafrica/2014/07/new-scramble-africa-2014723203324932466.html [accessed 08/11/2015].

Turse, N. (2014) "U.S. military averaging more than a mission a day in Africa", TomDispatch.com [accessed 10/02/2015].

Turse, N. (2015a) "American Special Operations forces have a very funny definition of success", *Nation*, 26 October, at http://www.thenation.com/article/american-special-operations-forces-have-a-very-funny-definition-of-success [accessed 08/11/2015].

Turse, N. (2015b) "The United States is training militaries with dubious human rights records—again", *Nation*, 10 September, at http://www.thenation.com/article/the-united-states-is-training-militaries-with-dubious-human-rights-records-again [accessed 08/11/2015].

van Klinken, A. (2016) "Christianity and same-sex relationships in Africa", in E. F. Bongmba (ed.), *The Routledge Companion to Christianity in Africa*, London: Routledge.

Vine, D. (2015) *Base Nation: How US Military Bases Abroad Harm America and the World*, New York: Metropolitan Books.

Walker, T. (2014) "How Uganda was seduced by anti-gay conservative evangelicals", *The Independent*, 14 March, at http://www.independent.co.uk/news/world/africa/how-uganda-was-seduced-by-anti-gay-conservative-evangelicals-9193593. html [accessed 08/11/2015].

Whitlock, C. (2012) "Leader of Mali military coup trained in U.S.", *Washington Post*, 24 March.

Windrich, E. (1992) "Savimbi's image in the U.S. media: a case study in propaganda", in B. Hawk (ed.), *Africa's Media Image*, New York: Praeger.

Xie, S. & Boyd-Barrett, O. (2015) "External–national TV news networks' way to America: is the United States losing the global 'information war'?", *International Journal of Communication*, 9(1), 66–83.

Xin, X. (2009) "Xinhua news agency in Africa", *Journal of African Media Studies*, 1(3): 363–377.

Chapter 28

Nollywood news

African screen media at the intersections of the global and the local

Noah Tsika

In the Summer of 2014, Nollywood, southern Nigeria's prolific commercial film industry, became a trending topic on Twitter as numerous users alleged that it was morally bankrupt and downright ridiculous for hastily producing dramas about Ebola. Among the most popular of these anti-Nollywood tweets identified the industry's perceived opportunism – its alleged shamelessness – in dramatising the virus's effects on West Africa. These tweets did not, however, evince even a rudimentary familiarity with Nollywood's contours, suggesting that their authors had not, in fact, seen any of the films that they were so passionately denouncing. Nollywood's actual industrial boundaries appeared to be beyond the grasp of these tweeters, with many of them misidentifying a Ghanaian film, Samuel Ofori's *Ebola: The Blood on African Soil* (2014), as a Nollywood production. Whatever their awareness of industrial distinctions, however, these tweeters appeared to share an investment in critiquing aspects of Africa's self-produced media image – and also in remaking that image in the name of something "respectable". Such a flagrantly condescending, boldly prescriptive approach to Nollywood is not limited to Twitter and other social networking sites, nor is it a new phenomenon. Rather, the opprobrium that the Twittersphere momentarily reserved for Nollywood merely reflects, in digital form, longstanding, largely Western conceptions of African cinema and media that dogmatically valorise retrospection in place of topicality, and "authenticity" at the expense of commercial savvy (see Diawara 1988; Murphy 2000; Tcheuyap 2011). Since its emergence as a bona fide commercial force in the early 1990s, Nollywood has combatted this fetishistic conception of "traditional" African storytelling through the rapid, relatively inexpensive production of an abundance of genre movies, becoming a major producer of crime films, horror films, action films, and family melodramas, initially for local, market-driven consumption on home video and later for global export via a range of streaming services, both licensed and pirated. While Western media outlets such as CNN, which offered an analogy between Ebola and ISIS, and *Newsweek*, which revived the rhetoric and iconography of "the dark continent" in a controversial August 2014 cover story, have rightly been critiqued for the perceived racism and ethnocentrism of their coverage of Africa's most recent Ebola outbreak – for, that is, imposing a confining and even misleading and alarmist set of representational conditions (see Tesfaye 2014; Seay & Dionne 2014) – Nollywood has been condemned for generating its own accounts of the virus, enfolding useful public-health information into the generic fabric of the family melodrama and the village comedy (see Ekpo 2014).

Nollywood's controversial depictions of such newsworthy topics as the Ebola outbreak and the acceleration of the Boko Haram insurgency raise pressing questions about the intersections between reportage and melodrama, between pedagogy and opportunism, and between therapeutic engagement and cruel exploitation. As illiteracy rates remain relatively high throughout Nigeria, Nollywood maintains a commitment to public outreach that is, in many instances, inextricable from sheer commercialism. With its embrace of multiple African languages in addition to English, Nollywood recalls Ousmane Sembène's description of his own filmmaking practice as a sort of "night school" for linguistically diverse Africans (Ukadike 1994). At the same time, however, Nollywood films are travelling to multiple diasporic locations, becoming truly transnational products, and thus contributing to the global complexity of Africa's media image. This chapter considers Nollywood's responsiveness – its popular yet contentious dramatisation of current events – as a function of economics, audience demand, political engagement, narrative convention, and new technologies of production and distribution.

Released in 2014, a number of Ebola-themed Nollywood films represent complicated contributions to the village genre – a demonstrably popular category of production that spans multiple African film industries. Perhaps unsurprisingly, global coverage of these rapidly produced Ebola-themed films has tended to pivot around suggestions of opportunism. In an article on Ebola's devastating effects on West African economies, *The New York Times* suggested that comic actor Sara D' Great, one of Sierra Leone's biggest media stars, had made three Ebola comedies in an effort to turn a profit – to personally benefit from a deadly outbreak (Gettleman 2014). Predictably, *The Times* did not position Sara's three films – whose titles in English are *Ebola's Arrived*, *Balance Ebola*, and *Ebola is Crazy* – in relation either to the dozens of other Ebola-themed films produced in West Africa in 2014 or to the rich history of African comedic engagements with deadly viruses. This history includes Henri Duparc's remarkable 1993 film *Rue Princesse*, from Cote d'Ivoire, which is a comedy about HIV/AIDS that Duparc designed to be an agent both of pedagogy and catharsis. Duparc based the film, in part, on clinical research on HIV/AIDS, and hoped that it would convey accurate and useful information about HIV prevention to illiterate local filmgoers. He felt that comedy – and "crazy comedy" at that – would be the best vehicle for his message, explaining, "I set out from the idea that a sense of humor always overcomes intolerance" (in Barlet 2000: 136). Equally worthy of consideration, in this respect, are the words of the Congolese poet Tchicaya U Tam'si, who writes that satire "produces an urge to laugh in order to conceal the urge to cry" (in Barlet 2000: 136). The Ebola-themed comedies produced in West Africa at the height of the outbreak might be seen as serving an analogous function, invoking the therapeutic potential of laughter while simultaneously contributing to an immensely popular film genre.

Nollywood's Ebola comedies are hardly unique in contemporary African screen media; not only are filmmakers in Ghana, Sierra Leone, and Liberia making their own Ebola comedies, but many of Nollywood's Ebola-themed films are, in fact, remakes of comedies about malaria, HIV/AIDS, and other afflictions. It is possible to view all of these Ebola comedies, however silly or offensive they may seem, as examples of resistance to the miserablism with which the news media have been known to depict Africa and Africans, particularly when couching the Ebola outbreak in Afro-pessimist terms – a reflection of the "inevitability" of disease on the continent (as in Bernard Goldberg's October 2014 report for Fox News, in which he invoked a land of "backwards people" and tragically ineffective "witch doctors" (see Tesfaye 2014)). If the notion of an Ebola comedy is anathema to Westerners, in some African contexts it is quite at home among an array of boldly satirical approaches. Consider, for instance, Evans Orji's *Ebola Doctors* (2014), an ensemble comedy produced in Enugu, Nigeria. Featuring three men – played by the Enugu-based Nollywood stars Stephen Alajemba, Chiwetalu Agu, and the late Dede One Day – who overreact to the threat of Ebola, donning increasingly ludicrous "protective" gear (including cellophane wrap) and using their hypochondria as a pretext for expressions of regionalism and misogyny, *Ebola Doctors* employs many of the tropes of the village film in satirising a certain anti-Lagos prejudice. Instructively, *Ebola Doctors* suggests that the news media – and television broadcasts in particular – help to promote this prejudice, albeit in complex and often contradictory ways.

The film examines the localisation of media, offering a brief re-enactment of a typical "ethnic" television broadcast in which an Enugu-based reporter positions Lagos as one of the cosmopolitan "sources" of Ebola – one of the big African cities to which "big men" repair after their morally suspect excursions into the global North. In contrast to the frequently alarmist, seemingly xenophobic approach of the global media establishment (Flückiger 2006; Shohat & Stam 2006; Tesfaye 2014) – an approach that is all too familiar to Africans with daily access to satellite television and thus to CNN and the BBC – the local broadcast policy depicted in *Ebola Doctors* emphasises the virus's threat to rural Africa, comprising an implicit critique of Western media's tendency to consider the vulnerability to Ebola of such "First World" metropolitan centres as New York and London. In keeping with the image of Africa advanced through the localisation of media, *Ebola Doctors* presents the African village as both an actual and a potential victim of the virus, offering a crucial counterbalance to the national–cultural chauvinism that may inhere in the global media establishment (Shohat & Stam 2006). As over two hundred prominent writers and academics alleged in March 2015, in an open letter of complaint to the American broadcast television network CBS, Western accounts of Ebola tend to exclude the experiences of people of black African ancestry. Instructively, however, local broadcasts, particularly in Nigeria and Ghana, provide their own resistant figurations, opposing, for instance, the infamous *60 Minutes* broadcast of 7 November 2014, in which correspondent Lara Logan travelled to Liberia to address the risks posed to those who, like Logan herself, had made the "perilous" trek to West Africa (see French, in this volume). The globally syndicated *60 Minutes* thus occluded the very experiences with which, in however "crude" or nakedly commercial a manner, Nollywood and other popular African film industries have engaged through the production of Ebola-themed comedies and dramas.

Like a number of other Nollywood films, *Ebola Doctors* directly depicts the Enugu-based consumption of "ethnic" broadcasting, offering a realist basis for its satirical extremes. In other words, the film gains in verisimilitude by having its protagonists repair to a bar where they can watch a local news broadcast rather than the umpteenth CNN or BBC special; what they do with the local newscaster's accurate, Ebola-related information is another matter entirely, and it speaks to the film's broadly comedic intentions. Ironically, the localisation of media has been part and parcel of the processes of liberalisation that have led to the transnational expansion of CNN, the BBC, and Al Jazeera, the African consumption of which must be situated alongside that of privately owned local or "ethnic" broadcasting services (Zeleza 2009). Nollywood's Enugu-based Ebola comedies, of which *Ebola Doctors* is but one, are less about Ebola than about the dichotomy between village and city, and in examining this dichotomy, they tend to suggest that Africa's media image is split between the distortions of the global media establishment and the immediately relevant lessons of local broadcasters. However, the mere fact of their existence has rendered these films morally suspect throughout the blogosphere (see Ekpo 2014), suggesting that, when Nollywood and Ebola come together, the result is necessarily risible. Upon closer consideration, however, a Nollywood film like *Ebola Doctors* seems less an opportunistic response to current events than a standardised extension of a popular, transnational African film genre – one that, undoubtedly, has roots in other media, including television sitcoms and newspaper fiction.

In addition to shedding some light on the localisation of media in Nigeria, *Ebola Doctors* and its comedic counterparts provide vital public-health information to viewers in and beyond Enugu. *Ebola Doctors*, for all its silliness and "shoddiness", is full of incontestable facts about Ebola transmission – facts that the film relays in multiple ways, including through an opening series of graphics, a recurrent title song, as well as the afore-mentioned, re-enacted local news broadcast. Even if one concedes that these Ebola comedies are not, strictly speaking, ripped-from-the-headlines docudramas – even if they seem strictly generic – it is still possible to per-ceive and even laud their apparent commitment to public health. Still, the threat of Ebola is, in *Ebola Doctors* especially, very much a pretext for the demonisation of the "been-to" – the African who has been abroad and who returns only to condescend to fellow Africans and constantly perform a certain cosmopolitan panache. Ebola narratives are especially conducive to this demonisation, given widespread concerns about the epidemiological effects of transnational travel, and *Ebola Doctors* offers, among its characters, a particularly pompous young man who, arriving in Liberia from London, later travels to his native Lagos, where he begins to experience symptoms of Ebola, collapsing in his fancy clothes, his gaudy "bling" jingling as he falls.

Released during a period marked, in part, by increased border patrol (particularly between Guinea and Sierra Leone), *Ebola Doctors* would seem to endorse the notion of a nationwide lockdown, such as Sierra Leone experienced for three days in late March 2015. But the film takes such isolationism one step further by depicting the dread of Lagos that several characters experience in Enugu. If the film's obviously satirical intentions help to militate against the notion that it is an agent of anti-urban prej-udice, then no such alibi is offered in Nollywood films that depict Boko Haram, and that, in the process, underscore the Afro-pessimist conception of a hopelessly divided Nigeria. Thus far, these films have generated at least as much negative attention – at least as much bad press – as Nollywood's Ebola comedies. One film, Pascal Amanfo's *Nation Under Siege* (2013), was rejected for exhibition at Silverbird Cinemas, a multiplex chain in Ghana and Nigeria, because of its representation of Islamist terrorism. One among a proliferation of popular films that reference the Boko Haram insurgency, *Nation Under Siege* is singular in some ways, and broadly emblematic in oth-ers. Amanfo's film follows the efforts of a counterterrorism expert to pre-vent the members of an Islamist insurgency from detonating a car bomb that will kill thousands of people, most of them students. In melodramatic, multi-character fashion, the film includes a series of intersecting sub-plots, one of which involves a young terrorist (played by Amanfo himself) who engages in a battle of wills with the Christian prostitute he has been ordered to murder as a sort of warm-up for suicide bombing. Hearing her impassioned pleas on behalf of peace and religious tolerance, the terrorist has a partial change of heart; the film implies that he does indeed carry out the execution of the prostitute, but it ends with him strapping a bomb to his body and detonating it in front of the leader of the Islamist insurgency (played, in a cameo, by the Ghanaian superstar Majid Michel). *Nation Under*

Siege thus draws upon the tropes of conversion and redemption familiar from American television dramas, especially Showtime's *Sleeper Cell* (2005–2006) and *Homeland* (2011–), but, unlike its Western counterparts, the film has not been met with much enthusiasm. Indeed, *Nation Under Siege* has received its share of bad press (see Hirsch 2013), which places it firmly in line with any number of other Nollywood films, the global flow of which often feeds broadsides against the alleged intellectual and aesthetic shortcomings of African popular media.

Just as there appears to be a certain global artistic consensus surrounding the cinematic representation of African civil wars – a certain agreement about the requisite themes and motifs (Harrow 2013) – there appears to be an equally stable approach to depicting Islamist terrorism. Jihad is jihad, whether executed by Al Qaeda in Algeria, Ansar Dine in Mali, or Boko Haram in Nigeria. Operating in largely allegorical fashion, *Nation Under Siege* contributes to this growing global consensus, abstracting Boko Haram into a jihadist sect that goes by multiple fictional names, but whose violent methods reflect those of any number of insurgencies operating in Africa and the Middle East. At one point, the film's counterterrorism expert – clad, tellingly, in a uniform that evokes Detective Olivia Benson of the globally syndicated NBC television series *Law & Order: Special Victims Unit* (1999–) – refers to one suspected insurgent as "the head of the Boko Katika clan", which she defines as "a group of immigrants occupying land in the far north." At other times, the film's active insurgents salute one another, and seemingly honour their shared cause, with the curious phrase "Rama Boko". Evoking the Hindu deity of the same name, "Rama" contributes to the syncretism of the film, which, even when alluding to Islamism, complicates the ideology – perhaps most powerfully when examining Islamist efforts to exterminate Muslim populations. From this perspective, it is instructive that the filmmakers retain the word "boko" but jettison the word "haram". While "haram" has its roots in Arabic and Hausa, and offers a relatively stable set of connotations centred on Islamic proscriptions, "boko" has both a murkier provenance and a more nuanced contemporary purview, complicating the film's allegorical operations.

Visually, *Nation Under Siege* is steeped in painfully familiar images – the sort of images that have comprised the global media establishment's sporadic coverage of Boko Haram – including those of men gunning down large groups of students, or those of car bombs being detonated outside churches. When the film's characters claim that Islamist insurgencies lead to genocide, they mean to convey the indiscriminate operations of those militants who seek to eliminate all opposition. When others refer to the holocaust of Africans, they provide crucial reminders about the victims of terrorist attacks being both Christian and Muslim, but they also employ the term "holocaust" in a cautionary capacity, warning government officials about the killings to come. Elements of the generic here include the terrorists' oft-articulated claim that they're operating in the name of "the most high God" – a construction that is no less familiar for being so theologically fuzzy – as well as the numerous references to terrorist activities in an ill-defined "northern region". Indeed, in the global imaginary, the geographical north is increasingly metonymic of Islamist militancy, whether the individual country in question is Nigeria or Mali. In addressing this imaginary, *Nation Under Siege* places a striking emphasis on the role of media technologies in shaping popular opinion. The film's striking self-reflexivity can be seen in its iconographic reliance on various recording and playback devices, which frequently become prominent aspects of Amanfo's mise-en-scène. In an early sequence, a radio remains sharply in focus in one shot, its clarity achieved at the expense of the image of the man who wields it. He may be blurry, but the radio – the source of a sermon about the dangers of ethnic nationalism – maintains its clearly defined contours. The film underscores the consensus-building operations of popular media by cutting from the shot of the radio to a shot of a woman who, holding a microphone and gazing into the lens of a camera, seemingly completes the radio announcer's sentence. Reinforcing the film's allegorical function, the woman identifies herself as reporting from a fictional state "in the northern heartland", and the name of her network is "the NTV". While the name certainly evokes the Nigerian Television Authority (NTA), it is important to recall that the NTA has not been known as the NTV since 1977. Broadcasting nearly forty years later, Amanfo's television reporter is clearly an agent of allegory – akin, perhaps, to the local newscaster in *Ebola Doctors*, who puts an "ethnic", Enugu-based spin on global coverage of a deadly outbreak.

By so consistently examining media technologies, *Nation Under Siege* conveys the complexity of discourses surrounding terrorism, including those that centralise questions of national belonging. The preponderance of shots of recording equipment recall a comment that Jonathan Kahana (2008) makes about such "specular images": "Revealing the presence of competing documentary sources [makes] two points: that the mere recording of events [isn't] enough to guarantee the truth of their representation; and that all representation, including the film in progress, comes from a particular position. Showing other means of recording within the frame of the film [is] a way of making the limits of that frame, in a manner of speaking, visible" (160–162). Like any allegory, *Nation Under Siege* is particularly invested in the limits of representation, and what, to the anti-Nollywood crowd, might seem sloppy, stupid, or simply accidental is, conceivably, a measure of Amanfo's syncretic methods, which blend not just competing definitions of terrorism but also the mixed metaphors, discrepant sign systems, and discordant voices so beloved of postmodern thought. Dismissing *Nation Under Siege* on the basis of its deviations from fact – as in mainstream coverage of the film – is to suggest that Boko

Haram is remotely "knowable". However tempting it may be to reduce the insurgency to a "coherent" Islamist extremism – a reduction so beloved of the global media establishment, which often ignores the gendered and socio-economic realities that feed Boko Haram (see Coles et al. 2015) – it is perhaps more appropriate to contextualise the insurgency in terms particular to Nigeria, which would account for a number of specific state failures and environmental catastrophes as well as the diminishing career opportunities and intensifying penury of young men. It is in relation to these national particularities that *Nation Under Siege* might seem confused and contradictory, at once embracing the generic aspects of Islamism and avoiding any attempt to pigeonhole Boko Haram. However, these very confusions and contradictions – like the paradoxical relations between global and local media images traced in *Ebola Doctors* – suggest the resistance of contemporary African screen media to some of the homogenising tendencies of the global media establishment.

The persistent topicality of African screen media needn't be seen strictly in terms of commercial opportunism, nor should it be elevated according to any one theoretical rubric. It is necessary to recognise the sheer diversity of African filmmakers' approaches to apparently ripped-from-the-headlines productions, which reveals as much about specific and divergent industrial factors as about discrepant authorial intentions. To suggest that *Nation Under Siege* bears a family resemblance to Kenyan popular films about the Westgate mall attacks would be to tell only part of the story. Certainly such Kenyan productions as *Westgate Under Siege* (2013) and *Terror Attack at Westgate* (2013) are just as topical as *Nation Under Siege*, but they differ from Amanfo's film in countless ways, including in their reliance on documentary footage of the attacks, culled from security cameras, citizen journalists, and professional television productions. *Nation Under Siege* is, by contrast, evocative of Nollywood standard practice through its reliance on location shooting and an original theme song, as well as through its depiction of prostitution, Igbo widowhood, and a mother who is in touch with the occult and can predict the future. Such canny combinations could not guarantee a theatrical run for *Nation Under Siege*, however, as the film was denied a public commercial exhibition on the basis of its "divisive" subject matter. Its fate thus suggests the transgressive potential of African screen media, the present complexity of which is deserving of serious attention.

References

Barlet, O. (2000) *African Cinemas: Decolonizing the Gaze*, London and New York: Zed Books.

Coles, A., Gray, L., & Momsen, J. (eds) (2015) *The Routledge Handbook of Gender and Development*, New York: Routledge.

Diawara, M. (1988) "Popular culture and oral traditions in African film", *Film Quarterly*, 41 (3): 6–14.

Ekpo, N. N. (2014) "Ebola virus movie released to mock Nigerians?" NigeriaFilms. com, 24 August, at http://www.nigeriafilms.com/news/28647/10/ebola-virus-movie-released-to-mock-nigerians.html [accessed 31/07/2015].

Flückiger, K. M. (2006) "Xenophobia, media stereotyping, and their role in global insecurity", Geneva Centre for Security Policy (GCSP) Brief No. 21, 6 December.

Gettleman, J. (2014) "Ebola ravages economies in West Africa", *The New York Times*, 30 December, at http://www.nytimes.com/2014/12/31/world/africa/ebola-ravages-economies-in-west-africa.html?_r=0 [accessed 17/04/2014].

Harrow, K. (2013) *Trash: African Cinema from Below*, Bloomington, IN: Indiana University Press.

Hirsch, A. (2013) "Boko Haram gets Nollywood treatment as Nigerian films imitate life", *The Guardian*, 4 July, at http://www.theguardian.com/world/2013/jul/04/boko-haram-nollywood-nigerian-film [accessed 17/04/2015].

Kahana, J. (2008) *Intelligence Work: The Politics of American Documentary*, New York: Columbia University Press.

Murphy, D. (2000) "Africans filming Africa: questioning theories of an authentic African cinema", *Journal of African Cultural Studies*, 13(2): 239–249.

Seay, L. & Dionne, K. Y. (2014) "The long and ugly tradition of treating Africa as a dirty, diseased place", *The Washington Post*, 25 August, at http://www.washington-post.com/blogs/monkey-cage/wp/2014/08/25/othering-ebola-and-the-history-and-politics-of-pointing-at-immigrants-as-potential-disease-vectors/ [accessed 31/07/2015].

Shohat, E. & Stam, R, (2006) *Flagging Patriotism: Crises of Narcissism and Anti-Americanism*, New York: Routledge.

Tcheuyap, A. (2011) *Postnationalist African Cinemas*, Manchester: Manchester University Press.

Tesfaye, B. (2014) "Misunderstanding the Ebola crisis is worse than ignoring it", *Africa is a Country*, 17 October, at http://africasacountry.com/2014/10/misun-derstanding-the-ebola-crisis-is-worse-than-ignoring-it/ [accessed 31/07/2015].

Ukadike, N. F. (1994) *Black African Cinema*, Berkeley, CA: University of California Press.

Zeleza, P. T. (2009) "The media in social development in contemporary Africa", in K. Njogu and J. Middleton (eds), *Media and Identity in Africa*, Bloomington, IN: Indiana University Press.

Index

60 Minutes 8, 38–9, 77, 226

Abiola, M. 65, 66, 68
Abubakar, Abdulrasheed 201
Abubakar, Amina 207
academic writing–journalism comparisons 30–2, 33–7
Achebe, C. 36, 37
Achmat, Z. 141
Ademo, M. 5
Adichie, C.N. 3, 17, 36
Adorno, T. 49
advertising and marketing expats 148, 149–51, 153, 155
Africa Live 177–8, 180–7
'Africa Rising' narrative 3–4, 17, 114, 152; Ghana and 116–25
Africa24 Media 98
African diasporic press 61–70
African NGOs 147–57
African Voice 64–9
Africa's Media Image (1992 book) *see* Hawk, B.
Afro-optimism, 6, 26–27, 52, 116, 122 *see also* 'Africa Rising' narrative
Afro-pessimism 2, 3, 17, 18, 103, 117
Agence France-Presse (AFP) 18–19, 20–3, 26–7, 200
aid 5–6, 9, 58; Africa's development narrative defined by 129–31
aid agencies 5–6
AIDS/HIV 224–5; activism 137–8, 140; British media and 132–42; depoliticalisation of 139–40;

emerging pandemic 133–5; global crisis 135–9
Al Jazeera 5, 84, 205, 216, 226
Al Jazeera English (AJE) 96–7; and new imperialisms 218–20
Al Qaeda 200
Al Shabaab 56, 143, 181–3, 200–1
Alasuutari, P. 53
Aldekoa, X. 89
Allison, S. 197
Amanfo, P. 227, 229
Amin, Mo. 2, 96, 97
Angola 214
antiretroviral therapy (ART) 132, 135
Arab Spring 53
Ashesi University 119–21; Honour Code 119, 120
Associated Press (AP) 18–19, 20–3, 62, 100, 215
Astrid, Princess 59
audience: feedback from 92; Western correspondents' perceptions of 73–82
audio cassettes 203–4

Babangida, B. 204
Bach, D. 4
Badawi, Z. 83–5
Band Aid 30 video 160
Barker, M. 166
BBC 226; compared with CCTV 181–3; coverage of AIDS in Africa 132–40; *Focus on Africa* 178, 179, 180–7; new imperialisms 218–20
BBC World 84

Belgian television 52–60
Bell, E. 144
Bend in the River, A (Naipaul) 35
Biafra 201
blogs 162, 166–7, 169–71
Bohnstedt, A. 168
Boko Haram 10; media strategies
    200–10; Nollywood 224, 227–30
Bono 140
Boswell, A. 89
Bourdieu, P. 122
Braquehais, S. 89
BRICS countries 6, 194
BringBackOurGirls campaign 190
Broere, K. 90
Brookes, H.J. 1, 47, 48
Bunting, M. 167
business reporting 20–1, 22, 26
businessman (audience category) 74–5
Bussman, J. 6

C-130 aeroplane 55
Calhoun, C. 169
Camerapix 98
Carmody, P. 217
CBS, open letter to 8, 38–9, 77, 226
CCTV Africa 177–89, 196, 211, 212–13;
    comparison with the BBC 178, 179,
    180–7
celebrity-endorsed campaigns 139–40
cell phones 110 *see also* mobile
    telephony
Central African Republic 100
Chad 143
Champion, C. 105, 106
Chibook abduction of schoolgirls 200,
    202, 206
China 10; changing foreign policy
    186; Chinese media perceptions
    of the reporting of Africa 211–13;
    commercial imperialism vs US
    military imperialism 214–22; media
    relations with Africa 194–7; reporting
    by CCTV Africa compared with the
    BBC 185
China Central Television (CCTV) *see*
    CCTV Africa
Chop Cassava 191

Christian Science Monitor 143
Christianity 219–20; evangelical 192,
    217–18
citation practices (of researchers) 47–8
citizen journalism 89, 105
citizen participation 92–3
civil society 190–2
Clemens, M. 167
CNN 5, 97, 113–14, 115, 226; new
    imperialisms 218–20
collective culture 109–10
colonialism 59, 193; Ghana 118, 121
comedy films 224–7
conflict 7, 30–1; CCTV compared with
    the BBC 179–86; news coverage 21,
    23, 26
Conrad, J. 35
constraints (on journalistic work) 90–3,
    168–9
constructive journalism 178–9, 196,
    212–13
content analysis 17–29; tone 19–20,
    23–6; topics 18–19, 20–3, 26–7 *see also*
    Critical Discourse Analysis
Cook, C. 48
Cooper, A. 48
co-production 37
corporate social responsibility 149–51
cost of reporting 97, 101
crime 21, 23
Critical Discourse Analysis (CDA)
    53–60
cultural–behavioural lens 134–5, 139
cultural chauvinism 83–4
cultural intermediaries 122
culture: collective 109–10; national
    75; professional journalists' 88–90;
    promotional cultures 149–51; visual
    102–12

Daily Mail, The 133
Darfur 30, 143
de Witte, M. 217–18
defensive rhetoric 77
deference (as cultural value) 118
Democratic Republic of Congo (DRC)
    7, 99–101
democratisation 105, 193

demonisation of the 'been-to' 227
depoliticalisation of AIDS 139–40
development 9; Africa's development
    narrative defined by aid 129–31
development journalism 168, 196
DFID, *Viewing the World* 46
diasporic press 61–70
Diawara, M. 121
digital divide 103–4
digital technologies: foreign
    correspondents and 89–90, 90–2;
    Ghana 121–2; *see also* internet, social
    media
direct dropping media strategy 205–6
discourse analysis *see* Critical Discourse
    Analysis
discursive practice 54, 57–8
distance (of the audience) 77–8
domestic politics 21, 23
domestication 52–60
Donner, J. 110
dramatisation of reality 153–4
Duparc, H. 224–5
Duvall, C.S. 61, 62

Easterly, W. 165–6, 219
Ebo, B. 48
Ebola 38–9, 84, 140; Nollywood 223–7
Ebola: The Blood on African Soil 223
Ebola Doctors 225–7, 229
economic consequences 179–86
Economist, The 130; 'Africa Rising' story
    3
economists' clash of ideologies 165–6
education (of correspondents) 87–8
Egypt 56
El Zein, H. 48
elections 113, 182, 184
emergency fatigue 169
emotional bond/connection 54–5
empowerment (African) 152–3, *see also*
    'Africa Rising' narrative
Endless, B. 25
Entman, R. 179
Enwezor, O. 103
Ethiopia 27, 96
ethnic violence 113–14; Rwandan
    genocide 7, 22, 31, 59

evangelical Christianity 192, 217–18
Eveleens, I. 89, 92
Everyday Africa 105
evidence, interpretation of 45–7
evolutionary representations 34–6
expatriate bubbles 90
expatriate marketing executives
    149–51, 148, 153, 155
explanatory themes 133–40
eyewitness accounts 54–5, 57

Facebook 113, 118
Fairclough, N. 54
family member/common person
    (audience category) 74–5
'Feed a child' video 159
female circumcision 97
Fessy, T. 89
film industry 10, 223–31
filters 108–9
Financial Times, The 130, 133, 134–5
Focus on Africa 178, 179, 180–7
foreign correspondents 4, 86–95;
    constraints 90–3; decline in
    99–101; journalists' culture 88–90;
    perceptions of their audience 73–82;
    pressures towards repositioning 93–4;
    socio-demographics 86–8, 93
formats (of news presentation) 56;
    coverage of Millennium Villages
    Project 163–6
Fortier, A. 90
frames 63–4; *African Voice* 64–9
framing: categories 179, 180;
    comparison of CCTV and BBC
    179–85
freelancers 91–2
French, H.W. 8, 38–39, 77, 216, 220

Gabon 38
Gagliardone, I. 178, 180, 196
Garuba, H. 49
Gathara, P. 8–9
geographic distance 77–8
geo-politics 6–8, 10, 193–9
Ghana 116–25
global crisis, AIDS as 135–9
global public sphere 190–2

Globe and Mail 20, 23–6
Golan, G.J. 45–7, 47–8
Golden Radiator Awards 160
Gorin, V. 105
Great, S. D' 224
Gruley, J. 61, 62
Guardian, The 47; AIDS in Africa 133, 134; tone of articles 19–20, 23–6, 166
guerrilla media strategy 204–5
Guinea 121

Hannerz, U. 75, 77, 78
Harber, A. 196
harmony 179–86
Harrison, G. 48
Harrison, J. 134
Harry, Prince 140
hashtag movements 190, 191, 192; SomeonetellCNN 5, 79, 114, 131
Hasty, J. 168
Hawk, B. xvi–xvii, 1
Heart of Darkness (Conrad) 35
Henderson, G. 89
Himmelman, N. 49
Hinshaw, D. 90
Hirst, D. 140
Hitchens, C. 17
HIV/AIDS *see* AIDS/HIV
Homeland 228
Horkheimer, M. 49
Hovil, L. 30
Hu Jintao 179
Hubbard, G. 165
human interest 179–86
humanitarian assistance 55
humanitarian news 9; creating a market for 143–6; news agency reporting 20, 21, 22–3, 26
Hume, D. 129
humour 158–60
Hunter-Gault, C. 3

I See a Different You 106, 107
Ibelema, M. 62
Idris, H. 205
immersive reporting 99–101
imperialism 7, 35, 83–4, 193–7, 214–22; commercial 214–22

implications of African events for home countries 55–6
Independent, The 166
InstaCPTguy 106
'Instagenic #sontagged' exhibition 107, 108
Instagram 102–12
Instameets 109–10
Instawalks 109–10
insurgency *see* Islamist insurgency
International AIDS Conference 136
international media organisations 5, 218–20; *see also* Al Jazeera, BBC, CNN
international news agencies *see* news agencies
international NGOs (INGOs) 136, 147–8
internet 43–4, 90–2; access 104; Boko Haram 206–7; online news organisations and new imperialisms 218–20
Invisible Children 79, 80, 190
IRIN 144–6
Islamic State 200, 206–7
Islamic State's West African Province (ISWAP) 207; *see also* Boko Haram
Islamist insurgency 219–20; Al Shabaab 56, 143, 181–3, 200–1; BBC compared with CCTV 181–3; Boko Haram *see* Boko Haram
Izama, A. 79

Jacobs, S. 80
jihadi insurgency *see* Islamist insurgency
Jonathan, G. 191, 192
Joshua, T.B. 192
journalism–academic writing comparisons 30–2, 33–7
journalists' culture 88–90

Kagumire, R. 79
Kahana, J. 229
Kenya 5; Al Shabaab 56, 143, 181–3, 200–1; Twitter 5, 113–15, 131; Western correspondents 73–82
Kenyan Paraplegic Organization (KPO) photo 148–54
'Kenyans for Kenya' campaign 151

Kenyatta, U. 4, 181, 183
Kimotho, Z. 150–1, 153, 154
Klare, M. 216, 217
Kogen, L. 215–16
Kony 2012 video 79, 80, 190, 218

Lancet, The 167
leaflet dropping 206
Lessig, L. 109
'Let's Save Africa' parody video 158
Lewis, S. 139
Li Keqiang 177
Liberia 38–9, 226
literacy 114
local audiences 78–81
local crews 97
local journalists 4–5, 97
local sensitivities 80–1, 85
localisation of media 225–7
Logan, L. 38, 226
Lord's Resistance Army 79, 190
Luggage is Still Labeled, The: Blackness in South African Art 103
Lundy, C. 105

MacBride Report 8
Mahajan, V. 3
Mail and Guardian 109
Mail on Sunday, The 136
mainstream media coverage 61–3
mainstream media strategy 204
Malawi 182, 184
Mali 55, 56, 58, 59
Maloba, W. 207
Mandela, N. 102, 140
Mari, A. 204
Marshall, B. 211, 212–13
Mau Mau 201
Mbeki, T. 63–4, 136, 148
McGregor, E. 139–40
media freedom 196–7
media strategies 200–10
medicines for AIDS 132, 135; struggle over access to 136–9
middle class 6
migration 7–8, 182, 184–5
militarisation 216–17
military imperialism 214–22

Millennium Development Goals (MDGs) 162, 169
Millennium Villages Project (MVP) 9, 161–74; constraints and opportunities 168–9; formats of reporting 163–6; tone of reporting 166–7
mineral resources 7, 217
mirror image defence 62
mixed/neutral frames 63; *African Voice* 64–9
mobile telephony 7
Mohamed Amin Broadcast Training Centre 98 *see also* Amin, Mo.
Mohammadi, A. 203
Mohammed, B.F. 204
morality 179–86
Morland, A. 92
Moyo, D. 165
Mozambique 214
Mpantsha, V. 106
Mudibo, N. 62
Mugabe, R. 192
Mukheli, F. 106
Mukheli, R. 106
Mulholland, J. 168
Munk, N. 168–9
Mutharika, P. 184

Naipaul, V.S. 35
narrative and technical practices 56
Naspers 197
nation branding 119–21
Nation Under Siege 227–30
national culture 75
national identity 102–3
national narratives 113–15
negative frames 63; *African Voice* 64–9
negative reporting 2–3, 46; *see also* Afro-pessimism
neo-colonial narrative 129
neo-imperialism 7, 59, 215–16
neo-liberal globalisation 138–9
neutral/mixed frames 63; *African Voice* 64–9
New African Magazine 61–2, 64
new cultural elite 117
New Ghana 116–25

'New Ghana' Facebook group 118–19
New York Times 3, 62, 224; tone of
    articles 19–20, 23–6, 166
news agencies 87–8, 215, 216; topics
    18–19, 20–3, 26–7; *see also under*
    individual names
news agendas 84
news magazines 43, 44
newspapers/press: coverage of the MVP
    161–2, 163–71; tone of articles 19–20,
    23–6; UK coverage of Africa 42–3, 44,
    47; UK press and AIDS in Africa 133;
    US coverage of Africa 42–3, 44
Nigeria 2, 6; Boko Haram *see* Boko
    Haram; film industry 10, 223–31;
    OccupyNigeria campaign 191
Nigerian Television Authority (NTA)
    229
Nollywood 10, 223–31
non-governmental organisations
    (NGOs) 5–6, 9, 130; INGOs 136,
    147–8; story manufactured for a
    Kenyan NGO 147–57
non-official sources 65, 67–8
non-profit news services 144–6
Nossiter, A. 88
Nur, M. 203
Nyabola, N. 8, 30

Obama, B. 130–1
objectivity 88
Observer, The 148, 152–3, 153–4
OccupyNigeria protests 191
offical sources 65, 67–8
Ogilvy and Mather 151, 153
oil 217
Olopade, D. 3
one-dimensional coverage 30–1
O'Neill, J. 6
online media strategy 206–7
online newspapers 162, 163–71
Orientalism 8, 58, 60, 141, 195
Orji, E. 225

Palast, G. 138
PANOS 135
parody videos 158–9
patents, pharmaceutical 136–9

Patton, C. 140–1
peer-reviewed journal articles 40–51
personalisation 57
pharmaceutical corporations 136–8
philanthrocapitalism 140
plurality of perspectives 35–6
politician (audience category) 74–5
politics 10; domestic 21, 23; geo-politics
    6–8, 10, 193–9
positive frames 63; *African Voice* 64–9
positive reporting 3–4, 23–6, 178–9,
    196; *see also* 'Africa rising' narrative,
    constructive journalism
poverty 80; linking disease and 140–1
power of images 2–3
power relations 193–9
presentation of the self 109
press *see* newspapers/press
press releases 164
problematic discourses 48–9
professional culture, journalists' 88–90
promotional cultures 149–51
Pronyk, P. 167

Qaqa, A. (aka Abu Darda or Abu Zaid)
    203, 205

racial identification 75
'Radi-Aid': Africa for Norway' parody
    video 158
Radiator Awards 159–60
Radiatoraid 9, 158–60
radicalisation 203–4
radio 44, 204
'rainbow nation' 102; *see also* South
    Africa
rape, epidemic of 7
rebranding the continent 119–21
RedSky advertising 149–50, 151
reductionism 33–4
refugees 182, 184–5
rehumanisation 136
relevance 75–6
remittances 6–7
resources, natural 7, 217
respect hierarchies 118
responsibility 179–86
Reuters 18–19, 20–3, 26

'Rising Africa' narrative 3–4, 17, 114, 152; Ghana and 116–25
Rosen, A. 167
Rue Princesse 224
Rusty Radiator Awards 159–60
Rwanda 7, 22, 31, 59

Sachs, J. 162, 165–6, 167, 169
Safaricom 148, 149, 153, 155
Sahara Reporters 191
Said, E. 8
SAIH (solidarity organisation of students and academics in Norway) 158–60
Sánchez Abril, P. 109
satirical memes 192
Scangroup 148, 149–50, 155
'Sceptical Third World Child' meme 158–9
schistosomiasis 129
'School Year' radio project 80
Schraeder, P. 25
scoping review 40–5
Scott, M. 61, 62
Seay, L. 8, 73
self: branding 119–21; presentation of 109
self-help manufactured story 147–57
semantic categories 64–5
Semetko, H. 179
sexual promiscuity 134–5
Shekau, A. 200, 202, 203, 205
Sierra Leone 227
Silverbird Cinemas 227
simplification 76
Sleeper Cell 228
small media 203–4
Smith, D. 90–1
social media 5, 104; Boko Haram 206–7; campaigns and the global public sphere 190–2; Facebook 113, 118; foreign correspondents 78–81; Instagram 102–12; New Ghana 117–21; Twitter *see* Twitter; YouTube 206, 207
social movements 192
social networks 92
social practice 54, 58–9

social ritual 105–9
SomeonetellCNN Twitter campaign 5, 79, 114, 131
source diversity 64–9
South Africa 6, 38; battle over AIDS drugs 136–9; Instagram and visual culture 102–12; national identity and access to visual culture 102–3; Western foreign correspondents 73–82
South Sudan 31
sports reporting 21, 22, 26
Sreberny-Mohammadi, A. 203
stability 179–86
Star, The 168
stereotypes 17, 34–6, 117; challenging using humour 158–60; imperial 83–4; in reporting of neo-imperialism 214–22
Stiglitz, J. 138
structural inequalities 138–9
Swaziland 138, 139
Sydney Morning Herald 20, 23–6
Synagogue Church of All Nations 192
    see also evangelical Christianity

Talk Africa 211, 212
Tam'si, T. U 225
Tashlapics 108
teleconferencing 205
Telegraph, The 47
television (TV) 43–4, 45, 215; Badawi's reflections on TV reporting of Africa 83–5; Belgian TV 52–60
Tencent 197
Terror Attack at Westgate 230
Tesfaye, A.M. 47–8
text (in CDA) 54–7
Thamm, M. 196–7
'They Say We Say' image 117–18
TIME magazine 3
tone of articles: MVP 166–7; newspaper articles 19–20, 23–6
tourism 56
tourist (audience category) 74–5
trade missions 58–9
translation of otherness 89
Treatment Action Campaign 136, 137
trends in reporting Africa 215–16

trust 120–1
Turse, N. 216, 217
Twitter 78–9; Boko Haram 206–7;
    Kenya 5, 113–15, 131; Nollywood and
    Ebola 223

United Kingdom (UK) 1; African
    diasporic press 61–70; coverage of
    MVP 164–7, 169–71; media and AIDS
    in Africa 132–42; news coverage of
    Africa 41–7
United Nations (UN) 144; MDGs 162,
    169; Millennium Summit 162
United States (US): coverage of MVP
    164–7, 169–71; military imperialism
    vs Chinese commercial imperialism
    214–22; news coverage of Africa
    41–6, 215–16

Valkenburg, P. 179
van Dijk, T. 58
van Klinken, A. 217, 218
video recordings 205, 206
visual culture: Instagram and 102–12;
    national identity and access to 102–3
voicelessness 38–9, 113
Volman, D. 216, 217
VRT (Flemish Radio- and Television
    Network Organisation) 52, 54, 57–8
VTM (Flemish Television Company)
    54, 57–8

Wainaina, B. 2, 117, 129–30
Wall, M. 48
Walton, M. 103–4, 110
war crimes 100–1, 219
Washington Post 62
Wekesa, B. 178–9, 212, 213
Western foreign correspondents *see*
    foreign correspondents
Western gaze 4
Westgate shopping mall attack 75,
    230
Westgate Under Siege 230
'Who Wants To Be a Volunteer?'
    parody video 159
Wohlgemuth, L. 40
World Bank 138
World Wide Instameet 109–10
Wrong, M. 17

Xin, X. 216
Xinhua 5, 216

'YeBook Instagram' exhibition 107
young people 191–2
YouTube 206, 207
Yusuf, M. 201, 202, 203, 204, 205

Zerai, A. 40–1
Zhang, Y. 178–9, 212
Zimbabwe 76, 134
Zizek, S. 49

 Taylor & Francis eBooks

Helping you to choose the right eBooks for your Library

Add Routledge titles to your library's digital collection today. Taylor and Francis ebooks contains over 50,000 titles in the Humanities, Social Sciences, Behavioural Sciences, Built Environment and Law.

Choose from a range of subject packages or create your own!

Benefits for you

- » Free MARC records
- » COUNTER-compliant usage statistics
- » Flexible purchase and pricing options
- » All titles DRM-free.

Free Trials Available
We offer free trials to qualifying academic, corporate and government customers.

Benefits for your user

- » Off-site, anytime access via Athens or referring URL
- » Print or copy pages or chapters
- » Full content search
- » Bookmark, highlight and annotate text
- » Access to thousands of pages of quality research at the click of a button.

eCollections – Choose from over 30 subject eCollections, including:

Archaeology	Language Learning
Architecture	Law
Asian Studies	Literature
Business & Management	Media & Communication
Classical Studies	Middle East Studies
Construction	Music
Creative & Media Arts	Philosophy
Criminology & Criminal Justice	Planning
Economics	Politics
Education	Psychology & Mental Health
Energy	Religion
Engineering	Security
English Language & Linguistics	Social Work
Environment & Sustainability	Sociology
Geography	Sport
Health Studies	Theatre & Performance
History	Tourism, Hospitality & Events

For more information, pricing enquiries or to order a free trial, please contact your local sales team: www.tandfebooks.com/page/sales